# SERIES EDITORS' FOREWORD

The Histories of the Gothic series consists of four volumes: *Gothic Literature 1764–1824*, *Gothic Literature 1825–1914*, *Twentieth Century Gothic* and *American Gothic*. The series provides a comprehensive introduction to the history of Gothic Literature and to a variety of critical and theoretical approaches. Volumes in the series also raise questions about how the Gothic canon has been received and seek to critically challenge, rather than simply reaffirm, commonplace perceptions of the Gothic tradition. Whilst intended as an introduction to the history of the Gothic they thus also provide a rigorous analysis of how that history has been developed and suggest ways in which it can be critically renegotiated.

The series will be of interest to students of all levels who are new to the Gothic and to scholars and teachers of the history of Gothic Literature. The series will also be of interest to students and scholars working more broadly within the areas of literary studies, cultural studies, and critical theory.

Andrew Smith, University of Glamorgan
Benjamin F. Fisher, University of Mississippi

ACKNOWLEDGEMENTS

This book was written in a period of personal upheaval during which I transferred from Keele University, Staffordshire to Trinity College Dublin, which entailed moving country as well as house. That it was finished at all comes as something of a surprise to me. My thanks go to Ben Fisher and Andrew Smith for their encouragement and supervision as general editors of this series and the team at the University of Wales Press for steering me through the process. Many thanks also to the anonymous reader for the Press, who made some extremely pertinent criticisms of the original manuscript and helpful suggestions for revision.

I am in great dept to the very large number of critics who have written on the Gothic in general, and nineteenth-century Gothic in particular, from whom I have learned much. The Gothic attracts some of the very best critical minds around, and if this volume is useful it is only because it tries to distil the analyses produced by others in the last thirty years. As always, my family was supportive and I dedicate the book to my brothers: Michael, Peter, David and Paul. My colleagues in the School of English, Trinity College Dublin were immensely encouraging. I particularly thank Kate Hebblethwaite (a fellow cloak race enthusiast), Aileen Douglas, Eve Patten, Philip Coleman, and Stephen Matterson. The students in my seminars in Gothic Fiction in Keele University and Trinity College contributed in many ways to this book, and had to endure my endless ramblings on the issues and texts covered here. Particular thanks to my postgraduate students Valeria Cavalli and Paul Morrissey, and an undergrad Paula Keatley who contributed some of the ideas contained and acknowledged here. Darryl Jones as always has been a mine of information; he tolerated numerous conversations about the Gothic, and shared with me his wide reading in and theoretical

# GOTHIC LITERATURE 1825–1914

HISTORY OF THE GOTHIC

# Gothic Literature
# 1825–1914

*Jarlath Killeen*

UNIVERSITY OF WALES PRESS
CARDIFF
2009

*www.uwp.co.uk*


*British Library Cataloguing-in-Publication Data*
A catalogue record for this book is available from the British Library.


ISBN    978-0-7083-2070-9 (hardback)
          978-0-7083-2069-3 (paperback)
e-ISBN  978-0-7083-2244-4

Printed on demand by CPI Group (UK) Ltd, Croydon, CR0 4YY

# Contents

knowledge of the field. Many thanks also to Martha Fanning and Eoin Smith, Eimear McBride and William Galinski, Margaret Robson, Trish Ferguson, Antoinette Curtin, Marion Durnin, Jenny Brown.

My deepest debt is to Mary Lawlor. For everything.

Publication dates are those of first serial publication when appropriate.

*For my brothers*

# Introduction

## Declining Definition

This study is an introduction to the varieties of Victorian fiction implicated in the Gothic genre. Before turning to that fiction itself, however, it is important to acknowledge that the very application of the term 'Gothic' to Victorian literature is controversial. In a valuable study of '"Gothic" and the critical idiom' (1994), the influential critic Maurice Levy 'mourned' the devaluation of the term 'Gothic' in studies of the form. He pointed out that traditionally, in scholarly works of the early and mid twentieth century, the term 'Gothic' had been used to designate a body of literature published between 1764, the year Horace Walpole's *The Castle of Otranto* first appeared, and 1820, which marked the grand culmination of the form in Charles Robert Maturin's encyclopaedic *Melmoth the Wanderer*. Levy complained that since the 1970s, however, 'Gothic' had been applied to all kinds of texts written right through the nineteenth and twentieth centuries, texts which had formal and narrative features which were not common to the 'Gothic tradition'.[1] Levy's point is that imprecision has invaded critical writing about the Gothic, and that in using the term to cover writing so different in nature from the 'original' tradition, its 'fundamental' meaning is being obscured. His criticism is echoed by Fiona Robertson, who defines Gothic precisely as 'a type of fiction which invites readers' fears and anxieties in highly stylised mystery-tales, using a limited set of plots, settings, and character-types, and including an element of history'. She warns that 'a novel should not be categorised as Gothic if it makes no attempt to situate the events of its plot in a historical setting'.[2] Her definition means that she excludes as 'non-Gothic experimentation[s] with Gothic conventions' novels usually included in studies of the genre, such as William Godwin's *Caleb Williams* (1794), Charlotte Brontë's *Jane Eyre* (1847) and Daphne du Maurier's *Rebecca* (1938).[3] Robert Mighall likewise makes an investment in history fundamental to his definition of the Gothic, highlighting a 'concern with the historical past … [and] rhetorical and textual strategies to locate the past and represent its perceived iniquities, terrors, and survivals', on which basis he excludes Mary Shelley's *Frankenstein* (1818).[4]

Discursive imprecision is a perennial problem in literary critical history,[5] and it may well be that critics are far too quick to assign the term 'Gothic' to any literature which employs conventions or tropes tangentially linked to the original tradition. There is certainly a widely acknowledged difficulty distinguishing between the formal terms 'Gothic' and 'horror', and, as Clive Bloom has suggested, such terms are often 'interchangeable'.[6] Some early reviewers of the original tradition adopted a 'shopping-list' approach to defining the genre. The anonymous article 'Terrorist novel writing' appeared in 1797 with the 'following recipe' for a Gothic novel:

> *Take –* An old castle, half of it ruinous.
> A long gallery, with a great many doors, some secret ones.
> Three murdered bodies, quite fresh.
> As many skeletons, in chests and presses.
> An old woman hanging by the neck; with her throat cut.
> Assassins and desperados, *'quant suff'*.
> Noise, whispers and groans, threescore at least.[7]

Many subsequent critics have tended to read as Gothic literature which reworks some or all of these conventions, so that even a text which is predominately 'realist', such as Charles Dickens's *Little Dorrit* (1855–7), can, because of its presentation of state institutions as reconstructions of traditional Gothic castles, be seen as an extension of the Gothic tradition. What is certainly true is that while one manifestation of the Gothic came to an end with Maturin's magnum opus, the form and tradition did not simply die in that moment, but were reborn and revivified in new ways, so that, as Julian Wolfreys has explained, after the 1820s Gothic cannot be 'figured ... as a single, identifiable corpus'. The genre fragmented and took up ghostly habitations elsewhere, indeed everywhere, in nineteenth-century culture: 'Escaping from the tomb and the castle, the monastery and the mansion, the gothic arguably becomes more potentially terrifying because of its ability to manifest itself and variations of itself anywhere'.[8] From the realist to the historical novel, from the strictest of rationalists to the most credulous of believers, the Gothic became ubiquitous. Wolfreys calls this survival of the Gothic the 'haunting absence' of the genre as a body of works in and of itself. This study will adopt a very flexible and inclusive understanding of the Gothic; 'purifying' the genre, by ring-fencing it through a very strict definition and then evicting texts which fail to fit this definition, does not take full cognisance of the sheer generic openness of the Gothic and its ability to migrate and adapt to formal circumstances far removed from its 'original' manifestations in the late eighteenth century. In looking at nineteenth-century Gothic we must follow the traces of a tradition, delineating the means by which the Gothic travelled into and transformed other genres and narratives while maintaining its own cognitive implications and formal and thematic conventions.

### Gothic Victorian / Victorian as Gothic

That the Gothic lost generic focus and shifted from being a tradition in the modernist sense to being a collection of Victorian gestures, a sensibility, to inflections, traces indicative of a nineteenth-century mentality, is hardly surprising to a twenty-first-century reader. After all, while the eighteenth century is still considered to be the age of reason, dominated by neoclassical architecture and rational conversation, in which the Gothic could exist only as a dark counterpart to mainstream culture (a reductive view of the eighteenth century), the Victorian Age itself is, to the general public, a Gothic one. Robert Mighall points out that notions of a barbaric past are crucial to cultural understandings of Gothic;[9] for this reason it is not surprising that the Victorians and the Gothic have become so closely intertwined to twentieth- and twenty-first-century audiences. To us, the Victorian age is *the* Gothic age. Wolfreys claims that for the Victorians, the Gothic was literally everywhere: 'all that black, all that crepe, all that jet and swirling fog ... These and other phenomena, such as the statuary found in Victorian cemeteries like Highgate, are discernible as being fragments and manifestations of a haunting, and, equally, haunted, "Gothicized" sensibility.' [10] However, the evidence suggests that Victorian men and women were more likely to think of themselves as living in an age of civilised progress rather than Gothic barbarism. It was in the twentieth century that the Victorian 'era' was retrospectively homogenised and transformed into an age of sexual repression shadowed by perverse transgression, an age of hypocrisy and duality, where propriety and pornography existed side by side, an age to which a Gothic vocabulary could be aptly applied. To the popular mind, Victorian England is suffused in fog and threatened by Jack the Ripper, populated by Gothic churches and pervaded by sexual perversity, draped in Dickensian darkness and tracked by Sherlock Holmes. Indeed, the term 'Victorian' has become a shorthand way to describe anything negative about contemporary society, and this view of the Victorians is perpetuated by a hundred period costume dramas, particularly the stylish adaptations of the great nineteenth-century canonical novels, often by Andrew Davies, presented on the BBC. Whereas Davies's adaptations of Jane Austen are invariably suffused with light and laughter, revisions of the works of Charles Dickens and George Eliot often look as if they were shot in the dark (thus giving the impression of an England in perpetual moral night), or through a dirty lens.

These adaptations are themselves heirs to the films of David Lean, especially his renderings of *Great Expectations* (1946) and *Oliver Twist* (1948), which utilised the techniques of German expressionist film-makers to create a type of Victorian London straight out of a horror film, a suggestion picked up by the hugely successful versions of Victorian England found in the Hammer horror films of the 1950s, 1960s and 1970s. As Matthew Sweet has written, 'Hammer used the historical setting to tell parables about the pleasures of the Permissive Society, which it dramatized as a battle between the promiscuous Undead and the conservative Victorians'.[11] Victorian England became the horrific alter ego of the sexually liberated contemporary world. The use of Gothic tropes attempts to tell a comforting story about how far we have travelled from those times. If writers like Walpole tried to use the Gothic to emphasise the historical distance between the 'medieval' Catholic Continent and eighteenth-century Protestant England, then Lean and the Hammer horror directors looked to the Gothic mode to indicate how far the Victorian past was from the twentieth century. In the same way, stories are told of the repressed Victorians covering the legs of piano tables as fables of how sensible is our contemporary sexual maturity – despite the fact that this was a joke invented by the Victorians about puritanical Americans.[12] Michel Foucault tried to banish the 'repression hypothesis' from the annals of critical literature by demonstrating that, far from stifling sexual discussion, the Victorians made it mandatory[13]; his labours were in vain, however, so that now,

> When we see, for instance, David Lynch's *The Elephant Man* (1979) or one of David Lean's Dickens' adaptations, we congratulate ourselves for having escaped the feculent horror-show of the Victorian city – a black-and-white world of bad drains and brick alleys, which modern plumbing and sodium lights have successfully banished.[14]

Indeed, it might be true to say that we need the version of the Victorians we have invented in order to maintain a view of ourselves as liberated in comparison.

This interpretation of nineteenth-century England was partly created by the literary 'modernists', the very designation adopted by these self-conscious innovators suggesting that the Victorians they were reacting against were somehow as 'medieval' and anachronistic as the Catholic clergy who dominate *Melmoth the*

*Wanderer* (1820). Virginia Woolf bizarrely believed that the modern age began the day Lytton Strachey said the word 'semen' aloud in her London flat, linking together modernist literature and sexual liberation.[15] It is odd that we have accepted Woolf's view that a reluctance to discuss sex in public is an indictment of any civilisation – an opinion which would suggest that the relish with which we lapped up the Starr Report detailing President Bill Clinton's sexual peccadilloes is an indication of our advancement. Sexual freedom has become the means by which we rate the sophistication of a particular society. Michael Mason begins his valuable study of Victorian sexuality with the warning that 'in our culture the Victorian age has a special place: more than any other era it awakens in us our capacities to feel hostile towards a past way of life, to perceive the past as alien, unenlightened, and silly';[16] this appears to be a view we are loath to give up.

To the general public, then, the Victorian era is a Gothic one of public respectability disguising private perversity. The academic view has (with notable exceptions) not been much more sophisticated until recently. For many influenced by post-structuralist and postmodernist views of representation, the nineteenth century was dominated by the realist novel and a realist aesthetic which pushed more 'radical' kinds of literature, such as the Gothic, to the margins (this, we should recognise, is merely another version of public light matched by private darkness). The interpretative pervasiveness of this view meant that many academics perpetuated a version of Victorian literature as dominated by a 'conservative' realism immune to and repressive towards outbreaks of the Gothic, which was banished to the peripheries. There was a tendency in the 1970s and 1980s to view realism as profoundly ideologically regressive and Gothic as a mode of subversion; since the realist text was central to Victorian writing, Victorian society in general could be stereotyped as reactionary and dedicated to a conservative aesthetic. The dominant interpretation of realism was cogently calibrated by Catherine Belsey as the view that

> the strategies of the classic realist text divert the reader from what is contradictory within it to the renewed recognition (misrecognition) of what he or she already 'knows', because the myths and

signifying systems of the classic realist text re-present experience in the ways in which it is conventionally articulated in our society.[17]

Belsey at times seems to suggest that realism is a kind of ideological trick played by ultra-conformist forces to quell social revolution. Colin McCabe's argument that George Eliot's *Middlemarch* (1871–2) epitomised aesthetic and social conservatism, while James Joyce's *Ulysses* (1922) was a literary version of social revolution, did not help matters.[18] Likewise, Roland Barthes launched a celebrated attack on the master realist Honoré de Balzac, revealing just how politically constructed such putative narrative realists could be.[19] In an era defined by broadly left-leaning academics, and when versions of Marxism and post- structuralism became default critical positions, many writing on Gothic took the broad view that it operated as an alternative and a response to the dictates of realism (although, as I will outline in the final chapter, when it came to actual analysis of Gothic texts, these same critics were much more nuanced). Gothic was transgressive, and since the Victorians were 'against' it, academia was against them.

To their conservative aesthetic realism, the Victorians had the misfortune to add conservative social and political values also. The constant linking of Victorianism to a certain set of 'family values' by sections of the political world anathema to many within the intellectual establishment caused considerable difficulties for a more rounded view of Victorian society. The former Prime Minister Margaret Thatcher famously claimed to sympathise with 'Victorian values', thereby guaranteeing a whole generation of academics would be almost automatically hostile to these values and the era they supposedly stemmed from. Thatcher opined:

I was brought up by a Victorian Grandmother. We were taught to work jolly hard. We were taught to prove yourself; we were taught self reliance; we were taught to live within our income. You were taught that cleanliness is next to Godliness. You were taught self respect. You were taught always to give a hand to your neighbour. You were taught tremendous pride in your country. All of these things are Victorian values. They are also perennial values. You don't hear so much about these things these days, but they were good values and they led to tremendous improvements in the standard of living.[20]

In his study of Jane Austen, Darryl Jones writes of the 1980s as extraordinarily problematic for many academics who were institutionally and personally outraged by the political values of the Conservative Party under Thatcher, and her government's assault on the universities: 'Most academics within the humanities ... being of broadly liberal political sympathies ... found themselves positioned somewhere between unsympathetic and implacably opposed to Margaret Thatcher'.[21] Some of these academics went on to write about Gothic almost as if it were a response to this feeling of disenfranchisement, thus promoting the values of the mode of writing they believed had been marginalised by Thatcher's ideological progenitors, the Victorians. Hence, some of the most influential critical work on Gothic was produced in the 1980s and early 1990s, meaning that it was written either just prior to or during the Thatcher era, including David Punter's Marxist-inflected *The Literature of Terror* (1980) and Rosemary Jackson's politically radical *Fantasy: The Literature of Subversion* (1981). Raphael Samuel explains this confluence very well, pointing out that at the same time as Thatcher was promoting her version of Victorian values as a bulwark against the trade unions and socialism, a revival of interest in the unsolved Jack-the-Ripper crimes of 1888 occurred, so that Victorian England became simultaneously identified with both public moralism and hidden perversion; the same figures that would preach about self-control and sexual restraint in the daytime were likely to be found wandering around Whitechapel procuring prostitutes and possibly ripping them to pieces in a display of the repressed coming back to life at night. Perhaps the horrifically capitalist Thatcherites were merely another incarnation of these murderous prudes.[22]

The public tend to think of the Gothic as a mode of representation indicating backwardness, atavism, perversity, sexual repression, murder and abuse, and reject it for that reason as belonging to the past. The Victorians represent that past, as monsters of perversity who lived public lives of staid conformity but who came out of the closet nightly to perpetuate the most horrific versions of abuse. This is a Victorian Britain populated by grotesques and caricatures, psychotics and schizophrenics. We might call it the 'Dr Jekyll and Mr Hyde view' of the Victorians. Indeed, if one of the most popular complaints about the Victorians is their attendance at freak shows, then they have become a collection of freaks for us. Academics, on the other hand, see the Gothic as liberating and transgressive, and the Victorians as the arch-conservatives who repressed the Gothic because of its threat to the 'family values' they held so dear. Mrs Beeton becomes the average Victorian in this scenario. These potent interpretations have caused great difficulty in trying to come to grips with the Victorians in all their historical complexity.

As Alice Jenkins and Juliet John argue,

> if realism as an aesthetic mode looms large in twentieth-century discussions of the Victorians – and there is no doubt that it does – this perhaps says as much about our need to create 'straw men' against which to measure ourselves as it says about the Victorians themselves.[23]

The same is true of the view of the Victorians as sexually repressed, which really needs to be put to rest. Moreover, the division between conservative realism and subversive Gothic is much too simplistic. Far from being merely social and aesthetic conservatives, the realists were engaged in literary experimentation, attempting to diffuse a mode of representation which sees the world as it truly is, however uncomfortable that picture. Although the realist novel does tend to promote middle-class power, this was often a middle class intent on *undermining* the status quo rather than endorsing it, a middle class trying to understand change, not prevent change from taking place.[24]

Even more importantly for us, the Gothic can now no longer be seen as aesthetically subversive and transgressive, as if that designated political and social radicalism as well. As Robert Mighall and Chris Baldick note, the description of the Gothic as subversive tells us more about the critical consensus reached in the 1980s than the Gothic itself, since 'the cultural politics of modern critical debate grant to vindicators of the marginalized or repressed a special licence to evade questions of artistic merit'.[25] While an earlier generation of Gothic critics established the transgressive tendencies of much of this literature, a host of new studies have demonstrated that there are also profoundly conservative aspects to the Gothic, including its tendency towards hyperbolic and chauvinistic types of nationalism, extraordinarily reactionary views of sexual deviance, and rigid paranoid policing of the domestic space. Gothic is a mode of writing riven with ambivalence, articulating both disgust and desire. It is too common in criticism to find one aspect or another being empha- sised at the expense of an understanding of Gothic in the round – although a close reading of these critics demonstrate that the general views they express are always made more problematic by their textual analyses. Baldick and Mighall, two of the tradition's best critics, have, for example, consistently drawn attention to the tendency within Gothic fiction to express disgust for Catholicism, the medieval, the past, and believe that the Gothic is essentially an Enlightenment genre since it rejects and denigrates the values of the past in favour of more liberal values. Critics such as David Punter, Fred Botting and Rosemary Jackson, on the other hand, have emphasised the 'transgressive' nature of much Gothic fiction, its *attraction* to the non-conformist, the Catholic, the past (or at least the version of these things believed by a Puritan Protestant society).[26] However, rather than conforming to either a 'conserva- tive' or a 'subversive' orientation, the Gothic is, as Tzvetan Todorov explained, radically ambivalent, and fails to decide between these two inflections of desire and disgust, modernity and the medieval.[27] I suggest that we try to avoid designations of the Victorians or the Gothic as oriented by either conservatism or subversion, hypocrisy or liberation, and instead realise that part of the reason why Gothic migrated everywhere in the nineteenth century, and part of the reason why there is no 'pure' Gothic or realist tradition in the Victorian period – since the Gothic and the realist cross-fertilise each other – is because the Gothic is not an aesthetically or ideologically stable mode.

It may be best to envision Gothic as a reaction to the social drama that took place as the modern age was born. Victor Turner has pointed out that social dramas take place in four main stages.

In the first stage normal social relations are undermined and a breach occurs; this breach is then extended and exacerbated in the second stage, which leads to the introduction of new mechanisms and relationships to redress the crisis in the third phase, and finally to the repair of the breach or the recognition that the breach is irreparable.[28] Modernity involved breaches in every sphere of society, a shift from town to country, from the pre-modern, quasi-feudal, agricultural round to the modern, capitalist and commercial world, opening up profound divisions between the mentality of the pre-modern past and the cosmopolitanism of the future. The movement, for example, from an agricultural to an industrial workplace was not represented simply as a shift from one geographical zone to another, but was weighted with moral and ideological ballast: movement was configured as improvement, and an intolerance towards the older, popular and 'superstitious' culture was indelibly linked to an urban lifestyle. Leonore Davidoff and Catherine Hall have described this transition very well:

> Rural culture, often represented to the middle classes by their domestic servants, became the repository of 'folklore', 'fairy tale', the supernatural, and dark and local family histories. Similarly, elements of boisterous play and carnival were separated and circumscribed, appropriated only for children and the inferior who were childlike.[29]

There is a sense, however, in which most of the population undergoing these shifts remained in Turner's third stage of adjustment and redress, never fully relinquishing attachment to the pre-modern, never fully giving commitment to the modern. In this third stage of accommodation there is an emphasis on what Turner calls 'liminality', when normal roles and rules are temporarily suspended and old forms are broken down. Turner writes that: 'the liminal phase has frequently been likened to death; to being in the womb; to invisibility; to darkness, bisexuality, and the wilderness'.[30] It is no surprise to find that such liminality or 'hesitancy' is also endemic to the Gothic, as Gothic is a means by which the third phase of the social drama is articulated. It is a kind of literary 'emergency', mobilised to prevent the final loss of old forms and modes of life linked to the pre-modern past, while also allowing its readers to grope their way towards accepting the new mode of life in modernity. In its hesitancy between two historical phases it is a way of being modern without relinquishing the pre-modern.

## Gothicising the Metropolis

The liminality of the Gothic explains why the genre is particularly attracted to the zones and sites where modern and pre-modern energies clash, such as, for example, the city. The growth of the metropolis was part of the reason why traditional Gothic fast became obsolete after the early 1820s – it was hard to be so frightened of the Catholic Continent when it seemed that much more terrible things were happening in the dark alleys and lanes of the city in which you lived. Jane Austen's *Northanger Abbey* (1818) might have parodied the traditional Gothic fear of Continental Catholics and their nefarious activities, but she did so only to re-situate the Gothic precisely where she thought it belonged: in the English home. Domesticating the Gothic effectively released its energies, and the growth of the industrial city allowed the stock characters of the genre to rematerialise in a new place. If foreign Catholics were no longer so central to the Gothic, they had not gone away but were simply reformulated as the urban under-classes (Benjamin Disraeli did, after all, call the working-classes a separate nation in *Sybil* (1845)). The city served a dual function, as both a powerful representation of modernity and its horrific underside. Julian Wolfreys has identified a widespread 'citephobia' in much discussion of nineteenth-century London,[31] while Richard Lehan argues that, far from expressing a faith in the spread of civilisation, the representation of London in the nineteenth century demonstrates an increasing 'hostility in the literary imagination – a hostility that went hand in hand with a distrust of Enlightenment values'.[32] The city was the new site in which Gothic plots and characters could work out their destinies. Far from simply freeing the population from their imprisonment in the superstitious past, the city incarcerated them in new kinds of barbarity and tyranny.

In an important study of the metropolis in the Gothic imagination, Robert Mighall argues that nineteenth-century Gothic writers turned from the Catholic Continent to the urban slums of London because they were convinced that these places were the sites of a kind of medieval survival, places where modernity had not yet penetrated fully. He vigorously argues that

> Victorian Gothic fiction is obsessed with identifying and depicting the threatening reminders or scandalous vestiges of an age from which the present is relieved to have distanced itself. Where the 'vestigal' is found (in monasteries, prisons, lunatic asylums, the urban slums, or even the bodies, minds, or psyches of criminals, deviants or relatively 'normal' subjects) depends upon historical circumstances.[33]

For Mighall these writers blame not the forces of modernity, but rather the failure of modernity to penetrate all the dark corners of the cosmopolis and eradicate the medieval remnants that can still be found there.[34]

In this view, the East End and its environs become what Mighall calls the 'new regions of romance', where 'vestiges' of the medieval can still be found terrorising the masses.[35] To prove his argument Mighall turns to one of Victorian Britain's most ambitious and popular attempts to intellectually map the city, George William MacArthur Reynolds's *The Mysteries of London*, and its continuation *The Mysteries of the Court of London*, which appeared as weekly penny serials from October 1844 to 1856. Mighall contends that, for Reynolds, urban slums were old and ancient institutions left behind, rather than caused, by modernisation, since 'to acknowledge that some slums were modern … would inhibit his anachronistic emphasis, thus making the move from the castle or convent of the early tradition to its urban equivalent more difficult'.[36] However, I believe that far from being convinced that modernity is the cure for all ills, the *Mysteries* articulate not only a nostalgia for the pre-modern past but a conviction that new horrors are being created by the new city. Much in the *Mysteries* could easily be mistaken for sociological reportage, and Reynolds is far from consistent in painting the Gothic slum and villain as medieval remnants rather than as modern products. In his Prologue to *The Mysteries of London*, for example, Reynolds places the blame for urban depravity firmly on modernity and 'whig history', claiming that while 'the bounties of civilisation are at present almost everywhere recognised', the problems associated with civilisation have been ignored: 'for centuries has Civilisation established, and for centuries will it maintain, its headquarters in the great cities of Western Europe: and with Civilisation does Vice go hand-in-hand' (3).[37] Reynolds's point is precisely that as civilisation progresses, so too does sin. Vice is civilisation's handmaiden, not something by which it is banished or obliterated. If, for Reynolds, the labyrinth is the best image to represent the horrific Gothic confusion of London's poor districts, this is due to the fact that it is only in modernity that the city establishes itself as labyrinthine: the city as a physical and moral maze is directly related to the growth and intensification of the population, both of which are caused by industrialisation.

Certain characters in his novel do express their belief that civilisation has passed by certain areas, thereby allowing the medieval past to rear its ugly head in dens of vice and squalor, but these characters are invariably speaking from a naively myopic view. Walter Sydney, the woman who goes disguised as a man and whose horrifying near-death experience in an extraordinarily Gothic Old House in Smithfield opens the narrative, opines that

> it seemed to me that I was wandering amongst all the haunts of crime and appalling penury of which I had read in romances, but which I never could have believed to exist in the very heart of the metropolis of the world. Civilisation appeared to me to have chosen particular places which it condescended to visit, and to have passed others by without even leaving a foot-print to denote its presence. (29)

However, a few chapters later we are visiting 'the Hell', a horrific gambling den in which the well-to-do behave like disguised versions of the 'wild cats' Sydney encountered in Smithfield (31).

Our hero, Richard Markham, is horrified at the prospect that men of such character 'are such wretches' but is assured by his companion that 'they do not care a fig what may happen so long as they get the money'. This scene ends with the losing gambler blowing his brains out and his body being found 'upon the carpet weltering in his blood' (36–7). Reynolds moves the reader through one den of horrors to another – some exist in the East End, but others are fashionable places where the sophisticated gather. There is never any suggestion that what we find in 'the Hell' is a piece of pre-modern depravity: it is merely a civilised type of the money-grabbing that goes on in Smithfield and Whitechapel. They are both Gothic spaces produced by modernity.

Population density, one of the characteristics of modern city life, according to the sociologist Louis Wirth,[38] causes all kinds of problems with which the medieval city did not have to deal, and this is precisely what is highlighted by Reynolds' narrative as the source of horrific recreations of scenes once thought confined to medieval monasteries, such as the living and dead being confined together:

> in that densely populated neighbourhood that we are describing, hundreds of families each live and sleep in one room. When a member of one of these families happens to die, the corpse is kept in the close room where the rest still continue to live and sleep. Poverty frequently compels the unhappy relatives to keep the body for days – aye, and weeks. (38)

Again he complains that 'Fair and attractive as the mighty metropolis may appear to the superficial observer, it swarms with disgusting, loathsome, and venomous objects wearing human shapes' (46). It is the modern London that produces monsters, not its medieval counterpart, since 'The country that contains the greatest wealth of all the territories of the universe, is that which also knows the greatest amount of hideous, revolting, heart-rending misery' (92). Indeed, as Trefor Thomas has emphasised, both serials are written in the form of the modern city, incorporating the demotic styles and forms, such as street ballads, journalese and criminal biography, basic to working-class life there.[39]

Reynolds also appropriates information found in contemporary inquiries into the state of London's poor, such as the reports of the Commission for Inquiry into the Employment and Condition of Children in Mines and Manufactures (1842), whose descriptions of mining life reappear in the story of Meg Flathers, who tells of working in the mines from a young age. On her first journey down into the darkness she is disgusted by what she finds:

> There they were, as black as negroes – eating, laughing, chattering, and drinking. But, to my surprise and disgust, I saw that the women and young girls were all naked from the waist upwards, and many of the men completely so. And yet there was no shame – no embarrassment!. (176)

The report makes it clear that many children, some of only four years of age, were working up to sixteen hours a day; it speaks of men and women working naked and fornicating; illustrations depict their undressed condition and were considered semi-pornographic. Although, after the report, a bill outlawing the employment of girls and women in the mines – for moral reasons – was passed, boys' employment was still permitted. Reynolds's dependence on and incorporation of these reports suggests that these serials should be seen as, in part, sociological studies themselves. M. Christine Boyer points out that much of the discourse about London in the nineteenth century was produced in order that the 'invisible city' – the slums, the sewers, the mines – could be made visible through representation, a belief that Reynolds appears to share.[40] However, while sociological investigators accepted the city's depravity but believed that by bringing it to the surface it could actually be banished by modernisation and development, the *Mysteries* appears to have no such faith in the progress of 'civilisation' being matched by morality (285).[41]

The ambivalence towards modernity evident in the *Mysteries* repeats itself in Charles Dickens's *Bleak House* (1852–3) which is among the most important novels published in the nineteenth century; it ambitiously attempts to provide a reading of the entire city of London in one text, exploring every aspect of the metropolis in depth. Although clearly a 'realist' novel, Dickens employs

Gothic tropes and indeed a Gothic architecture to explain the metropolis. Alan Pritchard argues that *Bleak House* is a very successful 'adaptation' of the Gothic to the modern urban environment, in which every convention of the old tradition has an equivalent in the new, including goblins (Krook), vampires (Vholes) and ogres (Smallweed).[42] The narrative is famously convoluted, depending on two principal speakers, an unnamed and supposedly 'omniscient' male narrator, whose recitation is interrupted by the first-person narrative of Esther Summerton, a major character in the story being told. In other words, the means by which the story gets told has much more in common with *Frankenstein* (1818) and *Dracula* (1897) than it has with *Middlemarch* or *The Way we Live Now* (1874–5). In her study of the Gothic, Eve Kosofsky Sedgwick isolates it as a form dealing with repetition, multiple narrators, stories within stories, 'the difficulty a story has in getting itself told'.[43] This narrative echo of the Gothic form is repeated in the title of Dickens's novel, which suggests that in this text the reader will encounter the English equivalent of the Gothic castles which populated the novels of Ann Radcliffe and Horace Walpole.

Ironically, *Bleak House* might sound like a haunted palace, but it is London itself, the great cosmopolis, which turns out to be haunted. Mighall maintains that in Dickens's mapping of the city he effectively reproduces the geographical disparity of the early Gothic novels which were set on the Continent, arguing that Dickens ensures that the lower-class regions of the city, where the Gothic rears its ugly head, are kept apart from the more salubrious districts, where the respectable characters live and where modernity has thrived. Those who venture into 'darkest London' act as urban explorers, recreating at home what the early Gothic novelists represented abroad. The foreign may now be housed in the domestic, but it is no less outlandish and anachronistic for that.[44] However, *pace* Mighall, in the version of the city offered in *Bleak House* it is never clear that medieval 'survivals' account for modern monstrosity, particularly since the novel takes an ambiguous attitude to time itself. The opening salvo in this Gothic depiction of London sees a dinosaur trooping down the streets of the modern capital:

London. Michaelmas Term lately over, and the Lord Chancellor sitting in Lincoln's Inn Hall. Implacable November weather. As much mud in the streets, as if the waters had not but newly retired from the face of the earth, and it would not be wonderful to meet a Megalosaurus, forty feet long or so, waddling like an elephantine lizard up Holborn Hill. Smoke lowering down from the chimney-pots, making a soft black drizzle with flakes of soot in it as big as full grown snow-flakes – gone into mourning, one might imagine, for the death of the sun (ch. 1, 13).[45]

This is an extraordinary passage, and covers huge ranges of time, from the Flood to future cosmic disintegration. An atmosphere of apocalypse, rather than enlightenment, hangs over everything. Rather than an emerging utopia, we have a primordial monster covered in mud and fog. As Martin Tropp points out, the dinosaur suggests 'the pervasive influence of the past',[46] but it also indicates that this past cannot be eradicated by modernity and that the future will be much like the past, if the allusion to the 'death of the sun' is anything to go by. There is no escape from past sin, or, indeed, human nature, which is what is suggested by the reference to mud and dirt. This is the primordial slime from which the Creator made us, and because of which He sent the flood to wipe us off the earth. The story of the Noachian flood is a simple one of human depravity followed by the punishment of a righteous judge. The Lord God of the Genesis creation and flood is starkly contrasted to the 'Lord Chancellor', sitting on his throne in Lincoln's Inn Hall, who is unable to dispense justice because he is as corrupt as those he is judging. The Lord expunged evil humanity off the face of the planet; the Lord Chancellor perpetuates this evil, rather than punishes it. He is sitting in 'the very heart of the fog'. London is a nexus of the ages in which past and future, Genesis and Apocalypse, are refined and zoned, presided over by moral pollution, perpetuated by modern bureaucracy (ch. 1, 14).

Dickens constantly translates traditional Gothic tropes and props into modern realist terms, not to evacuate the Gothic or to strip it of its power, but to introject it into the institutions and the situations pervasive throughout England. In this way the Gothic becomes more realistic, but the real also becomes more like a Gothic nightmare. What Dickens does is reveal the Gothic as the basis of the real. Thus, instead of the 'found' document, the cliché of the Gothic, we have the missing wills and documents which could clear up the ancient Jarndyce and Jarndyce case; the labyrinthine dungeons of the Castle of Otranto and the monasteries of Maturin are replaced here by the tortuous and obscure nature of the suit in which all these characters are embroiled. The horrific thing about this labyrinth is that every character in the novel is in some way, however tangential, connected to the Jarndyce and Jarndyce case, and this novel contains so many characters that it is difficult to keep up. In this plot the universe becomes a vast maze in which everyone is trapped and to which there is one key, which has been lost. The court of Chancery is like a vast octopus with limbs everywhere in the land: it 'has its decaying houses and its blighted lands in every shire; its worn-out lunatic in every madhouse, and its dead in every churchyard' (ch. 1, 15). There is simply no escaping it, and it remains as potent and powerful at the end of the novel as it was at the start: it is like a monster in a horror movie which simply cannot be killed, no matter what local victories can be gained. The novel itself is as gargantuan and never-ending as the Gothic city it invokes, a city stocked with typical Gothic props at every turn. Wolfreys argues that Dickens's 'writing of the city covers so much that, like the city of London itself, it seems virtually endless, infinite', a statement that is especially true of *Bleak House*.[47] Mr Krook and his house is the most obvious case of a Gothic villain and setting being transposed into a realist novel. As Tropp points out, Krook lives in 'a charnel house of waste',[48] stuffed with sacks of women's hair and old documents with secrets gathering dust, where Krook himself is like a walking skeleton, 'cadaverous and withered; with his head sunk sideways between his shoulders, and the breath issuing in visible smoke from his mouth as if he were on fire within' (ch. 5, 68). We find out later that he is indeed internally burning – he spontaneously combusts. Although Dickens gallantly sought to argue that this was a completely realistic moment and that the most up-to-date science supported him, it is clear that this is, in fact, the most Gothic element of the text.

*Sensationalising Modernity*

The transfer of Gothic devices from the Continental castle to the British home is most evident in the development of the genre of Sensation Fiction, a term first applied to novels published in the 1860s, beginning with Wilkie Collins's *The Woman in White* (1859–60), a genre best thought of as a kind of 'suburban Gothic', and which eventually segued into the emerging genre of the detective story. Just as the development of urban Gothic shows how modernity is considered to produce horrors of its own not reducible to the anachronistic or to history, so the suburban thrills of Sensation Fiction demonstrate categorically that, far from bringing enlightenment, modernity produces monsters. Jenny Bourne Taylor claims that:

> Sensation fiction ... drew on and broke down distinct methods of generating strangeness within familiarity, of creating the sense of a weird and different world within the ordinary, everyday one ... And it was through these intricate interactions that its appeal to sensation, to 'nerves', had both such psychological resonance and social complexity, providing it with the means that enabled it to explore 'those most mysterious of mysteries, the mysteries that are at our own doors'.[49]

Rather than needing the trappings of the ancient past, Sensation Fiction locates horror inside the houses and the bodies of respectable men and women, often of the middle classes, the most modern of peoples, and the appearance of the sensation and detective novels was implicated in the increasing interest in crime and sexual and family scandals in the Victorian press.[50] The modernity of Sensation Fiction was noticed by most of its critics in the 1860s and 1870s, one arguing that

> A writer who takes boldly in hand the common mechanism of life, and by means of persons, who might all be living in society for anything we can tell to the contrary, thrills us into wonder, terror and breathless interest ... has accomplished a far greater success than he who effects the same result through supernatural agencies.[51]

While the attempt to excavate the Gothic spaces of the domestic was praised by some, others were concerned about the effects this scepticism about suburbia would cause. The Archbishop of York complained in 1865 that

> [Sensation novelists] wanted to persuade people that in almost every one of the well-ordered houses of their neighbours there was a skeleton shut up in some cupboard; that their comfortable and easy-looking neighbour had in his breast a secret story which he was always going about trying to conceal.[52]

Mary Elizabeth Braddon's *Lady Audley's Secret* (1861–2) is a brilliant example of this geographical and physical shift from the past, the anachronistic, to the present, the modern. Although much of the action of the novel is focused around Audley Court, an ancestral mansion, as pointed out by Nick Daly, the crimes committed by Lady Audley are permitted by the railway network and the anonymity of modern cosmopolitan life.[53] The narrator, indeed, warns those who think that geographical and social distance from the 'primitive' orders provides any protection from crime:

> We hear every day of murders committed in the country. Brutal and treacherous murders; slow, protracted agonies from poisons administered by some kindred hand; sudden and violent deaths by cruel blows, inflicted with a stake cut from some spreading oak, whose very shadow promised – peace … No crime has ever been committed in the worst rookeries about Seven Dials that has not been also done in the face of that sweet rustic calm … (57)[54]

In linking the railway network with moral and intellectual degeneracy Braddon echoed Lord Shaftesbury's warning that 'the very power of locomotion keeps persons in a state of great nervous excitement', and his complaint that many who use the rail network 'have been obliged to give it up in consequence of the effect on the nervous system'.[55]

Modern infrastructure is not the only focus for withering evaluation here. Modern discourses of psychology are also critiqued as helping to hide rather than truly explain criminal passion. Lady

Audley conjures up the old image of female hysteria as the cause of her crimes, but the doctor attending the 'case' admits that 'there is no madness in anything that she has done … She employed intelligent means, and she carried out a conspiracy which required coolness and deliberation in its execution' (vol. III, ch. 5, 370). Yet, despite his conviction that there is no real madness in the case, he is prepared to allow the vocabulary of the psychologist to be used to lock Lady Audley up. What is done to Lady Audley by contemporary psychology is shocking: instead of incarcerating her in a convent to expiate her moral crimes, as is the fate of Agnes in *The Monk* (1796), she is confined to a Belgian asylum, a place where the best modern psychological medicine is offered. In other words, the punishment is the same, but the rhetoric surrounding it has changed. A Belgian asylum is the equivalent of a Spanish convent in all but name; modernity has not produced means by which to end the abuse of women but merely provided new means of perpetuating this abuse. The doctor's actions are more despicable, given that he certainly does not subscribe to the notion that insanity is a peculiarly feminine trait, insisting that 'Madness is not necessarily transmitted from mother to daughter' (vol. III, ch. 5, 370). Despite this, he conspires with other men to have Lady Audley confined in order to spare the blushes of her new husband. The modern medical establishment turns out to be as complicit with power as the old monastic ones. This is not a case of a medieval vestige, but simply of modern perpetuation of the crimes of the past, and is part of a (proto-feminist?) critique of the instruments of power: medieval or modern, the control remains in the hands of men who will use whatever rhetoric at hand to justify oppression. This is essentially the same moral as is preached in Joseph Sheridan Le Fanu's *The Rose and the Key* (1871), in which the heroine Mathilda is also confined to a private asylum – purely so that her evil relatives can claim her property. In an era when men often had their wives declared insane and incarcerated when they became too difficult to handle, that Braddon should have turned her destructive scrutiny on this practice is significant.

The novel as a whole is certainly not sympathetic to modern asylums, the narrator opining that

Madhouses are large and only too numerous; yet surely it is strange they are not larger, when we think of how many helpless wretches must beat their brains against this hopeless persistency of the orderly outward world, as compared with the storm and tempest, the riot and confusion within. (vol. II, ch. 6, 206)

The novel appears to be divided as to whether 'madness' is a label attached to women who transgress versions of the feminine deemed orthodox, or whether madness in women is actually caused by the kind of life a normal Victorian woman is expected to live. It poses a disturbing possibility to its Victorian readers, warning that the versions of femininity deemed most respectable could be used as disguises for female criminals, but also that these versions actually cause such female criminality. This was especially troubling since, as Anthea Trodd has pointed out, the angel-in-the-house was also the person in charge of protecting the skeletons in the cupboard: 'The heroine of the period was expected to be the soul of candour but also to preserve the family secrets; crime plots expose the contradictions involved in those demands.'[56]

Crime plots also expose the means by which modernity can produce ghouls of its own rather than relying on medieval remnants. In this novel the modern as well as the medieval is a world of male power; rather than attack Lady Audley as a despicable monster, the novel understands what has driven her to act so transgressively. Braddon herself was living with, and having children by, a man whose wife was confined to an asylum in Ireland – although this kind of detail may not have been known to very many of her readers – so the link between female insanity and infidelity would have been difficult for her to tackle, and what is detectable in the novel is a central ambivalence between resentment of her 'insane' love rival, and outraged sympathy at her plight. This contributes to the conflicted versions of the 'heroine' offered to its readers. Elaine Showalter points out that

Lady Audley's unfeminine assertiveness ... must ultimately be described as madness, not only to spare Braddon the unpleasant necessity of having to execute an attractive heroine, with whom she in many ways identifies, but also to spare the woman reader the guilt of identifying with a cold-blooded killer.[57]

In the homosocial Victorian world women needed to become ever more resourceful to preserve their space; Lady Audley has found the perfect means of manipulating the stereotypes of femininity (she is so good at playing the angel-in-the-house that she is almost ethereal at the start of the novel) produced by men to contain and possess women (rather than give them the vote, men would prefer to worship at their feet), while exposing its limitations. We are told at the start of the novel that:

> Wherever she went she seemed to take joy and brightness with her. In the cottages of the poor her fair face shone like a sunbeam. She would sit for a quarter of an hour talking to some old woman, and apparently as pleased with the admiration of a toothless cone as if she had been listening to the compliments of a marquis; and when she tripped away, leaving nothing behind her … the old woman would burst out into senile raptures with her grace, her beauty, and her kindliness, such as she never bestowed upon the vicar's wife, who half fed and clothed her. (vol. I, ch. 1, 11)

Lady Audley looks and behaves like a perfect example of what has been termed the 'proper' feminine, although there is an 'improper' one lurking underneath her performance.[58] If this is what the angel-in-the-house can do, then how is it possible for men to trust them and get on with creating a homosocial network from which women are excluded?

This possible 'feminist', 'subversive' reading would go some way towards explaining the novel's depiction of Robert Audley. After all, rather than heroic, Robert starts out as a man acting extremely suspiciously, at least in terms of conventional codes of male behaviour. A 'handsome, lazy, care-for-nothing fellow, of about seven-and-twenty', he is described as possessing a 'listless, dawdling, indifferent, irresolute manner'. Although he is a qualified barrister, he 'had never either had a brief, or tried to get a brief, or even wished to have a brief in all those five years' (vol. I, ch. 4, 35). Completely lacking a Protestant work-ethic, he is also rather effeminate in both characteristic and behaviour, often acting as if he is auditioning for the role of decadent aesthete. He spends most days sitting around smoking and reading French

novels with his 'shirt collar turned down and a blue silk handker-
chief tied loosely about his neck'. He may also be squandering his
time reminiscing about his days in college spent in the company
of George Talboys, for whom he possesses an interest threatening
to spill over into love. When George disappears, Robert is
apoplectic and cannot accept the loss of his friend. At one point
he despairs 'I have never eaten a good dinner at this table since I
lost George Talboys' (vol. I, ch. 19, 154). The novel revolves
around male loyalties and friendships, primarily that of Robert
and George, but also of Robert and his uncle, whose codes are
epitomised by the doctor's willingness to ignore his professional
judgement so that a man with a good name is not tainted by association with a criminal woman. Lady Audley is a threat to these
homosocial relations, not only because she is loyal to herself, but
also because she threatens to reveal them for what they possibly
are: homosociality bordering on the verge of homosexuality. Of
course, Eve Kosofsky Sedgwick has long pointed out 'the potential unbrokenness of a continuum between homosocial and
homosexual'.[59] Robert's obsession with George cannot, of course,
be acknowledged for what it is and must be contained within a
more acceptable version of masculinity. George's sister Clara thus
serves as the perfect foil, especially since she looks exactly like her
brother, 'so like the friend whom he had loved and lost, that it was
impossible for him to think of her as a stranger' (vol. II, ch. 6,
203). Sedgwick argues, in *Epistemology of the Closet*, that

> because the paths of male entitlement, especially in the nineteenth
> century, required certain intense bonds that were not readily distin-
> guishable from the most reprobated bonds, an endemic and
> ineradicable state of what I am calling homosexual panic became
> the normal condition of male heterosexual entitlement.[60]

While Lady Audley poses a threat to any recreation of the male
bonds George and Robert had created in Eton, and indeed pushes
them towards a more explicit confession, Clara Talboys serves as a
means of preserving these bonds within an outwardly heterosexual
economy, and this is demonstrated when they all live happily ever
after in a rural idyll together at the end of the novel.[61]

In this Introduction I have suggested that while Gothic certainly expresses antagonism towards pre-modern forms of living, it also harbours a desire for them, so that as a mode it walks a tightrope between being a force for modernisation and performing a bitter critique of such social transformations, especially as it relates to the migration from a rural to an urban environment. In the four chapters which follow I will attempt to follow this Gothic uncertainty as it manifests itself in a number of different sites through a number of different themes. Chapter 1 will look at how time was given a Gothic make-over in the nineteenth century, understandable when ideas about time were being challenged so seriously by the disciplines of geology and biology. Chapter 2 focuses on the figure of the child, long recognised as central to Victorian culture. This child is both beset by Gothic monsters and threats, and is itself configured as a monstrous threat to its parents and to society in general. Given the colonial expansion experienced in the nineteenth century, chapter 3 concentrates on how Gothic imagery was used to portray marginal ethnicities within the Empire and terrifying foreigners outside it. Chapter 4 examines occult themes and props that crop up repeatedly in Victorian culture and literature, from spectres to Satan, and argues for the centrality of the Gothic in negotiating new religious roles for a century tracked (though not overcome) by doubt and despair. While I have tried to cover as much Gothic ground as possible, some texts can be referred to only in passing, while others have been passed over completely. This is unavoidable in tackling the mutating traces of the Gothic through a field as voluminous as Victorian literature, but I hope the survey will allow individual readers and researchers to begin their own work.

# 1

# *The Ghosts of Time*

## History and the Victorians

It has long been recognised that Gothic is in many ways a grappling with the forces of time and history. In one critical intervention, Mark Madoff argued persuasively that the eighteenth-century use of the term 'Gothic' is bound up with notions of 'ancestry' and inheritance, with establishing an imaginative connection to the now anachronistic past rather than the present or the future.[1] The investment of the Gothic in history has not always been taken seriously. There has been a marked tendency in literary critical terms to distinguish Gothic from the historical novel as it emerged in the writing of Sir Walter Scott. The Marxist Georg Lukács, in his *The Historical Novel* (1937), argued forcefully that fiction before Scott – particularly Walpole's *Otranto* – used history as atmosphere and costume, while Scott took historical knowledge seriously.[2] However, as Fiona Robertson has explained, the division between the historical and the Gothic novel 'did not seem obvious to Scott'. She insists that 'Gothic modes of history were not preparations for the real thing [the historical novel] but ways of presenting the past and imaginative responses to the past which survive in the Waverley novels'.[3] This helps to explain the continued relevance of Gothic tropes and themes in Scott's writing, and also dispels the suspicion that Gothic novelists were not 'serious' when they invoked the past;

both the historical novel and Gothic fiction ask important questions concerning the relevance of history to the present, and interrogate versions of legitimacy central to national mythology. There is no clear line demarcating the historical novel from the Gothic, and most Victorian writers with an investment in the Gothic, including Charles Dickens, Edward Bulwer Lytton, Wilkie Collins, the Brontës, Charles Reade, Arthur Conan Doyle and Thomas Hardy, also wrote historical novels. The relationship between these two genres was osmotic and cross-fertilising, and together they highlight the centrality of historical inheritance to the nineteenth-century mind.

In the Gothic the past is never completely finished with; instead, it has a nasty habit of bursting through into the present, displacing the contemporary with the supposedly outdated. Although time was a concern for eighteenth-century Britons, Victorians had even more temporal baggage to grapple with, for many reasons. In the first place, the Victorians were enthralled by the idea of Progress and, superficially at least, devoted to the notion of 'modernisation', self-consciously modern in social and cultural terms. In broad terms, 'modernity' is centrally concerned with both rejecting the past and laying it to rest. As Michel de Certeau has argued, 'modern Western history essentially begins with the differentiation between the past and the present'.[4] In this model the past is configured as a nightmare plagued by superstition, tyranny and backwardness, while the present is conversely thought of as enlightened, tolerant and progressive.

Raymond Tumbleson has traced how this credulous, autocratic past was identified as Catholic, while the progressive present resulted from the break with Catholicism in the Reformation. During the reign of the Catholic King James II, Protestant polemicists aggressively depicted Catholicism as a sink of superstition and idolatry and concomitantly praised the Protestant present as sourced in pure reason, a dichotomy seen in such significant Protestant exercises in apologetical propaganda as Edward Stillingfleet's *A Rational Account of the Grounds of the Protestant Religion* (1665) and *Originae Sacrae, or a Rational Account of the Grounds of the Christian Faith* (1662), Samuel Johnson's *The Absolute Impossibility of Transubstantiation Demonstrated* (1688) and

Robert Boyle's *Reasons Why a Protestant Should Not Turn Papist* (1687).[5]

Rejecting the Catholic past by configuring it as grotesque and monstrous is central to Gothic literature. In its fetishisation of the present and the future, the nineteenth century displayed an almost neurotic fixation on escaping the burden of the past, in which exercise the Gothic played no small part. The Industrial Revolution, with its accompanying transformation of communication and manufacturing technology, encouraged those living through it to see the age as 'modern', as never before. Jerome Buckley has called the belief in Progress 'a primary dogma of the Victorian period'.[6] For many, 'History' was concerned with the emergence of the modern, it was the history of progress, and historians like Thomas Macaulay emphasised the barbarism of the past and the progressivism of the present. His *History of England from the Accession of James II* (1849–61) is considered one of the greatest examples of what is called 'Whig' history, a reading of the past as a way to the present; indeed, a reading of the past as directioned towards the present, moving from medieval darkness to modern light. Macaulay believed that

> The history of England is emphatically the history of progress ... To us, we will own, nothing is so interesting as to contemplate the steps by which the England of Domesday Book, the England of the Curfew and the Forest Laws, the England of the crusaders, monks, schoolmen, astrologers, serfs, outlaws, became the England which we know and love, the classic ground of liberty and philosophy, the school of knowledge, the mart of all trade.[7]

To some commentators the Gothic aesthetic served to enunciate and confirm this general progressive spirit that can be sensed throughout the Victorian age. Chris Baldick and Robert Mighall argue powerfully that the Gothic is a mode centrally concerned with expressing antagonism towards the atavistic, Catholic past, and loyalty to the enlightened present and future. 'Gothic fiction', they argue, 'is essentially Whiggish ... [the Gothic] delights in depicting the delusions and iniquities of a (mythical) social order and celebrating its defeat by modern progressive values.'[8] This mythical anachronistic social order is precisely Catholic in culture, which explains the Continental location of many Gothic texts:

> For if the good characters are 'modern' types drawn from Richardsonian sentimental fiction, the villains are characteristically archaic, their principal function being to represent the values of a benighted antiquity. Modern values are confirmed and modern virtues rewarded in the denouement, when the heroine escapes finally from the clutches of the Inquisition and is allowed to marry the suitor of her choice as she takes up residence in a tastefully designed villa, allowing the feudal castle to fall into ruins.[9]

In his important study of Victorian Gothic Mighall extends this claim and insists that 'The Gothic dwells in the historical past, or identifies "pastness" in the present, to reinforce a distance between the enlightened now and the repressive or misguided then.'[10]

As rhetorically persuasive as this argument is, however, ultimately the Gothic does not work in precisely this way; for Gothic writers the past was a place which could also be used to highlight the existential emptiness of the present, rather than its optimistic plenitude. After all, Jerome Buckley has theorised that as well as being fascinated by the future, the Victorians were 'obsessed' with the past, an obsession he finds in places as diverse as John Henry Newman's attempt to trace nineteenth-century Anglicanism back to the primitive Church, Charles Darwin's musings over the 'origin' of species, the proliferation of memento mori, the public fascination with dinosaurs, geological investigation into the ages of rocks, and the development of photography.[11]

Rejection of the past, enchantment with the present and hope for the future was not the only attitude to time and modernity that can be detected in the nineteenth century, and the Gothic represents not simply a mode for ecstatic celebration but also one of melancholic warning. Many were concerned that there was something seriously wrong with modern culture, something missing, and they sought that lack in the ruins of the past and the Catholic culture that had been rejected. As well as denuding the world of 'magic' and 'superstition', after all, modernity was believed to have drained meaning and wonder from creation. The sociologist Max Weber has described modernity as bound up in a 'disenchantment' of the world, and this ontological bleeding left a spiritual, emotional, moral and psychological vacuum at the heart of 'progress'.[12] Peter Berger puts it like this:

> If compared to the fullness of the Catholic universe, Protestantism appears as a radical truncation, a reduction to 'essentials' at the expense of the vast wealth of religious contents ... Protestantism may be described in terms of an immense shrinkage in the scope of the sacred in reality, as compared with its Catholic adversary ... At the risk of some simplification, it can be said that Protestantism divested itself as much as possible from the three most ancient and most powerful concomitants of the sacred – miracle, mystery, and magic.[13]

As the burden of making-meaning of the cosmos fell on to the shoulders of modern man, the weight became increasingly difficult for him to carry with psychological ease. The expansion of human responsibility for the world turned out to be an existential load so evident in the anxiety characteristic of modern men and women. Berger calls modern man 'a very nervous Prometheus',[14] and this was certainly marked in Victorian Britain. While a belief in human potential seems to be liberating, social and psychological difficulties quickly emerge from such new pressures. This sense of national psychological trauma – the trauma of what the sociologist Emile Durkheim termed 'anomie'[15] – creates nostalgia for the pre-modern period. The development of Romanticism was the most important expression of this nostalgia for the things denied by modernity, but it also explains why much Gothic literature reverts to what Robert Miles calls the 'Gothic cusp',[16] the intellectual fault-line dividing the Protestant English present from the foreign Catholic past, not simply to re-inforce that boundary, but to breach it and allow the past to return and, in some cases, undermine and banish the present.

Nostalgia for a more spiritually coherent past became more important in the nineteenth century after the detection of what has been called 'deep time', the discovery of a much longer past for both humankind and the earth. Geological investigation in general, and especially the publication of Charles Lyell's *Principles of Geology* (1830–3), announced to the British public that the earth was of an extraordinary age – indeed, an age which, it is fair to say, is unimaginable. Lyell argued strongly against geological orthodoxy, which held that a series of natural catastrophes had produced the present shape and structure of the earth, and proposed instead that change had come about very slowly over mind-bogglingly vast periods of time, in a theory known as uniformitarianism. Whereas many had previously hung on to Archbishop Ussher's claim that the cosmos was created *ex nihilo* in 4004 BC, this now seemed not only outdated but positively naive. Given the remarkable age of the earth, the idea that humankind, never mind individual men and women, were of cosmic significance came under extreme pressure. If the breach with the pre-Reformation past had appeared such an intense one to the societies of the seventeenth and eighteenth centuries, it began to seem rather parochial when viewed against the vast background of geological history. The reinvestigation of human history was one means of reorienting the self within the vicissitudes and vastness of time, and the Catholic Middle Ages took on an increasing fascination as an era when stability and meaning, time and self, appeared to be in harmony.

The Gothic is always ambivalent about the Catholic past; it desires that which has been excluded, yet it must repulse it simultaneously to maintain the coherence of the present. Rosemary Jackson's important study of fantasy argues that non-realism serves an important function in demonstrating what 'realistic' accounts of the world leave out and marginalise, indicating what 'cultural order' rests on.[17] The fantastic is a means to examine questions in ways which are deemed inappropriate in more 'realistic' kinds of literature, because in fantasy the desire which haunts the forbidden can be fully explored. A desire for the past has always been an aspect of modernity (hence the proliferation of nostalgia), and can be seen most obviously in the rhetoric of medieval merry England that pervades much conservative thought. Protestantism has always also desired the Catholic past as the Mother Church into whose arms it wants to return, but which it simultaneously despises. For this reason, anti-Catholicism should be seen as a version of Orientalism, since in fantasising about the Catholic Other, the average Protestant can indulge in many kinds of transgressive creativity. To paraphrase V. G. Kiernan, the rhetoric of anti-Catholicism has constituted a Protestant wet-dream,[18] and has acted, in Edward Said's terms, as a 'living tableau of queerness'.[19] This transgressive desire can be found in the vehemence with which Catholicism has been characterised as a discourse of perversity. A good example of this can be seen in the accusation that Catholics were responsible for the Great Fire of London, with one writer in 1680 producing a vision of what an England overtaken by Catholics would look like:

> your wives prostituted to the lust of every savage bog-trotter, your daughters ravished by goatish monks, your smaller children tossed upon pikes, or torn limb from limb, whilst you have your own bowels ripped up ... and holy candles made of your grease (which was done within our memory in Ireland) ... foreigners rendering your poor babes that can escape everlasting slaves, never more to see a Bible, nor hear the joyful sounds of Liberty and Property. This, this gentlemen, is Popery.[20]

Sexual desire and sexual disgust shadow each other in Gothic discourse, so that the average Gothic text is both a rapprochement with the Catholic past and a horrified reaction against it. The psychological knot of the Gothic form in which it subversively reaches out beyond the Protestant Real to its cultural and temporal Other, while simultaneously re-enacting the expulsion of Catholicism from the nation-state, explains a great deal about the convolutions of the mode and its attraction for a wide variety of people, for whom it provides some kind of historical closure. J. M. S. Tompkins points out that

> [the literary men of Protestant England] are very conscious of the picturesque attractions of convents, vows of celibacy, confessions and penance; they are seduced by the emotional possibilities of the situations that can be based on these usages; but they seldom fail to make it quite clear that they regard the usages as superstitious and irrational.[21]

The Gothic writer attempts to both undo some of the religious consequences of modernity – the disenchantment with the world, the over-dependence on the individual making meaning for himself, cultural and spiritual anomie – while perversely remaining committed to the ideology which has caused this disenchantment (Protestant reason, the power of the state). Ian Watt has explained that 'etymologically the term "Gothic Novel" is an oxymoron for "Old New"'[22]; this oxymoronic complexity works itself out in the competing discourses of the past inherent in the form, so that the Gothic novel is ultimately a reconciliation of competing discourses of history, Protestant modernity and Catholic medievalism, while also being a re-establishment of that competition. This intellectual and literary rapprochement with Catholicism was, of course, enabled in part by political changes. Colin Haydon has demonstrated that by the end of the eighteenth century, with the Jacobin threat effectively eliminated, it became more acceptable to express nostalgia for the Catholic past,[23] and it is no coincidence that the erection of Horace Walpole's Strawberry Hill House – an architectural embodiment of the potential reconciliation with Catholicism – began in the year after the Battle of Culloden. Catholic Emancipation in 1829 opened the possibilities for cultural investment in the Catholic past even further.

## Gothicising the Past

As both a writer of historical fiction and a leading Gothicist, William Harrison Ainsworth is a crucial figure in the Victorian examination of the relationship between past and present, and the way in which modernity not only depends upon, but yearns for, and yet inherently fears and despises, the pre-modern past. In a very thorough recent book-length study of Ainsworth, Stephen Carver has argued convincingly that this often neglected writer is a central bridging figure between the old Gothic tradition of Walpole and Maturin, and the diffusion of Gothic in the writings of the Brontës and Charles Dickens – but he is also a figure who demonstrates, like Scott, how central Gothic tropes are to historical recreation, since his novels are heady mixtures of Radcliffean

Gothic, proto-sensationalism, romance and realism.[24] Ainsworth was enormously popular in the early- to mid-Victorian period, a friend of Dickens and Collins, a respected editor, prolific author and highly controversial figure. He became an 'overnight success' with *Rookwood* (1834), but his Newgate novel *Jack Shepard* (1839) was believed by many to be an incitement of criminal behaviour, since it appeared to glamorise criminality and banditry. A historical novel like *The Lancashire Witches*, serialised in the *Sunday Times* from 1848–9, is a good place to begin an examination of the function of the Gothic past in Ainsworth's work, and is often believed to be his best novel.[25]

The novel is concerned with the legends of Lancashire (where Ainsworth grew up) witches in the sixteenth century. It is a compelling account, based in part on records and newspaper reports of the time, detailing the legacy of King Henry VIII's conversion of the state to a form of Anglican Protestantism, and how this impacted on areas like Lancashire. It opens in the middle of a revolt by a number of distinguished Catholics, pre-eminently John Paslew, Abbot of Whalley. He and his men are captured by the forces of the Crown and sentenced to death, but not before Paslew enters into a theological and psychological duel with Nicholas Demdike, formerly a monk of the same order as Paslew, who had been driven into a compact with Satan after Paslew tried to have him executed for a crime he did not commit. Demdike has since married and had a daughter but Paslew refuses to baptise her and instead utters a malediction on both mother and child, condemning them and their descendents as witches doomed to suffer for the satanic crimes of Demdike. The story then moves to the period of the reign of King James I, a zealous persecutor of witches, and examines the fate of Demdike's descendants and the community in which they live, and the inability of the past to lie down and die. Demdike's daughter is now Mother Demdike, the chief witch in the region, and with her rivals, Mistress Nutter and Mother Chattox, she holds the entire area in what is effectively a reign of terror. The plot evolves around the fate of Alizon Device, ostensibly Mother Demdike's granddaughter, but in reality the daughter of Mistress Nutter. The forces of evil seem determined to gain hold of her and convert her into a witch also, and the forces of good, led by her lover Richard Assheton and aided by the ghost of the Abbot Paslew (the most obviously Gothic element in the novel), have a hard time keeping her safe. After numerous tremendous set-pieces both Alizon and Richard die, although they maintain their theological orthodoxy, and are buried together in one grave.

Witches were clearly in fashion. Elizabeth Gaskell's *Lois the Witch* (1859) centres around the seventeenth-century Salem witch trials, with her heroine, Lois Barclay, mistakenly believed to be a witch after she arrives in Salem from England, searching for her relations. Gaskell's story exposes the prejudicial and credulous thinking that led to the Salem catastrophe and tries to demonstrate the human cost involved in what she believes to be outdated belief-systems. Ainsworth's novel is also deeply implicated in the ideological battle taking place between modernity and its historical nemeses, 'superstitious' world-views, this time Catholicism rather than Puritanism. The tussle over whether witches actually exist takes up much of the early part of the novel; the question is framed in terms of a debate between ignorant superstition – which believes in a whole host of marvellous phenomena – and enlightened reason – which believes only in what is accessible to the reasoned mind. Ainsworth is here articulating a debate that had been constant in Britain since the Reformation, given that in attacking Catholicism Anglican theologians had argued that reason was in the service of Protestantism. Indeed, Mark Goldie argues that modern scepticism has its basis in the post-Enlightenment attack on Catholic 'superstition', an attack which eventually led to the questioning of religion in its entirety.[26] From the standpoint of the nineteenth century, in which Ainsworth is writing, of course, the question of the existence of witches has been resolved: they do not exist, and the witch-crazes have been rationalised as due to a number of factors, including general ignorance and personal animosity, whereby some accused their neighbours of witchcraft to gain a territorial or financial advantage over them. Many characters in the novel articulate what had become the common case against the existence of witches and the explanations as to why anyone ever believed in them at all. Richard Assheton is always on hand to dispute with other characters who automatically assume the presence of supernatural agencies. When one man is found unable to move most of his limbs, the comical attorney Potts claims that this is an obvious case of witchcraft. Richard demurs: 'I offer no opinion ... but a paralytic stroke would produce the same effect' (236).[27] Much earlier in the novel, during a scene where a suspected witch is 'tested' by being dropped into the water while tied up (the 'ordeal by swimming'), he is again a voice of 'sanity', offering what we could call a rational theory of accusations:

> And see you not how easily the matter is explained? 'Give a dog an ill name and hang him' ... So with Mother Demdike. Whether really uttered or not, the abbot's curse upon her and her issue has been bruited abroad, and hence she is made a witch, and her children are supposed to inherit the infamous taint ... [T]he prejudice against her is sure to convict and destroy her ... Her great age, infirmities, and poverty, will be proofs against her. How can she, or any old enfeebled creature like her, whose decrepitude and misery should move compassion rather than excite fear – how can such a person defend herself against charges easily made and impossible to refute? I do not deny the possibility of witchcraft, even in our own days, though I think it of very unlikely occurrence; but I would determinately resist giving credit to any tales told by the superstitious vulgar, who, naturally prone to cruelty, have so many motives for revenging imaginary wrongs. (107–8)

When Mistress Nutter's house is attacked by her neighbour Roger Nowell, whom she has just bested in a boundary dispute and who now accuses her of being a witch, Richard levels the charge that Nowell is motivated not by religious zeal but mercenary envy:

> The magistrate who uses the arm of the law for purposes of private vengeance, and who brings a false and foul charge against his enemy, knowing that it cannot be repelled, is not entitled to any particular respect or honour. Thus you have acted against Mistress Nutter. Defeated by her in the boundary question ... you instantly accuse her of witchcraft, and seek to destroy her. (288)

As the voice of reason, Richard Assheton is persuasive in expressing the settled view of the nineteenth century.

The important point, however, is that he is completely wrong on each and every occasion. Mistress Nutter is indeed a witch, and a very powerful one at that, who, in collusion with Mother Demdike, has caused the boundary marks to move and the topography of the area to change so as to secure her territorial claims. Mother Demdike is far from being a weak and vulnerable woman open to accusations of witchcraft by those who are either ignorant or in enmity against her. When she finally enters the novel, very late in the plot, her malignant appearance is unforgettable:

> a face appeared, so frightful, so charged with infernal wickedness and malice, that Richard's blood grew chill at the sight. Was it man or woman? The white beard, and the large, broad, masculine character of the countenance seemed to denote the former, but the garb was that of a female. The face was at once hideous and fantastic – the eyes set across – the mouth awry – the right cheek marked by a mole shining with black hair, and horrible from its contrast to the rest of the visage, and the brow branded as if by a streak of blood. (305)

The point here is that the rational views of the Victorian present about the superstitions of the past are suddenly turned upside down, and it is the superstitions which turn out to be accurate indications of the true make-up of reality. The past is revealed as a terrifying hybrid beast whose home is in the yawning depths. We later see Mother Demdike emerge from a trapdoor out of the subterranean passages under her home in Malkin Castle, a representative of the ancient past come to regain power and authority. When she is finally caught she has retreated under the ground into a 'cavernous recess', like some weird but horrifically powerful fossil (356).

Although the plot moves inexorably towards the destruction of the witches so that by the end they have all been killed, their very existence has a corrosive effect on the rationalised arguments put forward by Richard Assheton for their non-existence. Even if the monsters and witches are exorcised by the end of the plot, by calling them into existence in the first place Gothic novelists like Ainsworth threaten the very basis on which the rational present is constituted. By projecting this debate into the past, and situating it at the historical fault-line of the Reformation, Ainsworth could be read as trying to make Victorian England immune from the threat of the witches. In other words, if an examination of these issues should occur, it is surely better to conduct them in a kind of historical test-tube cut off from the rest of history: whatever happened in sixteenth-century England cannot happen now. However, and as Ainsworth is clearly aware, things are not quite so simple, if only because of the fact that Victorian England is ideologically dependent on the sixteenth century for its self-definition. If *The Lancashire Witches* is a narratological and imaginative re-creation of the battle between the forces of modernity and pre-modernity, the present and the past, the sceptical and the superstitious, that took place in the decades after Henry VIII's transformation of the English landscape, then it also has bearings on the nineteenth century. The entire narrative, after all, is punctuated by a heightened sense, not of repulsion for this past but of nostalgia for those superstitious days of yore, and a concomitant alienation from the disenchanted present. As Stephen Carver claims, Ainsworth's novels reflect 'an increasing nostalgia for a pre-Enlightenment past over an increasingly rationalist and secular present'.[28]

Long descriptions of the sixteenth-century landscape and the buildings embedded in that landscape act as a means of highlighting the ontological gap haunting the Victorian present, a gap in which meaning has been evacuated. Consider, for example, the description of Mistress Nutter's house and environs as a good example of this tendency towards a pathological nostalgia. This is the dwelling-place of a powerful witch and 'seemed exactly adapted to its owner, and formed to hide dark and guilty deeds' (266). Yet, although the

> scenery was stern and somber, the hills were dark and dreary … the very wildness of the place was attractive, and the old house, with its grey walls, its lofty chimney, its gardens with their clipped yews, and its rook-haunted trees, harmonized well with all around it. (267)

This kind of contrast between fear and comfort happens repeatedly throughout the story. The novel acts as a folkloric compendium and revels in the customs of the Lancashire past, customs under threat from censorious nineteenth-century Puritanism. Ainsworth bathes the entire period in a warm glow of partly sexual desire, and numerous scenes of the sun setting or rising cover 'Catholic' Lancashire in a holy sheen:

> Evening was gradually stealing on, and all the exquisite tints marking that delightful hour, were spreading over the landscape. The sun was setting gorgeously, and a flood of radiance fell upon the old mansion beneath them, and upon the grey and venerable old church, situated on a hill adjoining it. The sounds were in unison with the hour, and the lowing of cattle, the voices of husbandmen returning from their work, mingled with the cawing of the rooks newly alighted on the high trees near the church, told them that bird, man, and beast were seeking their home for the night. (392)

A deep melancholy pervades such scenes, as the narrator suggests that this kind of England in cosmic harmony is about to die and go out of existence, that the sun is setting on a world-view (harmonious) and an environment (sacred, sacramental) as the move towards a modern cosmopolis is effected. Again and again the fertility and fecundity of the sixteenth-century environment are emphasised. The forests 'abounded with game', 'in its chases ranged herds of deer', 'the streams and polls were full of fish' (2).

And, of course, the forces of the Catholic Church are actually benevolent powers in this novel. It is the dead abbot Paslew who comes to rescue Alizon from the forces of darkness. We first see Paslew as he attempts the reconstitution of the Catholic Church in England after the order of Henry to raze the monasteries to the ground, and it is clear that the ideological bent of the novel is entirely opposed to this de-sacralisation of the landscape performed by the dismantling of the monastic orders. The era of Henry VIII is, to Ainsworth, a kind of axial age, a period of great turning and change, when a new and less coherent dispensation comes into existence. Whalley Abbey, where John Paslew was abbot, stimulates the narrator's intense desire for things now gone:

A sad, sad change hath come over Whalley Abbey. The libraries, well stored with reverend tomes, have been pillaged, and their contents cast to the flames; and thus long laboured manuscripts, the fruit of years of patient industry, with gloriously illuminated missals, are irrecoverably lost. The large infirmary no longer receiveth the sick; in the locutory sitteth no more the guest. No longer in the mighty kitchens are prepared the prodigious supply of meats destined for the support of the poor and the entertainment of the traveller ... But, though stripped of its wealth and splendour; though deprived of all the religious graces that, like rich incense, lent an odour to the fane, its external beauty is yet unimpaired, and its vast proportions undiminished (18–19).

This, we need to remind ourselves, was written the year after Pope Pius IX had agreed to restore the Catholic hierarchy in England, a move that was greeted with an abundance of 'no-popery' rhetoric and agitation, and is, in fact, a kind of critique of such anti-Catholic bigotry.[29]

Ainsworth's oeuvre repeatedly investigates this period of transition between the past and the present, the transition from the Catholic Middle Ages into a Protestant modernity, but reverses the value usually placed on these respective eras. Indeed, it is useful to compare Ainsworth's Gothic novels and their emotional investment in the Catholic past with the architectural redeployment of the Gothic by Augustus Welby Pugin. In his *Contrasts* (1836) Pugin repudiates the neoclassical style associated with ancient Greece and Rome and promotes English Gothic as a means of reconnecting with a more authentic emotional past, in which not only was the individual cherished (difficult in an age of 'deep time'), but the poor were looked after, the traveller was respected, stability was evident. This is clearly the kind of community valued by Ainsworth in his description of Whalley Abbey. Likewise, in his *Essay on the Development of Christian Doctrine* (1845), John Henry Newman went deep into Christian History to examine authenticity and found it in primitive Catholicism, rather than Protestantism. Stephen Carver believes that Ainsworth is an ideologically ambivalent writer who tends to side with the apparent victims of historical progress, rather than

41

having any particular political stance.[30] However, many of his contemporaries actually believed that Ainsworth had converted to Catholicism, given his sympathetic portrayal of Catholic figures throughout his writing life, though it appears that toleration rather than an actual re-establishment of Catholicism in England was what he desired.[31] His ambivalence is very well highlighted in his 'Tudor' series, to which I now turn. To understand this series we need to grasp fully the problems Ainsworth faced in attempting to treat Catholicism sympathetically.

The dependence on Protestantism of English (and British) national identity is hard to overstate, and has been well described by Linda Colley in her seminal *Britons*:

> From the Act of Union to the Battle of Waterloo in 1815, Great Britain was involved in successive, very dangerous wars with Catholic France. At the same time and long after, it was increasingly concerned to carve out a massive empire in foreign lands that were not even Christian. In these circumstances of regular and violent contact with peoples who could so easily be seen as representing the Other, Protestantism was able to become a unifying and distinguishing bond as never before.[32]

One of the means by which this unity was perpetuated was through the dissemination of a historical memory in which Catholics played a disproportionate role as persecutors, bedevillers, traitors and usurpers. David Cressy's examination of the English calendar shows how closely it resembles a persecutionist's charter, in which a Protestant elect was always on the run from a Catholic horde ravenous for Protestant blood.[33] A central figure in this calendar was 'Bloody' Queen Mary Tudor; Elizabeth I's accession to the throne in 1558 was figured as a central rite of passage in which England was once again saved from the foreign domination of the Catholic Other. John Foxe's enormously popular *Book of Martyrs* (1563) was specifically about 'the sufferings and death of the Protestants in the reign of Queen Mary'; it was Foxe's aim to demonstrate that Mary Tudor was a monstrous harridan, and his account of the cruelty suffered by innocent Protestants during her reign of power was drawn in stark and bloody imagery. It is in this context that Ainsworth's novel *The Tower of London* (1840), should be judged, because it demonstrates the ability of the Gothic novel to celebrate and absolve the Catholic past, rather than merely continue in another guise the horrific imagery of the martyrologies. The novel revolves around the short reign of Lady Jane Grey and its aftermath, but the major portion of the book is given over to Queen Mary's reign and, indeed, her character, and it is here that the radicalism of the novel can be truly felt. If most people were aware of Mary as a version of the Catholic monster, Ainsworth's novel — while remaining anti-Catholic to an extent — is a major attempt to rehabilitate the Bloody Queen. Indeed, so far from depicting only those who suffered in Mary's reign as martyrs, this novel widens the notion of martyrdom to include those Catholics who had suffered in the reigns of Henry VIII and Edward VI.

In his Preface to the original collected edition of the novel, Ainsworth addresses the negative criticism he had to endure for his sympathetic treatment of Mary:

> To those who conceive that the Author has treated the character of Queen Mary with too great leniency, he can only affirm that he has written according to his conviction of the truth ... it is time that the cloud which prejudice has cast over her should be dispersed.

He adds a quotation from Griffet, who claimed that 'we may perhaps discover that the reproaches which Protestant writers have heaped upon her have been excessive' (vii).[34] Book the Second opens with a long and generally positive assessment of the character of Queen Mary, praising her 'beauty', and warning that 'no one has suffered more from misrepresentation than this Queen. Not only have her failings been exaggerated, and ill qualities, which she did not possess, attributed to her, but the virtues that undoubtedly belonged to her have been denied her' (145). Mary is more often displayed in this novel in the guise of merciful queen than bloodthirsty tyrant.

Ainsworth lays Queen Mary's faults at the door of Edward Courtenay, with whom she had fallen in love but who betrayed her by attempting to elope with the Princess Elizabeth, and who later joins the rebels against her. Hurt by his traitorous act Mary is tricked by the Spanish spy, Renard, into affiancing herself to Charles of Spain. Treachery is blamed, not on Mary but on her advisers and lovers, who are driven by personal ambition rather than duty to the state. Mary is quite clear as to where her loyalty lies. She characterises the population of England as her children, in a brilliant speech to calm the nation when rumours of her marriage are leaked: 'Never having been a mother ... I cannot tell how naturally a parent loves her children; but certainly a Queen may as naturally and tenderly love her subjects as a mother her child' (376). Mary has no desire to execute Lady Jane Grey, considering her 'very young – very beautiful. I would rather reconcile her to our Church than doom her to the block' (211). She is kind even to bizarrely zealous Protestants, including the 'hot-gospeller' Edward Underhill. Even after he tries to assassinate her, we are told that Mary has pity on him, and 'despite all his reasoning to the contrary, her generosity affected him powerfully' (241). The novel extends its sympathy for Mary to her supporters, so that those who rebel against Lady Jane Grey are not depicted uniformly as motivated by base concerns. Gilbert – the first rebel – and his grandmother Gunnora Braose are represented as saintly figures, who are martyred in their devotion to Mary.

In general terms this reconciliation with the Catholic past is part of the focus of the novel on an interpretation of the Tower of London itself. This is absolutely crucial, as it fits in with other movements within English intellectual history taking place contemporaneously, in which there was a general turning away from the eighteenth-century version of neoclassical rationalism which saw the Glorious Revolution of 1688 as the foundation of an entirely new England, and towards a view of England, and the English constitution, as a very old Gothic building, in which many changes had been made throughout the ages but which had to be taken as a whole. This shift can be detected as early as 1765 in William Blackstone's *Commentaries on the Laws of England*, where he made the link between English legal inheritance and a Gothic building:

We inherit an old Gothic castle, erected in the days of chivalry, but fitted up for a modern inhabitant. The moated ramparts, the embattled towers, and the trophied halls, are magnificent and venerable, but useless. The inferior apartments, now converted into rooms of convenience, are chearful and commodious, though their approaches are winding and difficult.[35]

This image of the Gothic constitution was a central one for Edmund Burke in his defence of England against social and political upheaval in the face of the French Revolution in 1789. In his *Reflections on the Revolution in France* (1790) he argued cogently that 1688 was an evolutionary development to be grafted on to a venerable and ancient institution deserving respect, rather than any real revolutionary transformation, as radicals like Richard Price argued. For Burke, aristocratic government, tradition, the rule of law, were not to be jettisoned for the sake of abstract 'rights', but were to be reformed gently and slowly. Medieval architectural sites and medieval institutions gained importance as zones of nostalgic desire, but also as sites of political stability on which the present generation could build. Indeed, as Markman Ellis demonstrates, Gothic buildings like the Houses of Parliament, Windsor Castle and the Tower of London were transfigured into transformative zones in the present.[36] It is no surprise that Ainsworth, a writer with an extraordinary investment in the past-in-the-present, should write significant novels centring on both Windsor Castle and the Tower of London. The latter is in one sense a kind of Gothic guidebook to the building, and it actually laments the newest architectural additions. As Carver comments, the Tower is 'the focal point' of the novel and the 'controlling metaphor for the nation's history'.[37]

Ainsworth conducted a huge amount of research into the Tower and into the history of the period in general, and includes a full index to the novel. Descriptions of the Tower take up an enormous amount of space throughout the narrative, interrupting the flow of events and concretising the Gothic in a unique fashion. Carver claims that 'Ainsworth's descriptions of church buildings, his architectural allegory, carry a code that his readers would instantly recognize as Catholic', and he links these

Tudor novels with the Gothic revival in architecture being spear-headed by Pugin.[38] Ainsworth's Preface insists that his purpose was 'to make the Tower of London – the proudest monument of antiquity, considered with reference to its historical associations, which this country or any other possesses – the groundwork of a romance', a mode which has itself strong links to medieval chivalry and courtly love (v): 'It is piteous to see what havoc has already been made by alterations and repairs … Let us attempt to preserve what remains' (vi). The novel is, in fact, an anti-revolutionary tract which condemns in its turn all constitutional innovation, from the accession of Jane Grey, to the usurpation by Mary, to the rebellion against her. Continuity and loyalty to tradition, rather than innovation, is praised. All of George Cruikshank's illustrations in the novel depict the Tower 'as it was' before modern innovations interfered with its venerable perfection. Indeed, the Tower is transformed in part into a fairy-tale castle. It is guarded by three giants – Og, Gog and Magog – and a dwarf – Xit, and is shrouded in an atmosphere of nostalgia. The Tower of London is a Gothic site like the Castle of Otranto, with mysterious subterranean passages and horrific rooms of torture, but is also a site for worship, a sacred place.

Ainsworth is less interested in the struggle between Catholic and Protestant power-groupings in Tudor England than he is in the struggle between Gothic continuity and the revolutionary powers of modernity. This continuity is insisted upon constantly. The revelations concerning the true parentage of Cicely – the 'heroine' of the novel – reveal that she is the daughter of two people who died under Henry VIII for their adherence to the Catholic Church, for which deaths the word 'martyr' is used on a number of occasions. Although their daughter remains a Protestant, the point here is that she does not renounce her parents or disown their sacrifice; she both devotes herself to service of Lady Jane Grey (the handmaiden of Protestantism), and is given special favour by Queen Mary (the bulwark of Catholicism). A form of bodily reconciliation thus occurs in Cicely herself; she is a place where the past and the future can be merged. Thus, she has two names: she is both Cicely for the Protestant present and Angela for her Catholic past. In her body,

Jane and Mary, Protestant and Catholic, past and future, can be reconciled. Nostalgia and reconciliation are focal themes of the text.

If 'Bloody' Mary is partly redeemed in *The Tower of London*, a daring and ambitious project for any English Protestant to attempt in the anti-Catholic hothouse of the nineteenth century, then in his next novel Ainsworth took on the even more courageous job of rehabilitating the hated figure of Guy Fawkes. For Carver, Ainsworth's tolerant and indulgent attitude to Catholicism was brave in a period when 'anti-Catholic feeling was still running high'.[39] In *Guy Fawkes* (1840) Ainsworth chooses as a hero the man who tried to blow England back to the Catholic Middle Ages. Indeed, Carver concludes that the argument of *Guy Fawkes* that Catholics had been persecuted in England is actually 'astounding', considering the period in which it was published.[40] The novel is delicately poised, as it not only revolves around figures anathematised in legitimate English history as monstrous – the transformation of the historical Guido Fawkes into the Fifth-of-November Guy effectively distorted him into something so horrific it required ritual repulsion every single year – but also moves along a trope central to both Gothic literature in general and also Protestant understanding of Catholicism in this period: the trope of the secret. The conspirators, of course, work in secret, but they also reside in zones of secrecy. The sixteenth- and seventeenth-century recusant priests are forced to inhabit gaps and spaces in the apparently solid walls of great houses in order to evade capture; the characters operate under assumed names and disguises; the plot eventually focuses on an empty cellar, in which a man and his explosives lie hidden away.

Eve Kosofsky Sedgwick has anatomised the cult of the secret in modernity as expressive of the fractures of subjectivity wrought by the fear of the sexual deviant,[41] but Ainsworth demonstrates that there was a far more basic fear revolving around secrecy – the fear of the covert Catholic. For example, anti-confessional literature of the nineteenth century was hysterical in its attack on the secrecy basic to the Catholic confession, which women entered alone and were examined in intimate closeness – both physical and psychological – by an unmarried man. This was seen as a usurpation of the authority of husbands and fathers, and was configured as a site of sexual, familial and theological corruption. Charles Chiniquy drew on these fears in his breathlessly entitled *The Priest, the Woman, and the Confessional* (1874):

> The husband respectfully requested the friends to leave the room with him, and shut the door, that the holy confessor might be left alone with his penitent during her general confession.

> One of the most diabolical schemes, under the cover of auricular confession, had perfectly succeeded. The mother of harlots, the great enchantress of souls, whose seat is on 'the seven hills', had, there, her priest to bring shame, disgrace, and damnation, under the mask of Christianity. The destroyer of souls, whose masterpiece is auricular confession, had, there, for the millionth time, a fresh opportunity for insulting the God of purity through one of the most criminal actions which the dark shades of night can conceal.

> But let us draw the veil over the abominations of that hour of iniquity, and let us leave to hell its dark secrets.[42]

Ainsworth takes the trope of the secret and invests it with a number of positive qualities. Indeed, rather than Catholic secrecy being configured as sexually dangerous, it is the interference with such secrecy that is rendered sexually suspect in this novel.

Early in the novel one of the characters describes how Protestant agents of the state seeking desperately for Catholic priests have completely divested themselves of all notions of propriety and decency:

> You have never witnessed a midnight search for a priest by these ruffianly catchpoles … The miscreants break into the house like robbers, and treat its inmates worse than robbers would treat them. They have no regard for decency, – no consideration for sex, – no respect for persons. Not a chamber is sacred from them. If a door is bolted, they burst it open; a cabinet locked, they tarry not for the key. They pull down the hangings, thrust their rapier-points into the crevices of the wainscot, discharge their firearms against the wall, and sometimes threaten to pull down the house itself. (30)[43]

The language here is close to that of Edmund Burke's description of how the French rebels entered the bedroom of Marie Antoinette and dragged her out naked at the point of bayonets and poignards. This is a quasi-sexual violation, partly because Ainsworth, like Burke before him, has described the violators in ultra-phallic terms, penetrating, breaching, breaking down sacred barriers like unwelcome lovers. It is not, in other words, the priests who are conducting an illicit sexual practice, but the Protestant searchers. Indeed, so safe are these Catholic priests with women that some of the hiding places are actually within the bedrooms of Catholic wives and daughters, and the priests hole up there with no hint of impropriety (31). But where the Catholic priest passes into this sanctuary invited, the agents of the Crown must use force and brutality to gain entrance. Ironically, and shockingly, these searches are termed 'inquisitorial', a direct reversal of the usual charge against the Catholic Church with its instrument, the Inquisition (41). The Catholic home is a virginal woman, now abused and practically raped by these barbarians at the gates.

This is, of course, an extraordinary turnaround, more so when we remember the sanctity of the ancient house for Ainsworth. That such miscreants would actually pull down a venerable home in search of a Catholic priest demonstrates their complete lack of decorum and honour. In this novel these Protestant agents of the state burn down part of Ordsall House, which is described as a hallowed place by Ainsworth's narrator. As always for Ainsworth, that which is old is to be respected, and here that which is old and venerable and that which is Catholic combine. We are told that 'among the Popish party of that period, as in our own time, were ranked many of the oldest and most illustrious families in the kingdom' (19). The apparent aside – 'as in our own time' – is a crucial time-disorientating device, as it insists that Catholic good-ness cannot simply be dismissed as a past anomaly. Moreover, the narrative invests heavily in a demonstration of the honour of the conspirators themselves, and Guy Fawkes in particular. Opprobrium is held out for those who would persecute Catholicism in England, rather than those who would uphold it:

And even in the seasons of the bitterest persecution, when every fresh act of treason, perpetuated by some lawless and disaffected individual, was visited with additional rigour on [the Catholic population's] heads, – when the scaffold reeked with their blood, and the stake smoked with their ashes, – when their quarters were blackening on the gates and market-crosses of every city in the realm, – when their hearths were invaded, their religion proscribed, and the very name of Papist had become a byword, – even in those terrible seasons ... they remained constant in their fidelity to the crown. (19)

There is a strong suggestion here that the blame for Catholic treason is not the inveterately treasonable nature of Catholicism itself, but the circumstances in which Catholics found themselves; the fault, in other words, lies at the door of persecution rather than theology. The Catholics in this narrative are invariably generous, forgiving, compassionate, loving, magnanimous, coura-geous, intelligent, attractive; the Catholic bogeyman has been banished.

*Guy Fawkes* could be read as a Catholic retelling of one of the most notorious incidents in English history. Included as epigraphs to its various books are the two sides to the debate, and Ainsworth quotes Catholic historians as authorities rather than as biased commentators. Book the First opens with a quote from Father John Gerard, one of the key Jesuits in the period, who rails against the indignities to which Catholics were subject, complaining

What a thing is it for a Catholic gentleman to have his house suddenly beset on all sides with a number of men in arms ... Then are these searches oft-times so rude and barbarous, that, if the doors be not opened in the instant they would enter, they break open the doors with all violence. (1)

In opposition Book the Third opens with a quotation from Sir Edward Coke, one of the chief prosecutors of the conspirators, who claims that 'these traitors have exceeded all others in mischief', and who praises the 'admirable clemency and modera-tion of the king' (298). There is a hollow ring to this, however, since the reader has already been exposed to the torturing of the heroine, Viviana, who has opposed the conspiracy from the start but did not reveal the plot to the authorities because of her love for Guy Fawkes and her compassion for her fellow Catholics. Viviana is presented as a saint throughout the text, yet the authorities treat her horrifically:

> the tormentor then turned a screw, which compressed the iron glove so tightly as to give her excruciating pain ... The tormentor then placed the hand which was still at liberty within the other gauntlet. The torture was dreadful – and the fingers appeared crushed by the pressure ... The tormentor took a mallet, and struck one of the pieces of wood from under Vivian's feet. The shock was dreadful, and seemed to dislocate her wrists, while the pressure on her hands was increased in a tenfold degree. The poor sufferer, who was resting on the points of her feet, felt that the removal of the next piece of wood would occasion the most intolerable torture ... The second block was struck away. She was now suspended by her hands, and the pain was so exquisite, that nature gave way, and uttering a piercing scream, she fainted. (234–5)

Horrible as this is, we are told that this is the mildest form of torture used and that something 'a thousand times worse' awaits her (235). The description of the interrogation and torture of Guy Fawkes himself is a sustained piece of brutality, and the aim of such descriptions is clearly to place the reader on the side of the victim rather than the 'tormentor': state power, not Catholicism, is revealed as monstrous. Indeed, after his capture Fawkes is transformed into a Christ figure, suffering the indignities Jesus suffered at the hands of the Roman state:

> Meanwhile several of the spectators, eager to prove their loyalty to the King and abhorrence of the plot, loaded the prisoner with execrations, and, finding these produced no effect, proceeded to personal outrage. Some spat upon his face and garments; some threw mud, gathered from the slimy steps, upon him; some pricked him with the points of their halberds ... (299)

The conspirators are designated 'men, for the most part, of high intellectual powers, of untiring energy, and unconquerable fortitude' (20).

Rehabilitating Guy Fawkes was a major feat. As recently as 1821, in an essay commemorating 5 November, William Hazlitt had claimed Fawkes was a 'pale miner in the infernal regions, skulking in his retreat with his cloak and dark lanthorn, moving cautiously about among his barrels of gunpowder, loaded with death'.[44] In 1857, a decade and a half after Ainsworth's account, David Jardine's *A Narrative of the Gunpowder Plot* reiterated the traditional idea that it was all down to the nefarious and satanic activities of the Jesuits – a position particularly rejected by Ainsworth, who pointedly insists that there was no diabolical Jesuit activity since they were sincere, if mistaken, holy men. In her sober history of the Plot Antonia Fraser comes to the conclusion that the conspirators were 'brave, misguided men' of calibre, 'driven by continued religious persecution to Gunpowder, Treason and Plot', but Ainsworth was there well before her.[45] The novel condemns 'the extreme severity of the laws ... the spirit of religious persecution then prevailing' (5) – but also, surely, prevailing in the atmosphere of the 1840s. The narrator explicitly complains that 'pressed down by ... intolerable grievances, is it to be wondered at that the Papists should repine, – or that some among their number, when all other means failed, should seek redress by darker measures?' (7).

## Gothicising the Future

Far from merely denigrating and exorcising the Catholic past as a source of terror, Gothic is quite often a means of examining and appropriating that past and attacking the present. However, if the past was a source of Gothic potential rather than just Gothic repulsion for Ainsworth, other writers began to look to the future in ways which suggested that ahead lay not the glorious and gleaming palace of enlightenment perfection – as Whig history would have it – but another kind of Gothic nightmare. While Ainsworth emphasised the positive and desirable side of the Gothic past, other writers focused on the horrifically alienating elements of the yet-to-come. Although George Eliot is usually considered an author heavily invested in ideas of progress and enlightenment, in *The Lifted Veil* (1859) she actually reveals a future in which horror and ennui predominate. As is well known, Eliot was profoundly influenced by the reading of history offered by the philosopher of Positivism, Auguste Comte, who theorised that human history moved through three stages: from superstition in the theological stage, through religion in the metaphysical stage, towards 'positive' science in the final stage. In the scientific stage material progress would be accompanied by ethical advancement: we would become better people as our knowledge increased; altruism rather than egoism would become a determinant in social relations, and greater sympathy with others would free us from the devotion to self-satisfaction that had bedevilled human history. The future was going to be a bright one. What we find in *The Lifted Veil*, however, is a floundering faith in human progress and a collapse in the belief that the future would be better than the past.

In *The Lifted Veil*, the narrator Latimer is given the power of prevision, the ability to see into the future, and also granted the unique ability to access the thoughts of others – a kind of sympathy that would be looked on with envy by orthodox Positivists. Eliot herself had written of the importance of sympathy in ethical progress and had argued that the ability to enter as fully as possible into the minds of our fellow men and women was important to developing a truly altruistic personality. Sympathy with others was the means by which egotistic division could be broken down. In an 1859 letter to Charles Bray, Eliot claimed that 'the only effect I ardently long to produce by my writings, is that those who read them should be better able to imagine and feel the pains and joys of those who differ from them'. Having quoted this letter in her introduction to the tale, Sally Shuttleworth points out that *The Lifted Veil* is precisely an attempt to imagine what a person who could do this perfectly would be like, so that, in Latimer's ability to actually experience the feelings of others, we are given an opportunity to see first-hand what the Positivist future holds.[46] However, the experience – ironically – is horrifying rather than consoling. After all, what is revealed to Latimer in his interior journeys is not the perfectibility of human nature, but rather the true depth of human depravity. Access to otherness reveals how petty others really are. He realises, in other words, that hell is other people.

If some dewy-eyed optimistic believers in human progress thought that the next phase of human and social development would lead to the heightening of intellectual powers through the activation of hidden faculties of the mind (such as psychic abilities), Eliot's novella exposes these hopes and desires as hubristic and deluded. Such intellectual developments may lead, as Latimer shows, only to a world in which egos clash and where a struggle for power and influence is enacted.[47] If Latimer's prevision grants him the ability to see how disgusting others are, as readers we are shown what Latimer's mind is like through his first-person narration, and if he is the most fully 'developed' of humans because of his remarkable mind-reading abilities, then he is also the most objectionable. In a story populated with thoroughly unlikeable characters he is the most unsympathetic. Latimer's gift has not made him more altruistic but more ego-driven, and he hates all the others he meets, with the exception of his wife, who is plotting to kill him. Gazing into the future, all Latimer can see is his own destruction, and indeed the entire story is predicated on his imminent death. His first words are the ominous: 'the time of my end approaches' (3).[48]

Eliot was well aware that many Positivists held that prevision was important in the full development of the positivist future. Kate Flint notes that George Lewes, Eliot's partner, had pointedly emphasised this in his writings on Comte, and quotes the final chapter of *A Biographical History of Philosophy* (1845–6), where Lewes claims that

> the positive Method is the only Method … on which truth can be found … on it alone can *prevision* of phenomena depend. Prevision is the characteristic and the test of knowledge. If you can predict certain results and they occur as you predicted, then are you assured that your knowledge is correct.[49]

For these thinkers, naturalised and secularised versions of what had previously been considered religious and supernatural ideals were central; Eliot's own belief was that a secular Religion of

Humanity, which preserved much of the teaching found in Jesus' Sermon on the Mount, was vital to ethical progress. Preservation of the ethical truths of religion was crucial to these thinkers, and attempts at secularising the 'supernatural', especially as it manifested in the Gospels, could be found everywhere in the nineteenth century. Eliot's intellectual mentor, David Strauss, cautioned that

> Christ's supernatural birth, and his resurrection and ascension, remain eternal truths, however much their reality as historical facts may be doubted. Only the certainty of this can give our criticism calmness and dignity, and distinguish it from the naturalistic criticism of the last century, which thought the religious truth was destroyed with the historical fact.[50]

The Resurrection could be used as a metaphor to speak of the glorious future in which all things were to be renewed, and 'explaining' the secular meaning of the resurrection was central to the new secular gospels.

It is this secularised version of a future, metaphorical Resurrection that implodes in *The Lifted Veil*. The brilliantly realised scene in which Mrs Archer is 'resurrected' by Doctor Meunier is basic to understanding the tale, and is brought about through blood transfusion combined with artificial respiration: 'I could see the wondrous slow return to life; the breast began to heave, the inspirations became stronger, the eyelids quivered, and the soul seemed to have returned beneath them'. When she momentarily awakens Mrs Archer accuses Bertha of slowly poisoning her husband; she then passes out of this world again, leaving Latimer with some speculations: 'Great God! Is this what it is to live again?' (40–2). This is the first time Latimer has invoked God in the entire story, in a hideous reversal of the Christian theology of the Resurrection. After all, a central proposition of the Creed is the belief in 'resurrection of the body', the conviction that in some future state body and soul will be reunited. If Positivists hoped to achieve this on a secular plane, this hope is punctured by Mrs Archer's bodily revival, at which, as Latimer notes, 'the soul seemed to have returned'. Secular resurrection is futuristic dystopia. Eliot may have been partly inspired in her account of the resurrected body by a scene very similar in Ainsworth's *Guy Fawkes*. There, the occult Doctor Dee disinters the 'prophetess' Elizabeth Orton and, in the presence of Guy Fawkes, 'resurrects' her in order to ask her important questions. As in *The Lifted Veil*, blood is also required to effect the resurrection properly, this time the blood of Fawkes himself. Orton is awakened briefly and she foretells the failure of the plot: 'The end will be death … to the conspirators' (63). The future is not bright for Catholics in Ainsworth's account; in *The Lifted Veil* it is the secularists whose prospects seem bleak. Yet another monstrous resurrection takes place in W. W. Jacobs's story 'The Monkey's Paw' (1902), where a couple, using the enchanted appendage of the title, wish for the return of their son who has died in a machinery accident, only for him to climb out of his grave, still mangled, and knock on their front door in the dead of night.

John Henry Newman had long warned that 'Progress is a slang term',[51] and in *The Lifted Veil*, George Eliot reveals a Gothic intensity motoring the supposedly 'progressive' future. H. G. Wells took this one step further in *The Time Machine* (1894–5). By the time Wells came to write his masterpiece, the notion of progress and history going hand in hand had become rather less believable, and many thinkers were pointing out that the future might not hold the ethical and technological enlightenment so desired. If the past was a Gothic nightmare, then perhaps it would actually follow us – perhaps, in other words, horror is simply an aspect of what it means to be human. In his study of the relationship between *Progress and Poverty* (1879), for example, the economist Henry George set about troubling the English imagination by suggesting that, far from the march of time bringing greater improvements, it could in fact have devastating effects on the human race. He pointed out that while the cities were the crucibles of modernity, they were also the sites of appalling poverty, disease and loneliness. Material progress – so visible in these modern metropolises – ran side by side with destitution and horror:

> Where the conditions to which material progress everywhere tends are most fully realized – that is to say where population is densest,

wealth greatest, and the machinery of production and exchange the most highly developed – we find the greatest poverty, the sharpest struggle for existence, and the most of enforced idleness.[52]

In *The Time Machine* Wells projects this nightmare scenario into an imagined future where something called 'progress' is indeed discernible. When the Time Traveller moves into the year 802,701 he discovers a race of beings, the Eloi, who have become so refined and 'spiritual', so inured to manual labour, that they are physically attenuated and ethereal – they have progressed beyond physicality itself and become pure mind. The Eloi are the descendants of those best placed to benefit from the increasing wealth of the nineteenth-century city, the wealthy middle class who have, in effect, become a new aristocracy. Deep in the bowels of the earth, however, lurk the remnants of those left behind by the progress of history, the Morlocks, the descendants of the working classes who slaved in coal mines and quarries, and who have biologically regressed to a form of primordialism. Science has certainly 'progressed', as disease has been practically wiped out; however, since neither disease nor manual labour is required of them any more, the bodies of the Eloi have reverted to childhood frailty. If the Eloi are a kind of purely 'spiritualised' human, the Morlocks represent the human species at the level of pure physicality. The Eloi made the great mistake of thinking that the struggle between the intellectuals and the masses had ended in their favour and that the future was utopian; however, the masses had merely made a strategic retreat and now have re-emerged, after the full biological impact of decadent leisure has destroyed the Eloi's ability to form an effective opposition. *The Time Machine* at times reads like a compact version of Edward Gibbon's *The Decline and Fall of the Roman Empire* (1776–88), where Rome is destroyed not simply by the barbarian Goths at the gate, but also by the decadent indulgence of those who hold the reins of political and cultural power. The Morlocks are the futuristic Goths who will take advantage of this weakness and emerge as the new rulers, harvesting their former masters for food.

Wells's novel is also a development of an idea discernible in Richard Jefferies's *After London* (1885) which draws a picture of a denuded England destroyed by tidal waves, where those who survive have split into masters and slaves, and where all have basically degenerated into bestial conditions from which humans emerged: 'For all the rottenness of a thousand years and of many hundred millions of human beings is there festering under the stagnant water, which has sunk down into and penetrated the earth, and floated up to the surface the contents of the buried cloacae'.[53] Wells personifies this human excrement as the Morlocks, but, worryingly, appears to take great pleasure in the idea that in 'progressing' to this degenerate level, they will then enslave the descendants of middle-class Londoners (Wells's own peers). Running through the novel there is a sense that the human race itself is a kind of environmental pollutant that deserves to be wiped out. The future may be a Gothic nightmare for humanity, but a world without mankind may be a utopia for Wells the eugenicist. Indeed, a general death-drive can be detected deep within the novel, partially influenced by Lord Kelvin's Second Law of Thermodynamics (1868). This law postulated that the heat of the universe was slowly diffusing and that eventually the universe would be reduced to a huge heat dump in which life was impossible. If history was headed anywhere, it was not towards incremental increases in human happiness but annihilation. The Time Traveller confirms this 'cosmic pessimism'[54] in his final journeys into the very distant future, where he finds a world almost completely desolate in which mankind is no more, an earth left only to a ghastly mass of tentacles living in the sea: if life emerged into sophistication and complexity from a primordial Darwinian soup, it has returned there at the very end of history. In a horrific version of the 'End of History' as envisioned by Francis Fukuyama, all that remains is a tentacular horror. The novel converts the entire universe into a vast cosmic Gothic castle populated by monsters both human and subhuman, a universe composed of monstrous consumers; not only are we all heading towards a cosmic crunch, swallowed up by nothingness, but everything else is out to eat us up as well, including our cannibalistic selves. The Traveller is attacked by the Morlocks 'nipping at my neck' (74); the crab that attacks him is a slavering maw, 'the many palps of its complicated mouth [were] flickering and feeling as it moved' (83).[55] Ironically, of course, the human species is made up of monstrously hungry creatures, too. The first thing the Traveller does when he gets home is tuck into a hearty mutton meal, exclaiming gleefully 'what a treat it is to stick a fork into meat again' (15). The problem with the Eloi is at least partly that they have lost the feeling for both meat and death – and indeed, murder. They are vulnerable because they have not tasted blood. The narrator, on the contrary, has a very healthy appetite, which may be one of the reasons he survives;[56] this survival is only local, however, since the future is an open mouth into which we are all going to be plunged.

This chapter has tried to demonstrate that Gothic is far from being dedicated, in any simple way, to enlightened progress or retrogressive nostalgia, and is instead caught up in a hesitancy between these two modes, Ainsworth's novels brilliantly highlighting the beauty that has been lost in modernity, the novels by Eliot and Wells worrying about the threat of the future. Of course, the romanticised and Gothicised past could also be identified with the figure of the child, and it is to this figure I now turn.

# 2

# *The Horror of Childhood*

## *Constructing Childhood*

The emergence of the modern child has been traced in detail by a number of significant sociologists and historians, so need not be gone into in detail here. These studies have demonstrated that both children and childhood have been conceptualised and experienced in very different ways in different periods and geographical zones, so that it is difficult to speak of them as transparent or self-evident. Moreover, childhood has not been defined by children themselves, but by adults, so that, as LuAnn Walthers argues, 'Childhood ... reflects adult needs and adult fears quite as much as it signifies the absence of adulthood. In the course of history children have been glorified, patronised, ignored, or held in contempt, depending upon the cultural assumptions of adults.'[1] The seminal historian of childhood Philippe Ariés exaggeratedly claimed that childhood did not exist in the Middle Ages; instead, the child was seen as a potential adult rather than as occupying a time-period special in and of itself. Indeed, in medieval Europe 'as soon as the child could live without the constant solicitude of his mother, his nanny or his cradle-rocker, he belonged to adult society'.[2]

From the eighteenth century we can trace a growth in utopian thought concerning children, an increasing feeling that there was something special about the child, the emergence of what Hugh

Cunningham has called the 'middle-class ideology of childhood'. With the 'spiritualisation' of the family and the domestic sphere during the Reformation, and the apparent waning of the belief in original sin due to the influence of the educational writings of John Locke (whose suggestion that the child's mind was a blank slate was rather misunderstood) and Jean-Jacques Rousseau (who theorised the child as naturally innocent rather than corrupt), the increase of literacy (which required a long period of training for the young), and the expansion in house size (which allowed children to have rooms of their own in middle-class families), the child became an altogether different subject from her medieval counterpart.[3] Rousseau's was the dominant voice in this reassessment of the child as an innocent angel beset by the corruption of adult civilisation, under constant threat from the forces of grown-up power. Although the initial reaction to Rousseau's views was hostile, his conceptualisation of the 'innocent, natural child' was channelled into the writings of the Romantics, particularly of William Blake and William Wordsworth, and began to infiltrate general views about childhood in Britain. Romantic writers postulated a sacred and pure child, which appeared at odds with the child in dire need of socialisation, as propagated by the Puritan writers of the sixteenth and seventeenth centuries, so that 'from being the smallest and least considered of human beings, the child had become endowed with qualities which make it Godlike, fit to be worshipped, and the embodiment of hope'.[4]

This creation of a zone of innocence located in and around the child effectively allowed for the presentation of wider adult society as a space in which lurked monstrous threats to this innocence. 'Female Gothic' has been defined as a version of the Gothic depicting the vulnerable and sexually naive woman vigorously pursued by the forces of lust and emotional avarice, as personified in the villain of the tale.[5] What happens in the nineteenth century is that this innocence and vulnerability is translated wholesale to child figures, and society itself configured as the male villain out to get her. That the child was generally gendered female/feminine anyway enabled this translation of the terms of the female Gothic into the literature of childhood to be even more successful.[6]

## The Child under Threat

Charles Dickens is a central figure in the propagation of the modern myth of childhood as a zone of innocence besieged by malevolent Gothic threats from the family and from social, religious and political institutions. Dickens's fascination with childhood may have stemmed from his own experiences. His family famously slipped down the social ladder, due to his father's profligacy, until they all ended up living in a debtor's prison. The ten-year-old Dickens had by this time taken up work in Warren's Blacking Factory in Hungerford Lane in late January 1824, an experience that appears to have traumatised him for life: 'My whole nature was so penetrated with the grief and humiliation of such considerations, that, even now – famous and caressed and happy – I often forget in my dreams that ... I am a man – and wander desolately back to that time of life.'[7] Dickens' oeuvre is replete with references to this period in the blacking factory, as if, in revisiting the trauma in fictional terms, he could exorcise his personal demons. Recently, the critic and novelist Alison Lurie has theorised that certain writers, including Lewis Carroll, James Barrie and Edith Nesbit, never really left childhood, and for some critics Dickens's career is an illustration of the accuracy of Sigmund Freud's postulation that early childhood experiences determine the patterns for maturity.[8] Angus Wilson famously claimed that 'the work of Dickens's whole career was an attempt to digest these early shocks and hardships, to explain them to himself'.[9] In his writing, Dickens often transforms the adult world into a Gothic nightmare surrounding and threatening the angelic innocence of the uncorrupted child, as a way of explaining what happened to himself.

*Oliver Twist* (1837–9) is an examination of the view of the child as an innocent blank slate, except that, unlike Locke's hypothetical child, Oliver is incapable of actually learning anything from his experiences. He is simply an uncomplicated organ of goodness and innocence. Although the story of which he is the protagonist is apparently concerned with explaining that social conditions rather than biology determine the behaviour of men and women, Oliver directly undermines this polemical point, since no matter what happens to him he remains incorruptible and pure. Despite having a childhood so horrific that it hovers on the edge of parody, and despite living with a gang of thieves, he still reacts with 'horror and alarm' when he realises that they are pickpockets (ch. 10, 114), and becomes 'mad with grief and terror' when forced into involvement in a robbery (ch. 22, 211).[10] His incorruptible nature also means that he is essentially incapable of character development or growth. Dickens often displays a propensity to kill his child characters before they enter adolescence, in order to preserve their purity, but here he saves Oliver, perhaps because Oliver is dead already. Photographs of dead children became fetishised objects in this period, partly because the dead child in the coffin was an object of an innocence that could never be corrupted by bad behaviour. Although the Victorian public complained about and mourned vociferously the deaths of Paul Dombey (in *Dombey and Son* (1846–8)) and Little Nell (in *The Old Curiosity Shop* (1840–1)), they also eagerly consumed the episodes in which these deaths took place, suggestive of a general cultural fixation on killing the child as a means of protecting her. Before he got around to murdering both Paul and Nell, Dickens essentially killed Oliver by rendering his psychological and moral growth unachievable. Instead of Oliver learning to mature when he encounters evil instead, every time he is faced with a new challenge, he ends up in the sickbed.[11]

This innocent child is embedded in the Gothic metropolitan nightmare of London. Everywhere in London other than Mr Brownlow's house is depicted by Dickens as a space in which child abuse in all its forms takes place. The middle-class readers encountering Oliver's story near the safety of the comfort of the hearth can thus congratulate themselves that they live in the very space from which the Gothic threat to children has been banished. Indeed, the novel is a major accomplishment in that it manages to simultaneously indict the Victorians for neglecting children *and* displace that guilt on to a sacrificial ethnic group – the Jews – projected as living in the world outside the middle-class home. Indeed, *Oliver Twist* is partly a Victorian version of the medieval legends which imputed a blood libel on the Jews, and continues a rather scandalous tradition of presenting Jews as villains throughout the Gothic novel.[12]

Although Harry Stone has claimed that Dickens is simply reflecting the banal anti-Semitism of his society,[13] the Gothicising of the Jewish Fagin is not an accidental feature of the narrative but is fundamental to its symbolic architecture. The belief that Jews were involved in child kidnap and sacrifice has a long and pernicious history and is echoed repeatedly in the novel, especially, as Stone himself has pointed out, in the first scene between Oliver and Fagin. There, a half-asleep Oliver spots Fagin greedily poring over stolen jewellery; when Fagin notices Oliver is awake he holds a bread-knife over him as if about to perform a sacrifice, thus deliberately invoking the blood libel.[14] The central drama the novel presents us with is the struggle between an innocent Christian child and a monstrous demon-like Jewish figure, a struggle deep at the heart of Christianity itself.[15]

In this scene Dickens reworks the traditional image of the monstrous Jewish father-figure determined to sacrifice the innocent Christ-like child, an image which depends on two moments from the Bible to be intelligible: in Genesis, the great Jewish patriarch Abraham is ordered by God to sacrifice his son Isaac to demonstrate his obedience to God's commands. At the last possible minute, when the knife is raised above the prostrate figure of Isaac – just as the knife is raised by Fagin over the prostrate figure of Oliver – God sends a ram to be used as a substitute. In the second moment, in the New Testament, God the Father sacrifices his son Jesus to the Jews for the forgiveness of sins. In Fagin, Dickens reconfigures both of these Biblical moments. That Fagin is quasi-supernatural has long been recognised and, as Stone points out, 'he carries with him the sinister aura of medieval legends, Renaissance plays, and terrifying nurses' stories'.[16] Descriptions of Fagin as, for example, a 'hideous old man' who 'seemed like some loathsome reptile, engendered in the slime and darkness … crawling forth by night in search of some rich offal for a meal', make it clear that he is more than simply a criminal (ch. 19, 186).[17] The novel as a whole is constructed on a symbolic nexus in which the old dispensation (here represented by the Jewish Fagin), is destroyed by the new (the Christian Oliver).

Like much Gothic fiction, then, the novel operates on the logic of the scapegoat, whereby a selected person or group is held responsible for the ills of society and punished. As Richard Kearney has argued, these 'alien fictions' are useful in uniting the host community against a common enemy and help concretise patterns of what the anthropologist Mary Douglas has called 'purity and danger', whereby an 'alien' figure(s) is considered in bestial and metaphysically evil terms, to the extent that they become horrifically liminal monsters.[18] This Gothicising of the threat to the innocent child, the sacrificial displacement of Gothic features on to the criminal underclasses, racial minorities, 'child-abusing' institutions like the school and the workhouse, is a typical manoeuvre in Dickens's work on childhood. In *Great Expectations* (1860–1) the innocent Pip encounters the Gothic on the moors where the 'ogrish' criminal Magwitch lurks,[19] and also in the home of Miss Havisham, whose inability to let go of her own child-abused past when she was abandoned at the moment of adolescent transition into adult maturity (her wedding day), makes her into another version of the child-abuser of both Pip himself and Estelle. The novel opens with Pip on the graves of his parents, and expands into a spectral scene where the convict Magwitch apparently emerges from one of these graves – like a ghost of his father – to grab Pip and 'imprison' him in his iron grip (ch. 1, 35–6).[20] Magwitch later becomes a mysterious 'godfather' to Pip – a masculine mirror to the equally Gothic godmother Miss Havisham, who is actually a living cadaver. All the clocks in Satis House where she lives are set at twenty minutes before nine on the morning of her aborted wedding. The table on which her wedding cake rests has become a slab, the cake a festering corpse. She is literally the past haunting the present, and her design to make Pip bear the punishment she really wishes on her absconded fiancé is a vivid representation of the means by which adults work out their own traumas on children. This is illustrated when Pip helps this corpse walk across the room of death in which she resides. Their circular motion suggests the perpetuity of death rather than the linear motions of time; she places her white arm around him and traps him beneath her like a vampire. As Stone indicates, their *danse macabre* effectively becomes an occult ritual, and its magic force opens Pip up to the corruption which blights him for most of the novel. He can only be saved by the grown-up child, Joe, who has never left behind his own childhood, and who acts as a means of Rousseauvean transformation.[21]

In *The Old Curiosity Shop*, Little Nell is subject to the threat of Quilp, a man also out of a Gothic nightmare, as sexually interested in Nell as Fagin is in Oliver, requesting to sleep in her bed and promising to make her his second wife after the first one dies. As Harry Stone demonstrates, the central image of the novel is that of 'the lonely and beleagured child, wandering lost through the terrifying forests of the world, assailed by grotesque monsters and demons'.[22] Like Oliver, Nell remains morally impervious to the threats that try to molest her. Although she is first found wandering the streets at night like a prostitute, the reader is soon disabused as to any notions of her sexual ambivalence. Like a parodic Sophie she attracts wild animals and birds, she sleeps in a bed 'that a fairy might have slept in' (ch. 1, 14),[23] and she is so perfect she sets off rumours that she is, in fact, the child of royalty or the aristocracy. In the central image of the novel – Little perfect Nell leading her corrupted and weak gambling-addicted grandfather by the hand – is encapsulated Rousseau's notion that the child should be the teacher of the adult. Like Fagin's Jewishness, Quilp's dwarfish appearance marks him out as racially different. He has 'a few discoloured fangs' for teeth (ch. 3, 29), indicative of his vampire-like associations. When he smiles he 'looks like a devil', and though hideously ugly he is also monstrously attractive to women (ch. 3, 32). His wife confirms that despite his grotesque unsightliness, he 'has such a way with him when he likes, that the best-looking woman here couldn't refuse him if … he chose to make love to her' (ch. 4, 38).[24]

The pattern of innocence surrounded by Gothic danger is recreated in *Dombey and Son* (1846–8). Paul Dombey is rendered so pure by Dickens that, against the weight of Christian tradition, even baptism is unnecessary. Paul is even more a Christ-child than Oliver since his father translates 'A.D.' (Anno Domini – the year of Our Lord, the year of Christ) as 'Anno Dombei', the year of Dombey, explicitly linking Jesus and Paul (ch. 1, 2).[25] And Paul seems to deserve this, as he operates as a supernatural presence in the novel, first as a sickly, weak and preternaturally gentle child, and then as a ghostly presence after his death, a presence influencing all subsequent action. He certainly does not want to grow up, somehow sensing that it is in the adult world that the source of all danger lies:

> 'Shall we make a man of him?' repeated the Doctor.
> 'I had rather be a child,' replied Paul.
> 'Indeed!' said the Doctor. 'Why?' (ch. 11, 154)

James Kincaid points out that the novel constantly presents Paul in a passive stance, lying down, tucked up in bed, unable to speak, looking and batting his eyelashes at someone 'older' than him in body but unable to reach him in mind. 'What a pretty fellow he is when he's asleep', one character says portentously (ch. 8, 113), because there the adult world cannot get at him and destroy him – which is the reason he must die.[26] In their fevered consumption of Paul's pristine image the British public clearly implied that a grown-up and sexual Paul, a Paul with children of his own, a Paul whose innocence was to be lost, was completely unacceptable.

## The Threatening Child

The irony is that while superficially these novels try to protect the child, a closer reading suggests that something far more sinister is happening: the novels perpetuate the abuse of children Dickens is theoretically trying to stamp out, and this is partly because they see the child as a threat to adult integrity as well as the source of adult subjectivity; in other words, these novels both love the child and hate it, desire it and loathe it. This is an ambivalence central to Victorian society itself. As Hugh Cunningham argues, in Victorian Britain, 'we see children on the one hand protected by a formidable array of nannies and governesses, and on the other exploited to an extent previously unknown'.[27] The Victorians passed law after law to shelter children from abuse, and yet sent huge numbers of them up chimneys, down mines, into factories; they established the National Society for the Prevention of Cruelty to Children in the 1880s, but only after the Royal Society for the Prevention of Cruelty to Animals had been set up in the 1820s. In these novels, although the Gothic imagery surrounds the child and endangers them, it also, perversely, resides within them: the child is a Gothic figure in these texts as much as she is threatened by Gothic stereotypes. The child is both surrounded by death and actually comes to stand for death itself. It is appropriate that Mr Sowerberry finds Oliver Twist the perfect figure to accompany funeral processions, since Oliver's innate blankness is demonstrative of his closeness to the blankness that is death. This should not surprise us, since the belief in the child as innocent is a recent one in a Western history which has been dominated by the version of the child theorised by Saint Augustine, who believed that original sin rather than innocence infected each and every child from conception.

Famously, Augustine was the most important opponent of the heresy, propounded by Pelagius (*ca.*354–*ca.*420/440), that the whole of humanity was not implicated in the sin of Adam and Eve, a theology which implicitly denies the notion of Original Sin. Contrariwise, Augustine insisted that 'The whole human race … is bound to punishment'.[28] Influenced by Augustine's powerful argument, the child was seen as a figure in whom lurked all kinds of nasty sexual thoughts and desires. In post-Reformation Puritan theology this view was reinforced, since, as Lawrence Stone points out, 'The Reformation … drive for moral regeneration brought with it an increasing concern to suppress the sinfulness of children … [and there was] a deadly fear of the liability of children to corruption and sin, particularly those sins of pride and disobedience.'[29] For the Puritans, the child was a 'Dionysian' monster, who, as Chris Jenks puts it, 'enter[s] the world as a wilful material force … impish and harbour[ing] a potential evil'.[30] Julian Wolfreys correctly notes that Dickens's writing is radically ambivalent when it comes to the figure of the child, and that rather than simply innocent his children are also radically Gothic and malevolent.[31]

In *Dombey and Son*, for example, the constant linking of childhood and death is partly due, not to an excessive love of the child, but a fear of her. There is a crucial moment in the novel when Mr Dombey looks on his daughter Florence and realises that he is terrified of her, that, in fact, he despises her:

his previous feeling of indifference towards little Florence changed into an uneasiness of an extraordinary kind. He almost felt as if she watched him and distrusted him. As if she held the clue to something secret in his breast, of the nature of which he was hardly informed himself. As if she had an innate knowledge of one jarring and discordant string within him, and her very breath could sound it ...

She troubled his peace ... Perhaps – who shall decide on such mysteries – he was afraid that he might come to hate her. (ch. 3, 31)

In this passage the child is a fearful object of unknowable power. Florence appears able to see into Dombey, she seems to know something about him that he has concealed from the rest of the world. And this reminds the reader that Paul Dombey's emergence into the world caused a death. If Florence poses a psychic threat to her father, then Paul was physically disastrous to his mother. Kincaid points out that rather than being simply pure, Paul is also called 'precocious'.[32] The reader is specifically told that there is something frightening and disturbing about Paul: he is called a 'changeling', and a 'young goblin', and the narrator tells us that he resembles 'one of those terrible Beings in the fairy tales, who at a hundred and fifty or two hundred years of age, fantastically represent the children for whom they have been substituted' (ch. 8, 98). Carole G. Silver, a historian of fairy lore, has demonstrated that the fairies were viewed as terrifying rather than decorative entities by the Victorians, involved in child abduction, rape, murder, destruction and metaphysical evil, and these fears were often projected on to those believed to be their human equivalents, such as dwarfs or the mentally and physically handicapped.[33] Perhaps this is why Paul is referred to a number of times as 'sly' (ch. 8, 100); perhaps that is also why he is so 'old-fashioned' (ch. 8, 98) – because he represents an atavistic threat coming to claim a place in Victorian society.

Paul's identification with a changeling is significant since, as Silver points out, all Victorians knew that a changeling was a fairy replacement for an infant the fairies desired; they left in its place a child which was damaged in sometimes obvious, though sometimes more subtle, ways.[34] Changelings were greatly feared, and this helps to explain the discomfort that Paul brings to those around him. In his first (and only) school report, Miss Blimber records of him:

> It may generally be observed of Dombey ... that his abilities and inclinations are good, and that he has made as much progress as under the circumstances could have been expected. But it is to be lamented of this young gentleman that he is singular (what is usually termed old-fashioned) in his character and conduct, and that without presenting anything in either which distinctly calls for reprobation, he is often very unlike other young gentlemen of his age and social position. (ch. 14, 196–7)

Paul is a bizarre hybrid creature of age and youth from the very start. After his birth we are told that his face is 'crossed and recrossed with a thousand little creases', like an old man in a bonnet (ch. 1, 2). For Stone, he represents a space where youth and old age meet. Like Little Nell he is attracted by the old and the grotesque, such as Mrs Pipchin, a witch-like woman with a 'mottled face' and a 'hook nose', an 'ogress and child-queller' (ch. 8, 105–6). They are well suited and in the evenings sit by the fire together, contemplating each other intensely:

> The good old lady might have been – not to record it disrespectfully – a witch, and Paul and the cat her two familiars, as they all sat by the fire together. It would have been quite in keeping with the appearance of the party if they had all sprung up the chimney in a high wind one night, and never been heard of any more. (ch. 8, 113)

In his bizarre conflation of infancy and age Paul prefigures Thomas Hardy's Gothic child 'Little Father Time' in *Jude the Obscure* (1894–5), the 'boy with an octogenarian face' (part V, ch. 7, 381) who eventually murders Sue Brideshead's children before killing himself.[35]

Oliver Twist, too, despite his gravitation towards absolute purity, is always already contaminated because he is, after all, the result of an illegitimate relationship; in this, Dickens can 'safely' represent the polluting danger of the child while continuing to protest about his essential goodness and purity. Inheritance is a central issue in the novel, as much as it is a factor in Augustine's version of original sin passed through the father's sperm, and the angelic Oliver must therefore be infected with the depravity of his father, who not only made a bad marriage but then corrupted an 'innocent' girl, for which corruption he demanded that Oliver be morally perfect, as if to atone for the sins of the father in the saintliness of the son. Oliver is, therefore, 'Twist(ed)' – corrupted and pure, innocent and guilty, the source of redemption and yet the seat of sin. As Richard Dellamora reminds us, the word 'twist' has connotations of perversity.[36] The novel provides plenty of places where the Augustinian version of the child is articulated, since Dickens's children are frequently sublimated versions of the demonic. This is, perhaps, clearest in the description of the Artful Dodger, a twitching, malevolent monster from the very first moment we meet him:

> He was a snub-nosed, flat-browed, common-faced boy enough; and as dirty a juvenile as one would wish to see; but he had about him all the airs and manners of a man. He was short of his age: with rather bow-legs, and little, sharp, ugly eyes. (ch. 8, 100)

The Artful Dodger is a prototype for Quilp in *The Old Curiosity Shop*, whose deformity lies in his size. The point about these children is that they appear to be perverse combinations of the adult and the child, 'grown-up children'.[37]

The morally hybrid youth can be found everywhere in Gothic writing about childhood. The most famous incarnations of apparently innocent, ultimately malevolent children are, of course, Miles and Flora in Henry James's *The Turn of the Screw* (1898). While much of the critical discussion of this story has turned on the psychology of the governess, the two children are also morally and ontologically ambivalent, as is indicated from the start by Miles's expulsion from school.[38] This dual attractiveness is evident in a Gothic poem like Christina Rossetti's 'Goblin Market' (1862): these goblins may in some sense represent corrupt masculinity, but they are also inverse figures of the two children they harass. After eating the forbidden fruit Laura turns old and frail like a hydrocephalic and looks goblin-like. The poem is, in fact, the site of a parental fantasy in which the horrible child is punished for her misbehaviour by kidnap and abuse. The desire to punish the naughty child pervades Victorian literature;[39] here this pervasive desire is projected once more on to the foreign scapegoat. Laura is punished, not because she innocently stumbles upon a group of child molesters, but because she is too 'precocious' and has disobeyed the rules laid down by the adult world, so that she becomes a Victorian version of Red Riding Hood, who wandered off the correct path and spoke to the big bad wolf. As Silver explains, goblins have always represented the racially other, but they were also easily conflated with children since, according to some theories, the goblin was a remnant of the 'childhood of the species', a view intensified after the 1859 publication of Charles Darwin's *Origin of Species*. While there had been a traditional link between the dwarf, the folkloric hobgoblin and the fairy, with anthropological and colonial missions into deepest Africa and elsewhere, and inflected through social Darwinism, dwarves became configured as remnants of the primitive species of humanity, an original 'goblin nation'.[40] This explains why dwarves such as Mademoiselle Caroline Crachami (the 'Sicilian fairy'), and General Tom Thumb were put on display in Victorian freak-shows. These freak-show dwarves were not humans, but domesticated representations of the essentialised foreigner populating fiction about Gothic children. The discourse of fairyland was crucial in representing to the Victorians the strange new cultures with which they came in contact for the first time in the nineteenth century through imperial adventures. This was particularly true of goblins, of course, since they were considered a blend of biological and cultural oddness. In the 1870s and 1880s explorers came across tribes of African pygmies, thus apparently confirming the atavistic nature of dwarves. In this context, George MacDonald's *The Princess and the Goblin* (1870–1), in which a group of humans move underground (to protest at high taxes) and eventually devolve into grotesque goblins, seems more like an attempt at realism than fantasy. The notion of a fairy commonwealth (as seen in Robert Kirk's extraordinarily popular

*The Secret Commonwealth of Elves and Fairies* (1691)), in which fairies and humans lived side by side, the goblin world a close and uncanny companion to the real world, was easily translated into a reading of the colonial situation. And of course, these figures were most interested in abducting your children, so that they were Gothic child-abusers as well as bizarre foreign childlike others.

### Primitive Children

Emily Brontë's *Wuthering Heights* (1847) is a vivid demonstration of the general Victorian ambivalence surrounding the figure of the child. As Irving H. Buchen reminds us, 'the bulk of the story concerns itself with the infancy and early years first of Heathcliff, Catherine, Edgar and Isabella; and later of Linton, Cathy, and Hareton. And even when each generation grows up they are not so much adults as arrested children.'[41] Indeed, Cathy and Heathcliff are persistently represented as children in the bodies of adults, as a man and woman who have failed to grow up. This is why it is perfectly understandable that Cathy appears to Lockwood as a child in his nightmare during his stay at the Heights – after her death she has simply reverted to the form which articulates her nature most vividly, the figure of the homeless child. Lockwood's reaction to her is also telling since it exposes the hypocrisy behind the Victorian rhetoric of affection for children. Confronted by a child who has been abandoned and locked out of the safety of domesticity, Lockwood's reaction is not to comfort but to punish. His violence upon the orphan child is partly representative of the Victorians' violence against children in all their forms, a violence motivated in part by a fear of the Gothic they saw as manifest within the child. Letting the ghost of the child-Cathy into the house is a terrifying prospect for Lockwood because he sees her as an external threat to adult coherence. She also threatens because she exposes the hollowness of versions of the child as innocent. Far from being a Sophie or a Little Nell, Cathy is a good example of Augustinian child-as-terrorist.

All Brontë's children are clearly infected with the sin of our first parents. There is no sense of anything we might recognise as 'innocence' about any of the children in the novel. Even Edgar and Isabella Linton are first spotted attempting to tear apart a puppy. Far from being innocent and naive, we initially encounter Cathy asking her father to get her a whip when he goes to Liverpool – indicative of her general orientation towards cruelty, rather than benevolence.[42] Cathy spends most of her childhood delighting in making the adults cry. Her malevolence is also manifest in the fact that, in a couple of paragraphs, she (systematically?) annihilates almost the entire adult population of both the Grange and the Heights, terrifyingly dispatching those who might get in her way: she is the last person to see her father, tormenting him right up to his death, and she carries a fever to the Grange, infecting and killing both Linton parents. These children are constantly linked to death and destruction. Nelly reproaches Cathy's 'childish' attack on a bunch of pillows with a warning to 'give over that baby-work', and her narrative returns repeatedly to Cathy's infantile nature (160).[43] She tells Lockwood that Cathy 'seemed to find childish diversion in pulling the feathers from the rents she had just made' (160); another time she complains that Cathy is 'no better than a wailing child' (162). Hence, when Cathy is about to die her youth returns, and this is why she gives birth at this stage to a second version of herself.

This pattern repeats in the other children. As a young boy, Hareton is witnessed 'hanging a litter of puppies from a chair-back in the doorway' (217). Isabella's cruelty is manifested when, as a girl, she sees Heathcliff for the first time and cries out: 'Frightful thing! Put him in a cellar, papa' (91). As children both Heathcliff and Cathy liked to 'stand among the graves' at Gimmerton Kirk and dare 'its ghosts … to come' (164). The young Heathcliff, we are told, 'had a delight in dwelling on dark things and entertaining odd fancies' (354).[44] His childhood violence is never relinquished, and he behaves in horrifically cruel ways throughout the text, attacking practically all the major characters. Childhood is a zone of malevolent power which is why there is a strong connection between Cathy, Heathcliff, childhood and the demonic. This is most evident in Cathy's famous dream in which she imagines she is in heaven, finds it insufferable, and longs to return to the Heights, which we must imagine as a kind of hell:

Heaven didn't seem to be my home; and I broke my heart with weeping to come back to earth; and the angels were so angry that they flung me out into the middle of the heath in the top of Wuthering Heights; where I woke sobbing for joy. (120–1)

Desiring hell, she must be a type of demon-child.[45]

Heathcliff, of course, is not only a version of Satan,[46] but an inverse representation of the natural savage as described by Rousseau, a primitive beast, cannibalistic, atavistic, chauvinist, dangerous. In a perceptive article on the novel, Matthew Beaumont notes that in its constant linking of Heathcliff with the figure of the cannibal, Brontë's novel associates him with a whole discourse of primitivism and atavism, what George Boas has identified as a language of the 'childhood of the race'.[47] What the children invoke here is the primitive condition of humankind before the civilising values of Christianity were imposed. This 'childhood of the race' is not a benevolent society of equals living in harmony with Nature, as envisioned by Rousseau, but a society defined by a pagan orgy of violence, sexuality and cannibalistic ritual.[48] The child herself is pre-civilised and pagan. Since Cathy reverted to her girlish body after her death, there is no reason to believe that Heathcliff does not also become a child when he dies – or indeed, that Edgar and Isabella (who are 'shrieking as if witches were running red-hot needles' into them when first seen by Heathcliff (89)) have not also reverted to infancy. Heathcliff's barbarism is not simply uncontrolled violence, after all, and Beaumont argues that there is something of a ritualistic aspect to his constant calls for blood to be spilled (146). In reference to Edgar, Heathcliff announces that had he not been Cathy's husband, 'I would have torn his heart out, and drank his blood' (185). At another time while at tea with Cathy and his son Linton, he insists, 'Had I been born where laws are less strict, and tastes less dainty, I should treat myself to a slow vivisection of these two, as an evening's amusement' (302). Cathy, too, is a kind of cannibal, and Edgar is at one point horrified to see her with 'blood on her lips!' (157). Hareton enjoys torturing cats (and is reminiscent of his father who enjoyed hanging dogs), while Cathy's daughter and namesake enjoys torturing Hareton.[49]

The childhood these characters inhabit, then, is not a childhood of innocent joy and sanctity, but one in which the atavistic powers of the human savage are released. Childhood is terrifying. Indeed, the only way that the 'love' between Catherine and Heathcliff can be explained (or better still, explained away) is by referring it to a crucible of childhood where original sin, ritual sacrifice, cannibalism, paganism and atavism reign. Theirs is a love driven by original sin; they are Adam and Eve driven out of the Garden – only this, as Gilbert and Gubar argue, is a heretical version of the Book of Genesis. Strangely, some have actually seen Heathcliff and Cathy's relationship as sexless, as if their version of dependence and absorption is not sexual in itself.[50] To claim, as Cathy does, that she *is* Heathcliff, is to believe completely in the version of conjugal love found in Genesis in which two literally become one. Besides, their violence towards each other is suggestive of a desire which is channelled rather than sublimated, sadomasochistic rather than romantic.[51] Their desire is a primitive neo-pagan ecstasy at odds with the nineteenth-century domestic novel in which they find themselves, which goes some way to explaining how absolutely weird these figures are[52] – they often appear to have stumbled out of the poems of Percy Shelley and Lord Byron into a novel by Elizabeth Gaskell. It is no wonder that the other characters think that Heathcliff might have made a compact with the Devil – if he is not the Devil himself. Nelly speculates that 'it appeared [to her] as if the lad were possessed of something diabolical' (106), which, by the standards of the nineteenth-century child, he is – an earlier Puritan would have known what to do with the likes of Cathy and Heathcliff.[53]

*Perpetuating Boyhood*

Although Oscar Wilde is often considered to have been a worshipper of youthful beauty, a desirer of what James Kincaid has called 'erotic innocence',[54] *The Picture of Dorian Gray* (1890) is an indictment of the cult of youth rather than a celebration of it. Like a latter-day celebrity, Dorian wants to remain young forever, or, more accurately, to remain forever an adolescent, a liminal figure trapped between full manhood and childhood, and he is surrounded by men who also want him to achieve this wish. The picture Basil Hallward paints of him articulates the artist's desire for its subject, but it is this very picture which sparks Lord Henry Wotton's sexual gaze. The visual image of the erotic child was a common one in the nineteenth century. John Everett Millais's 1879 portrait of 'Cherry Ripe' images budding sexuality in a pre-pubescent girl, but there is a long tradition which depicted the adolescent boy as an image suitable for consumption. In Germaine Greer's controversial study *The Boy* (2003), she stresses that the sexually desirable adolescent boy, 'a male person who is no longer a child but not yet a man', is a traditional figure in Western art,[55] so that Basil Hallward is merely replicating previous great masters. The erotically charged image of the adolescent male allows those who consume it visually to re-enter their own youth in both nostalgic and sexual terms. The image of St Sebastian, his adolescent body pierced and penetrated with arrows, has been an icon of homoerotic passion for centuries, especially in the Victorian period.[56] Looking and gazing at versions of Sebastian and the portraits of other adolescent boys, the homosexual man can legitimately become involved in what is essentially a sex act, while also recapturing an aspect of lost youth. It is appropriate, then, that Dorian Gray possess a cloak on which 'medallions of many saints and martyrs, among whom was St Sebastian' are starred, and that in stabbing the portrait at the end of the novel he performs a version of the penetration inflicted on Sebastian by his captors.

This penetrated, martyred, eroticised adolescent boy stands at the centre of *The Picture of Dorian Gray*, a version of arrested masculinity that is both childlike and experienced, innocent and erotic, pure and corrupting. Masculinity is central to the entire novel, as has been pointed out by many critics, and Dorian's Apollonian child-man operates as the kind of masculinity apparently privileged by the text. This image should be contextualised against a period when questions of masculinity were central to public discourse. It was in the Victorian age that the Ancient Greek synonymy of the masculine and the athletic body was revived. As Brian Pronger explains, a masculine body is a hard, muscular, athletic body. Masculinity is power in the gender myth … Athletic competitions and the displays of the muscled athletic bodies at sports spectacles on the beach, in the gym, are among the strategies that the force relations of gender employ.[57]

In contrast with the image of the boy given in *Dorian Gray* – the image of a boyish and penetrated masculinity – another version of masculinity was becoming dominant all over Europe just at this moment in the figure of the first modern bodybuilder, the Prussian Eugen Sandow, who had become wildly popular throughout the Continent in the late 1880s, even being invited to Queen Victoria's jubilee in 1887. Sandow represented a version of masculinity as physically developed and powerful, a version consonant with that articulated in the 'muscular Christian' movement in the Britain of the 1850s and 1860s, now epitomised for us in Thomas Hughes's *Tom Brown's Schooldays* (1857), and the work of Charles Kingsley. Sandow was considered a perfect specimen of 'true' masculinity, and was hailed in the *Daily Telegraph* in 1889 as 'a short but perfectly built young man of twenty-two years of age, with the face of a somewhat ancient Greek type, but with the clear blue eyes and curling hair of the Teuton. When in the evening dress there is nothing specially remarkable about this quiet-mannered, good-natured youth; but when he takes off his coat'.[58] Sandow was the boy-child as bodybuilder. The image of the young, stripped-down, oiled-up and extraordinarily muscular Sandow soon came to challenge the effeminate and effete St Sebastian as an idealised image of male sexuality and maleness in general, and young boys were soon expected to imitate and model themselves after the muscular man rather than his more sensitive ethereal opposite.

In investing so heavily in the 'Sebastian-like' Dorian Gray, Wilde's novel could be read as offering a direct challenge to this new view of the male child as incipient Hercules. Sandow was the culmination of a history of display of the athletic body – boxing had long emphasised the view that physique and character were equivalents, which explains why the Marquess of Queensberry (the father of Wilde's 'friend', Lord Alfred Douglas), was one of the judges of some of Sandow's physique competitions. In one sense, Dorian's implied competition with Sandow prefigures Wilde's later confrontation with Queensberry. Significantly, the Muscular Christian and the bodybuilding man were also considered versions of the imperial self as ultra-masculine. Colonising powers were generally configured from the mid nineteenth century as aggressive in body as well as mind. In contrast, conquered or colonised people were configured as concomitantly female or effeminate: passive, backward, emotional, childlike, a primitive hangover from the childhood of the race,[59] clearly seen in the writings of the anthropologist David MacRitchie, who proposed that the fairy lore of Celtic countries should be seen as quasi-historical records of a now lost 'pygmy nation', a Palaeolithic population which eventually evolved into contemporary man. Some places had not managed to evolve from this beginning, however, and Ireland was often viewed as populated by effeminate male degenerates, for which Wilde came to stand, a view that can be seen in the caricatures of Wilde in *Punch*.[60] Wilde's family had a strong history of Irish nationalist activism in various guises so that, by embracing the version of masculinity and childhood found in images of Sebastian rather than Sandow, *The Picture of Dorian Gray* can be seen as part of the Celtic Twilight school of thought. Some Irish writers of the late nineteenth century believed that, by accepting and stressing the gendered difference between the Anglicised and the Celtic world, English colonisation had inadvertently given the Irish a discourse by which to emphasise the reasons why Ireland should be politically as well as culturally independent – the effeminate man was considered a more spiritual and cultured figure, open to truths cut off from the physical rationality of the Saxons. Dorian is, after all, a boy who has been translated to Tír na nÓg (the Land of the Young) – he is Ossian, a favourite figure for Irish mythologisers like W. B. Yeats, who reached into the misty and dreamy past for images of Irish masculinity to counter the muscularity of England.[61] Dorian feels that the youthful boy is a way back to spiritual superiority, which is why he spends much of his time contemplating the past: 'How well he remembered it all! Every moment of his lonely childhood came back to him as he looked around. He recalled the stainless purity of his boyish life' (104).[62]

However, if Wilde is a nationalist, he is not taking as unproblematic the version of childhood purity that can be found in some Celtic Twilight writing. Dorian is not, after all, an innocent Émile, but rather a version of a Darwinian child, red in tooth and claw. Jacob Korg has pointed out that in his devotion to sensual pleasure, Dorian takes on 'the identity of an animal', as he is effectively an experiment in what a Darwinian child would look like.[63] Getting back to Nature, returning to the childhood of the species, results in a hideous transformation, so that the beautiful boy hides the hideous beast: Dorian is Mr Hyde with a better profile. Lord Henry Wotton often sounds like a flower-power guru from the 1960s, urging Dorian to get back in touch with Nature, insisting that what is natural is also good: 'Pleasure is Nature's test, her sign of approval. When we are happy, we are always good' (67). Since, like Rousseau, Lord Henry thinks that what is natural, what is childlike, is also pure and guileless, it is no surprise that he cannot believe Dorian killed Basil: 'It is not in you, Dorian, to commit a murder' (179). Despite the decadence of his discourse, he is essentially taking a leaf out of Rousseau's book, and associating natural purity with Nature itself. The novel reverses this, so that the closer one is to Nature – the more one becomes the child – the closer one is to depravity.[64] The muscular man may be a more palatable alternative to the decadent child.

If some associated the primitive with the effeminate, other thinkers believed that a version of rampant ultra-masculinity was basic to the atavistic. This image of the beast within the man, of masculinity as an expression of primordial savagery, finds clear articulation in the tradition of the werewolf, the man whose suppressed desires find release in lupine transformation, an idea whose time had clearly come in the nineteenth century, where masculinity was considered such a threat. Early examples of werewolf literature include Sutherland Menzies's 'Hugues, the Wer-Wolf' (1838), and G. W. M. Reynolds's *Wagner, The Wehr-Wolf* (1846–7), though both distance the Victorian reader from the implications of the legend, Menzies temporally, by setting his plot in the Middle Ages (and by having his werewolf be a man whose straitened circumstances lead him to disguise himself as a wolf to frighten travellers into providing him with food),

Reynolds spatially, by setting his story on the Continent (other early treatments can be found in Frederick Marryat's *The Phantom Ship* (1837–9), and Clemence Housman's *The Were-Wolf* (1890–1), but both texts feature a female werewolf). In Rudyard Kipling's stunning 'The Mark of the Beast' (1890), a chauvinistic colonist, Fleete, slowly transforms into a wolf after he has been touched by the leprous 'Silver Man', in punishment for his cavalier treatment of a statue of the Indian ape god Hanuman. The best man-as-beast story is, of course, Robert Louis Stevenson's *Dr Jekyll and Mr Hyde* (1886), which powerfully illustrates the ambivalence which infects any nostalgia for the primordial, childish mysteries of humanity. Critics have pointed out that much of the language used to describe Hyde in this novel is linked to a Darwinian devolution, but it is crucial to recognise that Hyde is also depicted as a kind of child, a depiction made evident in the transformation scene:

> The most racking pangs succeeded; a grinding in the bones, deadly nausea, and a horror of the spirit that cannot be exceeded at the hour of birth or death. Then these agonies began swiftly to subside, and I came to myself as if out of a great sickness. There was something strange in my sensations, something indescribably new, and, from its novelty, incredibly sweet. I felt younger, lighter, happier in body; within I was conscious of a heady recklessness, a current of disordered sensual images running like a millrace in my fancy, a solution of the bonds of obligation, an unknown but not an innocent freedom of the soul. I knew myself at the first breath of this new life, to be more wicked, tenfold more wicked, sold a slave to my original evil; and the thought, in that moment, braced and delighted me like wine. I stretched out my hands, exulting in the freshness of these sensations; and in the act, I was suddenly aware that I had lost in stature (57).[65]

Hyde is a younger version of Jekyll, a childlike version unencumbered by the demands of the society in which Jekyll lives.

The relationship between childhood and *Jekyll and Hyde* was clear, even from the dream origin of the text. Stevenson's position as a man who was still living with his mother and involved in an at best problematic sexual relationship with his wife Fanny may have contributed to his vivid nightmare, in which he saw 'Hyde, pursued for some crime, t[ake] the powder and under[go] the change in the presence of the pursuers', a transformation Stevenson classified as 'a voluntary change becoming involuntary'.[66] Stevenson, of course, famously wrote up the dream the next day and showed it to his wife. She disliked it, however, and he threw the manuscript into the fire in a kind of childlike sulk. Although it is dangerous to psychoanalyse the dead, the image of a weak and vulnerable man (Stevenson had tuberculosis at the time) surrounded by strong and disagreeable mother-figures, reverting to childhood when criticised, is highly suggestive. The story that emerges from this dream concerns a transformation taking place inside a male body. James Twitchell brilliantly argues that Stevenson's dream is really about growing up and escaping from the mother's clutches, and that the bodily transformation undergone in the dream – and subsequently in the novel – concerns the exciting though also horrific metamorphosis of the physique undergone in puberty and adolescence.[67] *Jekyll and Hyde*, in other words, is at least partly about an attempt to reverse that transformation and revert to the period of youth before adulthood and its responsibilities are forced upon both Stevenson and Jekyll, before a voluntary change becomes one that is involuntary.

This all suggests, crudely, that Stevenson was, at the time of his dream, a boy in man's clothing, as Hyde is towards the end of the novel, when he arrives at Dr Laynon's door wearing Jekyll's oversized outfit. Laynon is a father-figure of sorts, a super-ego who displays patriarchal disapproval of Jekyll's activities, but who is there to bail him out when things go disastrously wrong. What is so interesting about the novel is that it reverses the expectations of its audience. After all, it was typically the grown man who was considered a beast in mid- to late-Victorian England, rather than the child. In much literature about sexual activity at the time, the assumption was that men constituted a problem in policing the purity of the nation which was embodied in women and children. As Claudia Nelson points out, after the 1860s many Victorians considered sexuality a threat to civilisation, and 'consensus located the problem in the male, the solution in the female: men were better able to feel and less able to control their lower natures than women'.[68] Many (though not all) widely published medical and religious experts expressed the view that women were spared too much sexual desire, but that men were overburdened with an abundance of it. Famously, William Acton authoritatively declared that 'the majority of women (happily for society) are not very much troubled with sexual feeling of any kind', and even Krafft-Ebing insisted in *Psychopathia Sexualis* (1886) that since the normal woman experienced little sexual pleasure, 'a predominating sexual desire in her arouses a suspicion of a pathological significance'.[69] Men, on the other hand, commonly suffered excess desire and were bestially prone to masturbation, adultery, prostitute-consorting and a variety of other sexual sins. Adult masculinity was configured as promiscuous and immoral, atavistic and monstrous. The male child was believed to be spared these desires until they were foisted upon him by Nature during his pubescent bodily transformation. The translation from boyhood to manhood constituted a sexual fall into immorality.

It is this version of growth into moral confusion that Stevenson challenges. The adult Jekyll is, of course, prone to immorality – but he has been programmed to be so from childhood. Utterson remarks that:

> Jekyll was wild when he was young; a long while ago to be sure, but in the law of God, there is no statute of limitations. Ay, it must be that; the ghost of some old sin ... punishment coming, *pede claudo*, years after memory has forgotten and self-love condoned the fault. (17)

Hyde is like Jekyll's childhood past coming back to haunt the adult present. Jekyll may have got away with things in his youth, but now a younger version of himself is returning to take revenge. And what Hyde does is attack father-figures. Sir Danvers Carew, the 'aged and beautiful gentleman' with a white beard (21), is an overdetermined version of both father and God-the-Father. The intensity of Hyde's attack on him seems unmotivated, unless there is an ulterior motive. When Jekyll comes to after the attack, he has a flashback to his youth, when he walked through the streets of London holding his father's hand, a memory which suggests that the murder of Sir Danvers had more to do with Jekyll's problematic relations to his father than with anything Danvers did himself. As William Veeder points out, Hyde also destroys a portrait of Jekyll's father at the same time as he effaces and writes blasphemies on the book of theology – a book of God-the-Father-speak – so that, together with the attack on Carew, these acts demonstrate 'Stevenson's rage toward the Fathers as well as toward father'.[70] In a prevision of Sigmund Freud's *Moses and Monotheism* (1939), which speculates on the origins of religion in the murder of the father by the tribal sons, and the subsequent transformation of the father into a totem, Jekyll uses Hyde to destroy his own father but then spends the rest of his life finding new versions of the Father in his 'friends', Utterson and Laynon.

If Hyde acts with what Veeder calls 'oedipal rage' against father-figures, acting like an orphan revolting against the patriarchs who have abandoned him,[71] Victorian literature is full of orphans menaced by father-figures – Oliver Twist's struggle with Fagin marked our entry into the Gothic world of childhood, but Bram Stoker's *Dracula* (1897) is also populated by orphaned men and women who have relapsed into versions of their own childhood, and who are desperately searching for substitute parents to comfort them in the face of a terrible new father. Indeed (as in *Wuthering Heights*), benevolent parents and parent-figures perish through the course of the plot. Lucy's mother is terminally ill from the start of the novel and expires when Dracula appears at the window. Her death is extraordinarily convenient for the Crew of Light, since had she not died, Arthur could not have got hold of Lucy's effects. Jonathan's quasi-father, Mr Hawkins, also (and very suddenly) passes away and leaves his worldly goods to his quasi-son. Jonathan is already a literal orphan when the story begins, as are Mina, John Seward and Quincey Morris. These deaths are indications that the novel is deeply involved in the metaphysical orphanage that nineteenth-century Britain had become, due to the crisis of faith and the apparent withdrawal of

God,[72] and that it is implicated in the most significant parental death of all – the death of God and the effect of this death on the forsaken children. This is made clear by the title of Arthur's father: Lord Godalming, Lord God-Alm-ighty, who is ailing and sick at the novel's start (perhaps having heard Nietzsche's declaration), and conveniently meets his end halfway through. God Almighty metaphorically dies, leaving Arthur to inherit his title – Arthur, the resurrected King of English legend, becomes the resurrected Lord God Almighty also. The novel enacts what J. Hillis Miller has called the 'disappearance of God', and resurrects in His place an ineffectual Son and heir. These heirs are all useless, since they lack the ability to grow up. Nietzsche's belief that the death of God, the death of meaningfulness, would induce a species of insanity in the forsaken orphan children is manifested in the novel, because as well as being orphans, all these characters are mentally unbalanced and suffer what can only be called a series of nervous breakdowns. Moreover, as well as being psychologically unhinged, they all appear to have arrested development, and lack the ability to grow up, beset by hypersensitivity, crying at the least provocation. At one point the entire room is drowning in tears. Seward records that 'we men were all in tears now. There was no resisting them and we wept openly … [Harker] flung himself on his knees beside [Mina], and putting his arms round her, hid his face in the folds of her dress' (ch. 23, 329).[73] With his grey hair and gaunt features, yet childlike dependency, Jonathan is a version of Paul Dombey and Hardy's 'Little Father Time'. All the men in this novel need counselling. Arthur at one stage looks to Seward for comfort: 'Here he suddenly broke down, and threw his arms around my shoulders and laid his head on my breast, crying … I comforted him as well as I could' (ch. 13, 180). He later breaks down again, this time with Mina:

> In an instant the poor dear fellow was overwhelmed with grief. It seemed to me that all he had of late been suffering in silence found a vent at once. He grew quite hysterical, and raising his open hands, beat his palms together in a perfect agony of grief. He stood up and then sat down again, and the tears rained down his cheeks. I felt an infinite pity for him and opened my arms unthinkingly.

With a sob he laid his head on my shoulder, and cried like a
wearied child, whilst he shook with emotion. We women have
something of the mother in us … I felt this big, sorrowing man's
head resting on me, as though it were that of the baby that some
day may lie on my bosom, and I stroked his hair as though he were
my own child (ch. 17, 245).

Mina holds the now-Lord God-alm(ighty)ing in her arms and
pets his head as he cries like a newborn. The new God is a big
baby. The old God is dead, and his orphaned children are
completely incompetent in confronting the alternative God that
wants to take His place – Dracula.

Dracula is a monstrous translation of God the Father Almighty,
whose desire is to make all the characters his 'children of the
night' (ch. 2, 25). His warrior past (Dracula has familial links with
'the berserker Icelander, the devil-begotten Hun, the Slav, the
Saxon, the Magyar' (ch. 18, 254)) suggests that he is an ultra-
masculine threat to his hysterically effeminate enemies. Like the
Jewish Fagin whom he reincarnates (indicated by his Semitic
facial features), he is a child-abusing patriarch. He is twice seen
bringing children back to Castle Dracula to feed his vampire
brides, and his victim Lucy Westenra becomes a serial paedophile
and child-abductor as the 'Bloofer Lady'. Moreover, like all the
other men, Dracula is a kind of lunatic – and also a malevolent –
child. Professor Van Helsing insists that all vampires possess a
'child-brain' (ch. 23, 322), a facet which associates Dracula with
the criminal classes, since much of Van Helsing's taxonomy of the
vampire is derived from Lombroso's theories of the criminal
mind, where the social deviant is figured as immature and
psychologically arrested. In such discourse the child and the
criminal mind become one and the same. Ironically, this ultra-
male does possess some feminine attributes. When Dracula forces
Mina to suck the blood from his chest wound, we are told she
looks like a kitten with its head forced into a saucer of milk – an
image which makes Mina into a child, and Dracula into her
monstrous mother, but also Christ.[74] He declares she is his
vampire bride (blood of my blood, flesh of my flesh), but this is a
connection as much parental as marital:

'And you, their best beloved one, are now to me, flesh of my flesh; blood of my blood; kin of my kin; my bountiful wine-press for a while; and shall be later on my companion and helper …'With that he pulled open his shirt, and with his long sharp nails opened a vein in his breast. When the blood began to spurt out, he took my hands in one of his, holding them tight, and with the other seized my neck and pressed my mouth to the wound, so that I must either suffocate or swallow some of the ——— (ch. 21, 306–7).

If the men of *Dorian Gray* are struggling with images of ultra-masculinity that had come to dominate discourse about male maturity throughout Saxon Europe, the warrior-figures in *Dracula* – the male Crew of Light – are struggling to become men but fail miserably, collapsing into hysteria, while a figure who has combined ultra-masculine soldiery with feminine maternity is slowly taking over the neighbourhood. Most importantly, Dracula's monstrous divinity tells us something about the nineteenth-century version of the death of God. Nietzsche was wrong when he announced God's funeral, because only a version of God had died, not the Christian God, but only the Christian God as understood by Protestantism.

As God the Father Almighty, the Protestant God, died, other occult and feminine versions of divinity were rising again and offering a serious challenge to the Established Church – including a rejuvenated Catholic Church. For Bram Stoker, devoted to an ultra-masculine version of Protestantism, this must have seemed like a horrific prospect for the future. The Catholic God is configured in his novel as Dracula, a man with feminine attributes: 'Mother Dracula' as a type of 'Mother Church', an inverted Jesus, whose belief in the Real Presence of Christ in the sacrifice of the Mass is so literal that he has taken to drinking the blood of men and women everywhere. Dracula has provoked a plethora of different critical readings from literary critics, who have seen him as everything from a Jew, to an Irish landlord, to an Irish rebel, to an incarnation of sexual perversity, to a primordial savage: he is all these things and more, because, in his status as a monstrous version of the Protestant divinity, he assimilates to himself everything that God the Father Almighty is not. The

Protestant God has died; Dracula has risen from the grave to take his place.

On to this scene comes Van Helsing, a Dutch Catholic. He is able to defeat Dracula because he believes in the same things as Dracula, and shares many other things with his monstrous enemy. In the first place, his 'Christian' name is actually Abraham, which confers upon him a Jewish aura: like the great Old Testament patriarch he is willing to perform a sacrifice for the greater good. Moreover, while the other characters are orphans, Van Helsing is actually a bereaved parent whose own son has died, and on his arrival in England he begins to adopt the orphans one by one. Bizarrely, Arthur looks exactly like his dead son, and Van Helsing goes on to convert all of the Crew of Light into his children, except John Seward, who becomes his 'partner' (a substitute for his wife who has been confined to an asylum – perhaps from having to listen for too long to Van Helsing's broken English?). Van Helsing comforts Quincey Morris with the words 'Good boy … brave boy. Quincey is all man, God bless him for it. My child …' (ch. 24, 349). He has earlier called Jonathan his 'child'. In other words, his duty is partly to relieve these children of their orphan status and take over where the dead Lord Godalming left off. By acting as a benign substitute father with more appeal than Dracula, he can also enable his adopted children to pass from childhood to full masculinity. He says about Quincey, at one stage, that he is 'a man and no doubt'. Of course, Quincey's tendency to burst into tears at the slightest opportunity would seem to undermine the insistence that there is no doubt that he is a man. However, Van Helsing's role is to reinforce masculinity, or indeed, to force these pathetic boys into becoming real men fit to take on the enemies of England, whether they be rivals for the now-dead God of Protestant Christianity, or simply challengers to the superiority of the British Empire itself.

This reading might make it seem that Dracula is a pro-Catholic novel; since Protestantism is ineffectual in the new dispensation, Mother Church (embodied in Van Helsing) should take over. Yet, to see the novel as asserting Catholicism as the antidote to the spiritual angst caused by the Death of God would be, I think, a serious misreading. This is a profoundly anti-Catholic novel, deeply suspicious of Catholic power.[75] Thus, the Protestant loyalist Stoker cannot afford to give the Catholic Van Helsing too much authority because his Catholicism remains a problem. Catholicism's only use is to defeat an extreme version of itself, in the guise of Dracula. When this rival God has been dispatched, when Dracula has been killed, Catholicism itself will also be defeated, and Protestant English masculinity must take its central place again.

After all, Van Helsing is not perfect. His familial skills are, at best, rather dubious – we are not sure why his son died, but that his wife has been committed indicates that life with Abraham might not be easy. He is as unstable as the other men, anyway. At one point Seward tells the reader that 'I thought that the Professor was going to break down and have hysterics' (ch. 25, 361), and this is after he has already gone into a notorious fit of mirth brought on by what he calls 'King Laugh' (ch. 13, 186). If Lucy is his quasi-daughter, she is also, incestuously, his wife, since, in giving her his blood he admits that he has committed polyandry. The Catholic Van Helsing is crucial to defeating the monstrous Catholic Dracula, but when that has been effected he must give way to the Protestant English again. He merely provides the Catholic means to exorcise demonic Catholicism; he really proves that Catholicism is a backward, superstitious relict which still has the power to threaten a weakened Protestant masculinity. The transition from pathetic childhood (the Crew of Light), and Gothic childhood (Dracula's child-brain) to grown-up imperial Protestant masculinity is what the novel really wants to achieve.

As this chapter started with the Gothic Jewish threats to the orphan child as figured in Charles Dickens's *Oliver Twist*, so it ends with an entire collection of orphans again threatened by a monstrous and partly Jewish Dracula. The quasi-father (yet also hysteric) who answers the threat of the absurdly grown-up, yet child-brained Dracula is Van Helsing, a Catholic Scientist from Amsterdam. This has a particular relevance for the Irish readership of the Irish author Stoker – after all, the final nail in the Irish Catholic coffin was hammered by William of Orange, so that in making his 'hero' a Dutchman but also a Catholic, Stoker is in effect rewriting the past. William of Orange was always configured in Unionist history as the saviour of the Irish Protestant Ascendancy from the Catholic menace; here, the Catholic Van Helsing comes armed with stake and Host ('I have an Indulgence' (ch. 16, 224)) to save the English Protestant middle classes.[76] In seeing these middle-class men as orphaned children Van Helsing infantilises the very group which originally produced the infantilising discourse of the Irish. In confronting Dracula and his child-mind, the Crew of Light confront the primitive and the atavistic, the very things which the 'nineteenth century up-to-date with a vengeance' have actually repressed (ch. 3, 43). Since childhood has been sterilised, the horrific child that is Dracula and his atavistic potency appears beyond them; the childish past has 'powers of their own which mere "modernity" cannot kill' (ch. 3, 43). The link between childhood and Ireland, suggested here in *Dracula*, provides the perfect way to move the discussion of nineteenth-century Gothic from the child to the regions, zones not only childlike but also backward, perverted and populated by monsters.

# 3

# *Regional Gothic*

## *Imagining the Ethnic Other*

Gothic writers have always held the colonial fringes to be particularly potent sources of horror for the English imagination, particularly those areas deemed part of the Celtic world. A view of England as surrounded, and concomitantly threatened, by the Celtic 'peripheries' transformed these regions into zones of radical indeterminacy and fertile sources for fears of ethnic infection and moral pollution. Samuel Johnson's *Dictionary* (1775) had long established that the term 'Gothic' described 'one not civilised, one deficient in general knowledge, a barbarian',[1] so it was a word easily applied to these fringe territories believed to be populated by primordial remnants. As the debate on biological evolution heated up in the 1870s the historical apprehension of racial and ethnic contamination was intensified, due to the unease generated by the discourse of racial hybridity as a cause of degeneration. Some elites had been coping with such worries for years before the Darwinian debate began, but discussion of evolution undoubtedly helped to fuel the forays into extremes of racial theorising, such as are found in the work of scientists and anthropologists like John Beddoes and John Knox. Fear now shifted, in Judith Halberstam's words, from a focus on 'corrupted aristocracy or clergy, represented by the haunted castle or abbey, to [that] embodied by monstrous bodies. Reading Gothic with nineteenth-century ideologies of race suggests why this shift occurs.'[2]

The question of race and ethnicity was approached through an anthropological framework which situated contemporary races, ethnicities, nations and cultures within a chronologically progressive view of history, where some cultures were viewed as historically 'behind' others, more atavistic. Anglo-Saxons were located at the highest point of the evolutionary scale and others were judged relative to that point. This view is particularly evident in anthropological studies from the 1870s onwards, and can be found in such seminal works as Edward Tylor's *Primitive Culture* (1870), which argued that chronology was insignificant in studying different cultures, since the job of the anthropologist was to place individual cultures on an evolutionary rather than a historical scale.[3] Ireland, Scotland and Wales were useful in that they operated as spaces harbouring the atavistic, thus bolstering English claims to evolutionary superiority, but they were also (geographically and ethnically) close enough to pose a serious psychic threat to Saxon minds nervous about the future. The Celtic fringes were spaces on the edge of the known world, straddling this world and the next, and it was easily imagined that weird and terrible things could happen there. This is why County Galway could serve so well as the setting for William Hope Hodgkins's *The House on the Borderlands* (1908), since the west of Ireland was literally thought to be a borderland between normality and the strange. This relationship between colonial 'centre' and colonised 'periphery'[4] also helps to explain why Gothic literature forms an important part of the story that Britain has told itself about its own identity, and is part of the reason why relations with the regions are central to the Gothic tradition. Peggy Phelan points out that 'identity is perceptible only through a relation to an other', so that Self and Other are perpetually bound up together.[5] Darryl Jones is perfectly correct to argue that 'modern Britain was conceived in blood', primarily through a series of long and protracted wars with Catholic France, but the tradition of 'hating others' had always been a central aspect of identity politics in the archipelago.[6] As the idea of Britain was being fostered and nurtured by political and

literary cultures, imagining it required imagining what its opposite would look like. The Continent was, of course, a ready-made
Other against which Britain could be made to look coherent
despite its clearly composite nature. The Catholicism of
Continental France and Spain (traditional enemies of England),
and of Italy (the seat of the Pope) helped to solidify this growing
imagined community called Britain. As Jones puts it,

> by imaging forth the European Other as Catholic, superstitious,
> barbarous, irrational, chaotic, rooted in the past, the Gothic novel
> allowed a British audience conversely to identify itself as Protestant,
> rational, ordered, stable and modern: Continental Europe is the
> domain of fantastic unreality, whereas England is rooted in
> contemporary realism.[7]

There is a danger in this sentence of ignoring the difference
between Britain and England, a danger of which Jones is well
aware. After all, Britain is and was an imaginary community with
extremely delicate fault-lines drawn along the borders with Wales,
Scotland and the Irish Sea.

Literature became one means by which these fault-lines were
examined. William Patrick Day argues that the romance genre
operates as a 'fable of identity' in which fractures are healed and
disharmony dispelled, self-identity and otherness reconciled in a
marriage of formal convenience.[8] The romance form was a
crucial one for Britain, given its status as a conglomeration of
competing and incompatible nations (and often kingdoms). In the
romances which flourished in the eighteenth-century work of
novelists like Maria Edgeworth and Sydney Owenson, figures
symbolic of these national identities would move through a plot
of confusion and love to reach a marriage in which the 'English'
male figure united with his 'Celtic' female equivalent and all difficulties were absolved.[9] The romance prefigured the kind of
political relationship held to be ideal by Matthew Arnold, who, in
*On the Study of Celtic Literature* (1866), argued that hybridity in a
'marriage of hearts' would solve the protracted political enmity
between the Celts and the Saxons.[10] Of course the English
figure always retained authority in this marriage, thus ultimately

reinforcing at the level of plot the hegemony already established in politics.[11] The colonial ethic of the romance is mitigated by the generally positive attitude taken towards the native cultures of the Celtic fringes, so that as well as marrying the Celtic female the English man usually learns to cast aside his previously disapproving attitude towards the Celtic zone and benefits from the Celt's feminine 'sensibility'. These English figures are often depicted as overburdened by an attachment to reason, while the Celtic female is portrayed as hovering on the edge of an overexcited emotionalism: in marriage the two extremes are moderated and the couple meet somewhere in the middle, producing a rationality leavened by the passions of the heart.[12]

An alternative means of examination of British fault-lines has been the Gothic novel of the regions, which poses a pathological account of the breakdown of identity and the collapse of personal and national integrity in the encounter with otherness; marriages of competing identities may be attempted but they are never successful and usually collapse, often into female madness and male symbolic impotence, usually into fragmentation of identity and narrative failure. The kinds of generic instabilities and disintegrations that Elizabeth Napier has diagnosed as symptomatic of the Gothic genre as a whole demonstrate what Day has termed a 'collapse of identity'.[13]

In the hands of writers emerging from the colonial centre – England – 'regional Gothic' can often demonstrate such a pathological fear of the regional Other that it verges on a paranoid nationalism or a reactionary and ultra-conservatism determined to police national boundaries.[14] Even here, however, the Gothic is infected by a desire for the Other disallowed within conventional culture, and this desire destabilises the narrow-gauge identities naturalised within the dominant culture. After all, for the metropolitan man suffering the agonies of modern ennui and angst in which self-identity became increasingly problematic, the Celtic fringes offered a means by which to recuperate and revive. If reconnecting with the 'inner child' was one pathway towards self-renewal, another was through connection to the 'real' via the zones of the natural and spaces of sensibility – the Gothic constituencies of the Celtic fringes. It was believed that these places possessed the ability to recall to truth the vitiated modern individuals thronging the cities of modernity. Celtic spaces could become places for reconstitution and revitalisation of the Self. Whereas the metropolitan centres were considered sites of manufactured and hollow identity, the regions were believed to be 'authentic' areas for the soul. Travels into the regions allowed the jaded cosmopolitan to shore up power and truth again for a return journey into psychic battle in the urban jungle of inauthenticity. The Gothic re-enacts this movement but undermines it; the union of Self and Other is always a nightmare rather than a romantic dream; authenticity is not discovered but is revealed as so horrifically Other that the cosmopolitan is completely undone in his encounter with it; moreover, desires felt by the centre for the exotic other are intensified until they become neurotic, leading to dissipation rather than sexual union. The typical Gothic novel is torn by competing impulses towards wholeness and fragmentation, and although the Celtic fringes operated most clearly as these problem regions, any major non-cosmopolitan area in Britain served equally well.

## Gothicising the Regions

The writing of Thomas Hardy is pervaded with a sense of the British regions as Gothic localities; his Wessex is a terrain of history, legend, portents, superstition, folklore, ghosts and fatalism, a place stuck in the past. Hardy's oeuvre includes some straightforwardly Gothic stories, including 'Barbara of the House of Grebe' (1890), and others resort to the grotesque and employ Gothic motifs in order to conjure up a specific atmosphere – as in the spectral attack in 'The Withered Arm' (1888) and the ghostly visitation in 'The Committee-Man of "the Terror"' (1896). More important than these obvious examples, however, is the constant depiction in Hardy's major novels of the countryside as an almost preternatural landscape of mystery and legend. As James F. Scott has pointed out, 'personal skepticism [about the supernatural] never reduces Hardy's enthusiasm for the mysterious dreams, strange portents, or dark curses and spells of Gothic fiction, all of which he parades in copious array', usually in connection with the Wessex world he envisions as running parallel to modern London,[15] and here the influence of writers such as Sir Walter Scott and Harrison Ainsworth is clear, as is Hardy's debt to Edmund Burke's description of the sublime as defined by terms such as 'obscurity', 'vastness' and 'power'. Typically, Hardy's characters are set in stark contrast to a bleak, pitiless and terrifying rural backdrop, such as the Vale of Blackmoor and Marlott in *Tess of the d'Urbervilles* (1891), or Egdon Heath in *The Return of the Native* (1878). Lord Cecil argues that 'Hardy's stories are full of relics of English popular superstition which played so large a role in the histories he listened to round the fire in the long winter evenings'.[16] Fearful that the lore and traditions of the rural past were fast disappearing and being forgotten he attempted to preserve them in his fictional depictions of the countryside. Not only do these landscapes abound in the paraphernalia of the Gothic – ruins, graveyards, corpses and psychic phenomena – but they come bearing the weight of the past impinging upon the present, and are therefore ghostly landscapes themselves. Throughout *Tess*, the characters travel through forests covered by mist and ruled by 'darkness and silence' (69), encounter a 'mouldy old habitation' in which are 'life-size portraits' of the d'Urbervilles which 'haunt the beholder afterwards in his dreams' (210), come across the 'green foundations that showed where the d'Urberville mansion had once stood' (352), the 'ancestral sepulchre' (353). Tess herself, at times appearing to be an embodiment of the landscape, is inscribed with the imagery and otherness of the Gothic:

> The spectral, half-compounded, aqueous light which pervaded the open mead impressed them with a feeling of isolation, as if they were Adam and Eve ... At this dim, inceptive stage of the day, Tess seemed to Clare to exhibit a dignified largeness ... and almost regnant power – possibly because he knew that at the preternatural time hardly any woman so well endowed a person as she was likely to be walking in the open air within the boundaries of his horizon (ch. 20, 120).[17]

In Arthur Conan Doyle's *The Hound of the Baskervilles* (1901–
1902), it is Dartmoor that is imbued with a Gothic sensibility.
However, *Jane Eyre* (1847) is a useful text in which to examine in
detail this internal struggle for national identity between the
centre and the peripheries, especially since Charlotte Brontë may
have been sensitive to the question of regionalism, due to her
father's Irish background. The spectre of regional Gothic looms
large over *Jane Eyre*. In addition, the novel is thematically
concerned with the child figure, threatened by external Gothic
forces, but also possessing an unsettling uncanniness in its link to
primitiveness and atavism. As was pointed out in chapter 2, it is
not unusual for childhood to represent the personal and cultural
past, so Charlotte Brontë's association of the child with folklore
and forgotten cultures is hardly unique. However, it is in the
correlation between childhood and the atavistic regional spaces of
the British Isles that the danger to cosmopolitan identity lies,
because these cultures are precisely what have been repressed and
displaced by the modern adult urban subject, so that to encounter
a child is also to encounter the return of the repressed, an
encounter often represented through the language of the malevolent supernatural. Jane herself embodies these subversive regional
and folkloric energies. Early in the plot, the heroine catches sight
of herself in a large mirror, and the child looking back at her is a
phantom representative of herself:

> the strange little figure there gazing at me, with a white face and
> arms specking the gloom, and glittering eyes of fear moving where
> all else was still, had the effect of a real spirit; I thought it like one
> of the tiny phantoms, half fairy, half imp, which Bessie's evening
> stories represented as coming out of lone, ferny dells in moors (ch.
> 2, 21–2).[18]

What Jane sees is an image of herself as located in the discourse
of the regions, since the folkloric stories she remembers are
directly related to the rural environment in which she grew up.
Moreover, she is called an 'imp', 'goblin', 'sprite', and 'changeling'
by Rochester, who constantly associates Jane with supernatural
forces.[19]

For Rochester, Jane functions as a piece of the Gothic past, an exotic space that will help him recover psychological wholeness, a virgin and wild land he needs to tame. That Rochester is suffering from modern ennui and angst is clear, and he appears to feel that an immersion in the Gothic may cure him. This alone would help to explain his first marriage to Bertha Mason, who clearly attracted him as much by her mysterious difference as her money. Jane is Bertha's double in this sense, since she also represents a repeat of the exotic otherness Rochester hopes will alleviate his metropolitan malaise, her supernatural qualities linked in some way to the folkloric properties located in her body and in her mind.[20] However, if Bertha Mason represents the kind of atavism that cannot be absorbed and which must instead be crushed if the Self is to survive contact with it, then Jane embodies a tamer and more pliable version of this same otherness, contact with which allows for recuperation of the Self rather than dissolution. Of course, it was completely normal for the regions to find themselves represented as split by a monstrous duality: tame and beautiful Hibernia was doubled by the ape-like and violent Paddy, the stately countered by the terrorist. Rochester's struggle between Bertha and Jane is symbolic of that taking place throughout Gothic texts emerging from the 'mainland' in the nineteenth century, where the regions are configured as spaces of self-rejuvenation for the vitiated metropolitan, and also terrifying places where horrific otherness resides.

Crucially, Rochester, too, is not securely English, and is not only described throughout the novel as dark and having exotic features, but is actually called a 'Paynim', a 'sultan' and a 'Grand Turk'; he is clearly meant to contrast with his 'double', the 'true' English man, St John Rivers, who is depicted as 'tall, slender; his face riveted the eye; it was like a Greek face, very pure in outline: quite a straight, classic nose; quite an Athenian mouth and chin … His eyes were large and blue, with brown lashes; his high forehead, colourless as ivory' (ch. 29, 386). Cora Kaplan points out that 'the constant evocation of Rivers' whiteness becomes increasingly ambivalent, then fully critical … Whiteness as frigid adult phallicism represents an aberrant extremity of the human.'[21] Pure whiteness and pure Englishness are not endorsed here, as both are merely recipes for impotence. Rivers is the walking, talking, neoclassical exemplar, a human version of the architecture considered so representative of the English style in the eighteenth century. In contrast, Rochester is a Gothic edifice, with a 'dark face', 'broad and jetty eyebrows', possessing a body with 'unusual breath of chest, disproportionate almost to his length of limb' (ch. 14, 151). As Elsie Michie points out, this sets Rochester apart as indicative of a more problematic, hybridised Englishness.[22]

It is St John Rivers's constipated version of Englishness that is ultimately condemned by the novel: he is incapable of opening up to allow the alternative spaces of either India, which he is going to try to completely civilise, or Jane herself to affect him in Arnoldian style. Instead, he attempts to crush their difference and make them reflect *his* identity. Rochester, contrarily, wishes to subdue but not destroy otherness and difference, uniting it to his own body, in his (eventual) marriage to Jane, and in the child that is the product of this union. This marriage succeeds partly because Jane is rather more like Rochester than she may at first seem. After all, as Michie points out, her early reading schooled her in colonial desires. She consumed *The Arabian Nights* and *Gulliver's Travels* as if they were stories of colonial endorsement, and they stoked her craving to visit different lands and possess them.[23] Although she has inscribed upon her some of the insignia of difference, hers is precisely a difference that can become sameness. Just as she has fantasies of colonial expropriation (which would explain her terrible treatment of Bertha), she has also a need to be conquered like a recalcitrant colony. She tells the reader of how she found Rochester's eyes fascinating, exercising an 'influence that quite mastered me – that took my feelings from my own power and fettered them in his' (ch. 17, 198). Jane's is partly a masochistic dream of slavery, of being enchained and rendered powerless by the superior mastery of her husband. She is, in other words, a pliable land in the way that Bertha could never be. Bertha is the only one who refuses to conform to Rochester's version of master–slave relations. She simply cannot be absorbed, and effects a terrible revenge on those who try to contain her threat. Rochester is scarred and almost killed by his encounter with the kind of total otherness she represents. Jane may have her moments of rebellion, but her desire for and marriage to Rochester ends that period of defiance. During her initial engagement to Rochester, Jane insisted that should he become a tyrant, like a sultan, she will 'go out as a missionary to preach liberty to them that are enslaved ... and I'll stir up mutiny' (ch. 24, 302), but when she actually discovers a enslaved woman on the premises, rather than protest at what has been happening to her effective double, she allows that slavery to continue indefinitely.

Despite Jane's palpable discomfort at Rochester's tendency towards the discourse of power, his 'smile such as a sultan might, in a blissful and fond moment, bestow on a slave his gold and gems had enriched' (ch. 24, 301), we discover that when he begins to recover his eyesight after their marriage the first thing he spots is a 'glittering ornament around [Jane's] neck', a kind of bejewelled chain (ch. 38, 501). Far from being the story of a woman's refusal to submit to the dictates of ownership and exoticism, *Jane Eyre* documents the transformation of two rebellious and exotic women from the colonial and regional peripheries from free agents into quasi-slaves, but also the transformation of an Englishman into a hybrid figure (although Englishness remains dominant). If, in Jenny Sharpe's judgment, colonialism 'is the discursive field in which Jane's struggle for self-determination is played out', that is a struggle which has well and truly come to an end by the close of the narrative, with Jane's capitulation to a version of Romantic Union in which her identity is preserved by subordination to Rochester's.[24] While it is certainly not fair to judge this compromise against a feminist paradigm of refusal that would only come to fruition much later, it is important to note that it does signify the novel's own ideological commitment to a form of metropolitan and colonial hegemony. The novel as a whole comes to endorse the kind of 'union of hearts' philosophy that would later be argued for by Matthew Arnold in his analysis of relations between Ireland and England, although in Rochester's near-death experience with Bertha, a coded warning to the Englishman about wandering too far from home for his sexual and cultural kicks may be encoded.

## Problematising Regionalism

In opposition to the compromised racial and ethnic hybridity examined in *Jane Eyre*, a competing discourse of total fear of biological pollution also characterised English Gothic writing on the 'regional'. *Jane Eyre* was written in a period of colonial confidence, when Britain was self-assured of its own power and authority, its ability to overcome regional and colonial defiance; towards the end of the century, however, this confidence began to evaporate, and Gothic writers explored what would happen if perspectives were altered and the colonial centre was threatened by invasion. In much the same way as regional Gothic posits the peripheries as zones of the bizarre ripe for the taking, in H. G. Wells's *The War of the Worlds* (1897) England itself becomes regionalised, a space ready to be invaded and appropriated. Rather than the centre of the universe, England (and ultimately the Earth) is simply a cosmic county to be exploited by alien invaders. The narrator constantly opines against the arrogance of human superiority: 'so vain is man, and so blinded by his vanity, that no writer, up to the very end of the nineteenth century, expressed any idea that intelligent life might have developed [on Mars] far, or indeed at all, beyond its earthly level' (8).[25] This sounds like a parody of English views of the Celtic fringes, which were considered exotic but in which the prospect of intelligent life was believed to be small. With the coming of the Martians things suddenly change for the cosmopolitan mind, since 'we men, the creatures who inhabit this earth, must be at least as alien and as lowly as are the monkeys and lemurs to us' (8). In the perspective of the Martians the English reader is as un-evolved as Celtic white chimpanzees. *The War of the Worlds* owes a great deal to Bram Stoker's *Dracula*, since that, too, is a novel of horrific reversals. The Count, as has been pointed out by Stephen Arata, is a 'reverse-colonizing' alien, intent on treating the middle-class Englishmen and women he encounters as fodder, in a horrific repayment for colonising attitudes.[26] Such fears abound in Gothic literature towards the end of the century. In H. Rider Haggard's *She* (1886–7), an occult African 'goddess' expresses a desire to visit and perhaps take over Britain, while in Richard Marsh's *The Beetle* (1897), a priestess of the Egyptian goddess Isis 'invades' Britain in order to get her revenge on the man who jilted her twenty years ago, and also to victimise white women in her pagan rituals. As Glynnis Byron notes, that this woman 'is both human and animal, animal and insect, male and female, and, perhaps most shockingly of all, heterosexual and homosexual' makes her threat to the integrity of the rational English body even more terrifying.[27]

The fear of reverse colonisation and invasion found in all these novels reflects a more general belief in late-nineteenth-century Britain that the era of colonial superiority had come to an end. Paul Kennedy has described the 'new imperialism' of post-1870s Britain as an 'imperialism of fear', motivated as it was by a belief that Britain's economic dominance of the world was over and that the United States and Germany were not only catching up, but would soon overtake it.[28] The Liberal MP Meredith Townsend articulated this increasingly pessimistic view of Britain's global power in 1888, declaring that,

> whether for good or evil, a great change is passing over Englishmen. They have become uncertain of themselves, afraid of their old opinions, doubtful of the true teaching of their consciences. They doubt if they have any longer any moral right to rule anyone, themselves almost included.[29]

There was a widespread belief that all empires ended in collapse and failure, fuelled by a voguish interest in Edward Gibbon's twelve-volume *The Decline and Fall of the Roman Empire*, which was read as a commentary on contemporary Britain rather than a piece of history. Gibbon blamed the collapse of Roman authority partly on its cultural decadence, as exhibited in over-indulgence, moral permissiveness and laziness, and many could trace such qualities in contemporary society. 'Decadence' was a term applied to the forces supposedly undermining robust colonial masculinity, such as aestheticism and the New Woman, the very forces seen as dangerous in texts like *The Beetle*, *Dracula*, and *The War of the Worlds*, where the Martians' appearance points up the vitiated masculinity of the previously smug and pompous Englishmen. The aliens are real men, possessing the ultimate male member, a penetrating nozzle that literally sucks the life out of the natives.

Moreover, they are also more evolved than the English. The Martians have brains that are so highly developed that they don't actually need bodies any more, and are more like minds with vampire-like penises: 'the Martians were heads, merely heads. Entrails they had none. They did not eat, much less digest. Instead they took the living blood of other creatures and injected it into their own veins' (125). Wells, deeply influenced by Darwin's bulldog Thomas Huxley, suspected that in the survival of the fittest, comfortable, middle-class Englishmen might actually come out a lot worse than the primordial foreign thugs to whom they believed themselves superior. Years of luxury had rendered muscle apparently unnecessary to the suburban Englishman, and he had grown weak and flabby; in contrast the colonial fringes had retained a masculine edge ready to be used in a final battle with their imperial masters. *The Time Machine* envisions middle-class England as so physically wasted that it had become prey to the reconstituted Eastenders living under the ground; *The War of the Worlds* warns that the danger to English hegemony might lie in its own self-satisfaction and moral indolence, as this smugness may encourage an actual invasion.

The Martians are horrific hybrids of brain, bacteria and phallus, pure Darwinian primitivism and masculine force. The English may have been reducing the colonised masses to beasts for centuries, but in this novel suddenly they are themselves seen as animals to be used as beasts of burden and as food: 'Yet across the gulf of space, minds that are to our minds as ours are to those of the beasts that perish, intellects vast and cool and unsympathetic, regarded this earth with envious eyes, and slowly and surely drew their plans against us' (7). Matthew Arnold had only been the foremost theorist of the English as awesome rational intellects with little sympathetic genius (for which quality they needed to absorb, amoeba-like, the Celts). In this novel it is the English who are absorbed and sucked up by parasitic brains. The idea of the alien absorption of the English puts the whole concept of allegorical union, which formed the basis of the Romantic novel, in jeopardy. Here the English characters meet with parodic yet terrifying versions of themselves: if the English were meant to be the ultra-rationalists, the Martians can trump them even in that.

When a delegation approaches the Martian ship carrying the white flag of peace the only reaction of the aliens is the profoundly rational one: the heat-ray comes out and roasts the white-flag carriers alive, as if on a barbecue.

Wells obtained a perverse pleasure from imagining his fellow-countrymen and women being set upon by a superior invading force disciplined by the rigours of Nature. Brian Aldiss details how, when writing the novel, Wells traversed his neighbourhood on a bicycle to gain a closer perspective on the place and people he was about to imaginatively obliterate: 'I completely wreck and sack Woking', he wrote, 'killing my neighbours in painful and eccentric ways.'[30] The Celtic neighbours of the English had been wrecked and sacked plenty of times, and it was now the era for a reversal of fortune. Contrary to some readings of the novel, which see it as cautioning against England's colonising tactics, it is in fact a warning to the empire to get its masculinity up to colonial scratch again. When he meets the annoying curate, Wells's narrator complains, 'Be a man!' (71) – the ultimate put-down here. This sentiment was hardly unusual in the 1890s, as critics like Patrick Brantlinger and Elaine Showalter have forensically shown.[31] Wells, who is often seen as a champion of human rights, is really a crusading little Englander. After all, the plot is propelled forward by the conviction that England requires a moral and biological Augean stable-clean, of a kind the Martians might be able to provide. The artilleryman articulates a view of English society as polluted by poets and aesthetes, and he delights in his vision of a world run by Martians in which only a hardy bunch of humans have survived: he is glad to announce that

> there won't be any blessed concerts for a million years or so; there won't be any Royal Academy of Arts, and no nice little feeds at restaurants … If you've got any drawing-room manners or a dislike of eating peas with a knife or dropping aitches, you'd better chuck 'em away. (154)

The invading foreigners represent a unique opportunity for the English to begin again. The artilleryman wants a human cull of what he believes are evolutionary ineffective members of the species, which includes not only biologically ineffective but also culturally and ideologically suspicious humans. Driven by this ideological vision, it is understandable why the novel appears at times lost in admiration of the Martians, and the famous first paragraph can be explained in no other way.

*The Island of Doctor Moreau* (1896) has also often been misread as a compassionate novel, campaigning against the horrors of vivisection and cruelty to animals. Yet Doctor Moreau tries to enact here a more vivid and bloody version of Matthew Arnold's programme for peace in the British Isles: Moreau is trying to graft on to beasts the minds of rational Englishmen, just as Arnold advocated a grafting of the English mind on to the exotic body of Celtic subordinates. If Moreau wishes to 'burn out all of the animal' in order to make a 'rational creature of my own' (78),[32] what he is trying to achieve is precisely what is argued for by Matthew Arnold in his study of 'The Incompatibles' (1881), which posited that the Irish and the English were not so incompatible after all, but could be united and hybridised. In the novel this hybridity fails miserably and Moreau is constantly frustrated in his (Frankenstein-like) attempt to create a beautiful rational creature out of base materials. There is something inherently wrong with these animals, so that the rational cannot gain hegemonic control over the emotional and instinctual. As he puts it,

> the least satisfactory of all is something that I cannot touch, somewhere – I cannot determine where – in the seat of the emotions. Cravings, instincts, desires that harm humanity, a strange reservoir to burst suddenly and inundate the whole being of the creature with anger, hate, or fear. (78)

To Arnold the Celt was profoundly emotional and irrational, and his faith in controlling these weird aspects through hybridisation was not, in fact, very deep. In 'The Incompatibles' he worries that the rational Englishman would eventually be polluted and overrun by contact with base Celtic emotions, so that rather than gain the upper hand, hybridity could well signal the beginning of the end for Anglo-Saxon superiority. *The Island of Doctor Moreau* effectively warns that the beast cannot be bred out of racial degenerates and suggests that it is best to simply wipe them out.[33]

It also continues the attack found in *The War of the Worlds* on vitiated English masculinity. The narrator, Prendick, is a comfortable idle Englishman who travels about on a ship appropriately named the *Lady Vain*, and lapses into pathetic hysteria when he is left on a raft alone for a few days. If this is what the Empire has to protect it, then the Empire is in trouble. Tellingly, Prendick is incapable of making a raft because he has never done 'any carpentry or suchlike work' (124); in other words, he is unqualified in normative masculinity. The narrative sets about acclimatising him to the horrors of vivisection and training out of him his initial (and, the novel suggests, effeminate) queasiness at the sight and sound of the puma being cut into by Moreau. When Moreau experiments on the puma, Prendick is initially driven wild:

> I found myself that the cries were singularly irritating, and they grew in depth and intensity as the afternoon wore on. They were painful at first, but their constant resurgence at last altogether upset my balance. I flung aside a crib of Horace I had been reading, and began to clench my fists, to bite my lips, and pace the room. (38)

It is, perhaps, the classical education which has made Prendick so sensitive to the cries of pain, rendering him something less than a man. There is little time to be reading Horace when faced with the future of mankind. What he must learn is how to face up to his responsibilities manfully. By chapter 17, as Lucy Bending argues, everything had changed: 'Scarcely six weeks passed before I had lost every feeling but dislike and abhorrence for these infamous experiments of Moreau's ... So indurated was I at that time to the abomination of the place, that I heard without a touch of emotion the puma victim begin another day of torture' (96–7).[34] That Moreau was actually driven out of England by a public unable to face up to its scientific responsibilities is crucial to the plot. How can an England ill-equipped in handling scientific experimentation on animals ever carry out what has to be done by an empire in order to survive? This helps explain why race is so central to the novel. Moreau wishes to take over the body

itself, and exert what can only be called a colonial mastery over it.
This is reinforced by the fact that all these experiments take place
on a remote island, and what Moreau creates look unsurprisingly
like caricatures of men-of-colour: it is an Ape Man that Prendick
first encounters, whom he calls 'a fair specimen of the Negroid
type' (76); another beast is described as possessing a 'black
Negroid face' (28), while another has a face 'ovine in expression –
like the coarser Hebrew type' (86). These are not simply animals,
but, rather, types of colonial subject which still require taming.[35]
The material bodies Moreau wishes to master are the science-
fiction equivalent of the colonial fringes found in more straightforward imperial texts. His mistake is in thinking, like Arnold, that
the ethnically and regionally Other can be tamed by hybridity
and miscegenation. He must learn that no matter what is done to
change these savages, the 'stubborn beast' will always re-emerge. If
the beast-men Prendick encounters on this island tell the reader
anything, it is that you cannot make Prosperos out of Calibans.

## *Writing Back?*

That the regional man may possess a robust masculinity was a
constant fear haunting the pages of the Victorian press, and it had
already appeared in Charlotte Riddell's 'The Banshee's Warning'
(1867), in which vivisection and the regional mind were also
associated. The story concerns a 'handsome' young Irish emigrant
surgeon, Hertford O'Donnell who lives in Soho in the period
before chloroform was used in operations (306).[36] His ability to
calmly cut into a screaming patient in agony makes his reputation
in London: compared to other surgeons Hertford is as 'hard as
steel', able to operate with extraordinary rationality in extraordinary circumstances (307). He has, in other words, surpassed his
colonial masters in combining a rational scientific mind with
muscular strength. Where anti-vivisectionists were busy warning
the public that a man who could cut into a unsedated animal
today without flinching should be under moral suspicion, because
tomorrow he may be cutting into human flesh, Hertford has
mastered the art of inflicting pain without concern since 'he

cared no more for quivering nerves and shrinking muscles, for screams of agony, for faces white with pain, and teeth clenched in the extremity of anguish, than he did for the stony countenances of the dead' (307). This is due to his ability to view the human body and its possessor as objects, rather than subjects; 'the human body was to him, merely an ingenious piece of mechanism', and he looked upon it as Brunel surveyed the Thames Tunnel (307). This immigrant has adopted the stereotypical stiff upper-lip of the Englishman; if Arnold believed that Irishmen were too prone to excessive emotion, O'Donnell is incapable of emoting at all, since 'he had no sentiment, he had no sympathy' (307).

Written in an era of unprecedented concern about medical ethics and the incapacity of doctors to see their patients as anything other than objects,[37] Riddell taps into the real concerns of the anti-vivisectionists about the extension of medical power. As scientific knowledge advanced the public was forced to rely increasingly on the professional specialism of the doctor, but this only amplified uncertainty because everyone knew that doctors were required to do apparently horrific things in their jobs. The fear was that perhaps some of them actually enjoyed these terrible acts. The idea of lying prone and vulnerable before a man with a scalpel is, understandably enough, likely to engender feelings of terror in even the most rational of us; suspecting that this same doctor might see you as some kind of 'engineering feat' rather than a fellow human is hardly likely to calm your nerves. The doctor was, in one sense, a parodic and horrific version of the ultimate and rational Englishman, so rational that feeling itself has been stifled. O'Donnell the immigrant has not only adopted English ways and customs, but has become the ultimate Englishman, in a nightmare version of what Homi Bhabha has called 'mimicry', whereby the colonised learn to parrot back the manners, language and customs of the coloniser in order to lull him into a false sense of security.[38] There is a thin line between mimicry and internalisation, however, and O'Donnell seems completely serious in his adoption of rational English attitudes; he 'never lost his temper, never muttered a surly reply to the gate-keeper's salutation' (307).

O'Donnell's peers are not convinced, however, and suspect that deep within him the Irish strain (the 'stubborn beast'?) has not been eradicated. To their judgement 'he was Irish – not merely by accident of birth … but by every other accident and design which is objectionable to the orthodox and respectable and representative English mind' (308). His professional orthodoxy hides an inveterate 'Irishness', expressed by 'living at an awful pace', which puts him in debt. The public Englishman is a private Celt. We learn that in his past he was indeed the stereotypical wild Paddy, 'who had ridden like a centaur over the loose stone walls in Connemara … who had led a mad, wild life in Trinity College', but who had, after coming into his inheritance, simply decided to flee Ireland and 'shook the dust from his feet' (311). There he determined to make his way up in English society, marry the wealthy heiress Miss Janet Price Ingot, and live richly ever after. Then his Irishness suddenly returns, in the shape of a banshee.

The unexpected appearance of a banshee in the middle of cosmopolitan London is a bizarre moment of uncanniness for the protagonist, since 'It's a mighty queer thing to think of, being favoured with a visit from a Banshee in Gerrard Street' (314). The banshee is a harbinger of family death, but also a messenger from another world entirely, a world as far away from the cosmopolitanism of London as the next world is from this. This is an invasion like that of Dracula into the 'nineteenth century up-to-date'. The banshee reminds O'Donnell of his familial duties. We learn that he had left Ireland after impregnating his secret lover, and that she has come to London to present him with their son. Unfortunately, both become involved in a motor accident and the boy requires O'Donnell to operate. The reappearance of his Irish roots so unnerves O'Donnell that his rational English front is taken from him and his Irish essence revealed to the world: 'I have seen to-night that which unnerves me utterly. My hand is not steady' (322). His public image is utterly eroded by the unearthing of an Irish past in a London present. Like Moreau's hybrids, the stubborn beast-flesh made itself appear again despite years of being denied.

In Riddell, then, we can trace the outlines of a regional response to the cosmopolitan treatment these places received in Gothic and Romantic literature, the version of the Celtic fringes as zones of the weird, as examples of an atavistic, irrational, primitive and child-like otherness out of step with modernity. Some on the Celtic fringes responded to this stereotyping by internalising many of the negative characteristics posited of them by racial theorists, but others reacted by writing back, challenging the very notion of such ontological boundaries between colonial Self and degenerate Other. Regional Gothic feeds on, even while challenging to the limit, the versions of historical progressivism emanating from cosmopolitan centres; if, in part, it endorses then, then it also operates as a warning that what has been lost is valuable, and that in losing it modernity has left its citizens open to invasions, reverse colonisations and 'degeneration'.

The great Welsh Gothicist Arthur Machen illustrates this ambivalence brilliantly in his 1890 novella *The Great God Pan*. It opens in the wild Welsh hills, where a scientist, Dr Raymond, operates on the brain of an orphan girl he has raised, called Mary, giving her the ability to see the god Pan. The operation is a success, but the encounter is so horrifying that Mary is reduced to idiocy. It later emerges that Mary was raped by Pan and has given birth to a daughter, Helen, a bizarre girl with extraordinary and dangerous gifts, who later moves to London. There she establishes herself as a centre of social life, but soon the men in her circle begin to commit suicide. It transpires that Helen has been giving them, too, glimpses of Pan. There is a sense here that something normally resident in the Welsh wilds has been let loose to run amok in modern London; if the metropolitan is afraid of his regional counterpart, he has good reason to be. The stereotypical depiction of the regions as spaces of weird sexuality is at least partly endorsed in Machen's novel: perverse sexuality follows Helen everywhere. As a young girl she is often seen in the woods cavorting with a 'strange naked man' (11),[39] and her friend Rachel is found 'half-undressed' and weeping in her room after having been visited by Pan (13). To Fred Botting the story concerns the dangers of female sexuality, since Helen 'reveals secret forces at the heart of things, forces that should, the narrator moralises, remain buried, no doubt because their sexual nature is linked to female desire'.[40] More than female desire, however, these forces speak clearly of regional chaos: the regions and female sexuality were closely linked in the colonial mind, so it is no surprise that our cultured narrator is horrified at the thought of Welsh deviance escaping across the English border and penetrating the heart of the metropolis.

The emergence of Welsh feminine evil in London is the Celtic equivalent of the appearance of the Romanian Count Dracula on the streets of the capital; this is reverse invasion, since it manifests as a kind of Welsh nationalist violence against London degeneracy. The link between perverse sexuality and the immigrant population was particularly strong in late-nineteenth-century London, and the Whitechapel murders of Jack the Ripper were believed by many to have been perpetrated by a foreigner, a belief Machen is clearly responding to here. The irony is that the whole train of events has been caused, not by the superstition generally thought intrinsic to the regional personality, but by 'modern' science. The body of Mary is of little concern to Dr Raymond as long as his experiment is allowed to take place. This is science up to date with a vengeance, as what Raymond is practising is a variety of vivisection. Despite the fact that he has spent years raising Mary, he sees her not as a daughter but always as a potential subject for his experiments. Metropolitan, rational, 'English' scientific endeavour, which reduces everything to an object for inquiry, is the cause of a chain of occult and bloody events.

## Irish Gothic

Joseph Sheridan Le Fanu is important to examine in relation to regional Gothic, since his fiction grapples powerfully with notions of hybridity and racial horror. Le Fanu is now considered the central figure in a tradition of Irish Gothic, a tradition which also encompasses writers such as Maria Regina Roche, Maria Edgeworth, Sydney Owenson, Charles Robert Maturin, Oscar Wilde, Bram Stoker, W. B. Yeats and Elizabeth Bowen.[41] Most of these writers belong to a 'class' (the 'Anglo-Irish') whose relationship to Ireland was conflicted. The 'Anglo-Irish' have generally been codified as divided in their allegiances and identities, attempting loyalty to both English ethnicity and Irish birth.[42] Many critics and historians have argued that these writers felt a loyalty to both difference and similarity, Ireland and Britain, nationalism and unionism. Julian Moynahan's description of this community as 'hyphenated' is very useful, as it captures something of the mental tightrope its inhabitants had to walk.[43]

For 'Anglo-Irish' writers the project of romantic union with England as found in the 'national tale' was problematic because it entailed accepting their loss of political power of Ireland after the Act of Union in 1801, when that power was transferred to the parliament in Westminster. However, the Union also, contrarily, became a bulwark of protection for the Irish Protestant community, since it meant that Irish Catholics would never be a political majority. After Catholic Emancipation (1829), the Union was considered to be the most important barrier to Catholic hegemony over the 'Anglo-Irish' community, many of whose members feared being completely overrun by primitive Catholic natives, despite a concomitant commitment by this very community to a version of cultural nationalism which distinguished the Irish from the English by virtue of conflicting customs, language and literature: cultural nationalism and political unionism ran psychologically side by side for many of the 'Anglo-Irish'.

Christina Morin has written that 'Superficially happy allegorical marriages aside, [Irish Gothic] texts ... illustrate the persistent fear that the authors' fictional attempts at identification and an ensuing symbolic national reconciliation will remain just that – fictional'.[44] For the Irish it was difficult to consider the union-as-marriage trope as anything other than a rhetorical smoothing over of inherent violence. C. L. Innes has usefully traced how allegorical marriage is usually configured in Irish texts as fraught and ambivalent, often closer to rape and violation than to companionate marriage, and Claire Connolly has demonstrated that political pamphlets, ballads, songs and speeches about the Union between Ireland and Britain failed to mention love or companionship.[45] Irish writers attempted to undermine the dominant model of the Union by emphasising the autonomy and self-authorisation of the allegorical female in the marriage. Kate Trumpeter has brilliantly detailed how early optimism about the possibility for a union of equals began to fade in the increasing adoption by writers of a paradigm of fracture rather than union, 'prolonged courtship complications, to marriage crises, and even ... to national divorce' and mental breakdown.[46] The romantic past is transformed into a perpetually repeating horror story, whereby contemporaries are forced to relive forever the nightmare mistakes of their ancestors. Unlike the romance, which sees the past and present reconciled in a forward moving narrative closure, the Irish Gothic ruptures the present by the re-entry of elements of the past that the present wants to forget, and effectively puts an end to the future entirely. The tension between past and present is not resolved but in fact exacerbated, and that past crucially includes the atavism that narratives of enlightenment nationalism imply can be eradicated and educated out of the system of the natives.

A text like 'Green Tea' (1869) illustrates Le Fanu's resistance to simplistic stories of modernity and progress, and his use of the scientific cutting edge to explain the continued hold the atavistic, colonial past has on even the most educated and up-to-date nineteenth-century figures. In the image of the tormenting monkey Le Fanu captures a number of competing problems for mid-nineteenth-century Englishmen. On the one hand, of course, there is the simple translation of this monkey into a reminder of the threat that Darwinian theory posed to the view of the human species as a special creation of God. The monkey is an indication of the bestial nature of humanity itself, our apish rather than divine origin. The monkey causes the Revd Jennings to suffer a crisis of faith typical of that experienced by some clerics, who tried to confront honestly the implications of recent scientific findings for theological thought. On another level, however, the monkey is emblematic of a national and political problem, rather than one that is only theological in implication. After all, the Irishman-as-ape was a familiar image to the English public, through the pages of *Punch* magazine.[47] If the monkey kingdom was the place from which the human species had evolved, many thinkers and a great many of the public assumed that some races and ethnicities had not yet fully emerged from this kingdom. Obviously, Africans had to endure the vast majority of these racial attacks, but there was a widely held view of Ireland as an atavistic playground suitable for those who had failed to drag themselves upwards on the evolutionary ladder by their own bootstraps. The tormenting monkey is, perhaps, a nagging reminder that there were a number of spaces on the British map which had yet to witness a complete decoupling of animal and human.

'Green Tea' was written during a period of increased Irish nationalist activity on the British mainland, when the public were becoming convinced of the inveterately violent tendencies of the Irish. Moreover, as in so many other texts we have encountered, the representative English figure, the Reverend Jennings, is no great epitome of masculine power, but is a figure of compromised, or at least ambivalent, masculinity. His manhood seems under threat from the very start of the story, his nervous excitability heightened through an encounter with Dr Hesselius, whose looks 'penetrated his thoughts' (9).[48] Their uneasy banter causes Jennings to behave more like a flirtatious girl than a muscular Christian: 'a sudden embarrassment disturbed Mr. Jennings, analogous to that which makes a young lady blush and look. He dropped his eyes, and folded his hands together uneasily, and looked oddly' (10). Helen Stoddart has argued that their relationship is explicable through Eve Sedgwick's notion of the Gothic as a genre of 'male paranoia' revolving around compromised versions of masculinity.[49] Haunted by a version of the ultra-masculine alpha male, the voices ordering suicide that Jennings hears are symptomatic of a more general feeling in English culture towards the mid to late century that imperial masculinity was on the verge of self-destruction. Jennings is clearly suffering from a form of hysteria, a condition previously thought applicable only to women;[50] this condition renders him unable to complete a romantic union with a feminised version of the Irish nation, and instead propels him into an eventually destructive and homoerotic union with the ultra-masculine simian-Irishman, in which the English figure is rendered completely impotent, and eventually defeated. Jennings's suicide may be a warning about the embattled condition of mid-century Englishmen, undermined from within by the forces of religious crisis and social and moral uncertainty, and from without by the resurgent masculinity of the regional male. It is a similar fear to that which pervades *Dracula*, of course, which finds a collection of near-hysterical empire boys trying to fight off the atavistic forces of the past (as represented by one single Eastern European man) in a battle for the very soul of the West. If Stoker's novel appears to end on a note of optimism about the possibilities for resurgence of the empire power, since the Crew of Light do defeat Dracula, Le Fanu's short story is much more pessimistic.

The narrative is, moreover, pervaded by an anxiety about authority in general. It poses as part of a collection of official case-files from the papers of the now-deceased metaphysical physician Dr Martin Hesselius (the forerunner of Sherlock Holmes, Stoker's Van Helsing, Algernon Blackwood's 'psychic detective' *John Silence* (1908), and William Hope Hodgson's *Carnacki the Ghost Finder* (1910–12)), being put forward for the perusal of the public by his one-time assistant and now literary executor. They have, then, the imprimatur of authority apparently stamped on them from the outset. Things are, however, a great deal more complicated. In the first place the Editor had also trained as a doctor but somehow managed to cut his own fingers off as a young man, an 'accident' which rendered him incapable of practising. However, his work as an Editor requires that he use his hands, yet we are expected to accept that he has not compromised himself in this task. After his 'accident' he fell into 'wandering' around Europe before falling in with Hesselius, a 'wanderer' like himself (5). Wandering is not a neutral activity for a text in a tradition which includes as one of its central masterpieces *Melmoth the Wanderer*, and it implicates both men in ambivalent, even satanic, behaviour. The implication, in other words, is that the Editor of these papers is (perhaps) a madman himself, and (possibly) a case-study of Hesselius's that went wrong (much like that of Jennings, who, like the Editor, also harms himself). We have to trust this (possibly insane) Editor who 'translates' these papers which are in a number of languages, and into which he makes interpolations (which he does not highlight) and from which he makes excisions (which he does not flag).

The good doctor Hesselius himself frankly undermines his own authority and medical credibility in 'Green Tea' by abandoning his suicidal patient at the first opportunity. His disappearance is the real cause of Jennings's suicide, since he clearly felt deserted by the very man who promised to help him. That Hesselius refuses to accept that Jennings was his patient in the first place (as such an admittance would jeopardise his so-far perfect record), and that he then puts forward at least four possible causes of Jennings's illness (some of them mutually contradictory), hardly instils in the reader any sense that this is a man in control. Such collapsing of authority may not seem to have anything to do with the colonial and regional implications of the story, but in fact is germane to them. As authority is deferred further and further away from the traditional sources (the medical and theological professions, editors and texts), all points from which a consolidated attack on the invading monkey/Irishman could be launched are undermined. If there can be no trust in traditional sources of authority, how could a moral, let alone a military case, be launched against those nationalities and regions which would threaten British integrity? In such a case of compromised authority the monkey will win.

Reconciliation between an atavistic Ireland and a colonial England, between the regional past and metropolitan present, is impossible to achieve in texts like this, and attempts to resolve tensions result only in suicide and internal psychological dissolution. Many have seen in the psychological deformities of his central characters an aspect of Le Fanu's own personality. After his wife died Le Fanu famously became increasingly withdrawn and solitary, becoming a virtual recluse. However, rather than reading this as demonstrative only of a personal pathology, it is possible to see in Le Fanu's withdrawal his response to his microscopic analyses of his own culture through his literary publications. In other words, Le Fanu's case may be one of cultural rather than (or rather than only) personal pathology. His withdrawal reflects the way Irish Protestants increasingly viewed themselves in Victorian Ireland. Roy Foster has outlined how, as the nineteenth century progressed, the Anglo-Irish came to feel marginalised by the government sitting in Westminster, and he suggests that many 'withdrew' into occult and Gothic activity and belief to find new sources of power.[51] The hyphenated existence of the Anglo-Irish attracted many of their writers to liminal states, such as vampirism, ghosts and the living dead, as a means of articulating the desperation and ennui felt in regard to their own waning power in colonial Ireland. Le Fanu's *Uncle Silas* (1864) is a case in point, a novel pervaded by an atmosphere of world-weariness and desperation. We now know that it was always meant to be an 'Irish novel'. Elizabeth Bowen argued that it should be read as a coded account of Anglo-Irish psychology, and this was confirmed by W. J. McCormack, who proved that the novel was originally set in Ireland and only transferred to England at the insistence of Le Fanu's publisher.[52] McCormack has, moreover, brilliantly anatomised Le Fanu's depiction of Silas Ruthyn, arguing that it is a portrayal of a man who is already dead, who is a kind of zomb-ified revenant, since 'virtually on each occasion when Silas appears he is described in terms drawn from the vocabulary of death':[53] Silas is described as an 'apparition', 'preternaturally soft … spectral … a shadow … dazzlingly pale … a ghost', he grows so 'very queer sometimes – you'd think he was dead a'most', with a 'death-like scowl' (205).[54] Indeed, for McCormack, 'we can hardly avoid the conclusion that the world of Bartram is the post-mortem recreation of Knowl, and that Silas in some way is the dead soul of Austin'.[55]

Silas's Swedenborgism, a religion which provides the believer with the tools to open up his 'second sight', allowing him to see the dead, is thus peculiarly appropriate, and operates as a useful instrument for a class losing power and visibility. The Anglo-Irish effectively felt themselves politically disappearing throughout the nineteenth century; Swedenborgism is a methodology which would render them visible again. The fears of the Anglo-Irish have been calibrated by Elizabeth Bowen, who argued that 'when Le Fanu wrote of hermetic solitude, the autocracy of a great country house, the demonic power of family, myth, fatalism, feudalism and the Ascendancy outlook, all part of the Anglo-Irish hybrid culture, he did so from innate understanding'.[56] Certainly, a fatalistic atmosphere dominates the narrative. Bartram-Haugh is overgrown and in danger of being lost to nature by the time Maud gets to it for the first time, and its isolated nature is reflected in the self-absorbed conditions of those who live there. Silas has turned inwardly upon himself, hardly venturing forth from his room to visit other areas of the house, and frequently retreats into a drug-induced catalepsy any time reality infringes too far into his self-obsession. He is, of course, merely living out a trait previously seen in his brother Austin, who could go for days without speaking to his daughter Maud, seemed incapable of expressing himself clearly, and talked continually in coded form as if initiating Maud into a language of secrecy and occlusion. When he speaks to her of going on a visit he means that he is soon to die, but he expects that Maud should be able to understand him. Towards the end of the novel, Maud in her turn expects the reader to be capable of deciphering the Swedenborgian language in which she has become fluent, especially when she begins talking of her dead children as if they are still with her.

The Anglo-Irish frequently immersed themselves in occult codes and practices, and a great many Ascendancy men were members of the Freemasons, as if they were trying to hermetically seal their own imploding and eroding society and protect it against extinction by translating it to a new language and dimension. If they were going to be wiped out politically in terms of material power, perhaps they could transfer themselves into another realm of power altogether and emerge victorious. When Austin dies he reappears as Silas; death is not the end, but the beginning of a new and more promising existence. In the new dispensation Silas can exert enormous power, despite the fact that he is (metaphorically) deceased. The mystery of the locked room is in part the mystery of how an enclosed, sealed-in group can continue to reproduce: the answer is by seeking out alternative means of reproduction. If, in Le Fanu's famous vampire story, Carmilla recreates new versions of herself simply by rearranging the letters of her name, so that she is reproduced as Millarca and Mircalla, here Austin can become Silas, and perhaps Silas can transfer himself into the mind of his niece, Maud. She has, after all, by the end of the novel, apparently become a convert to the Swedenborgian doctrines she had previously inveighed against. She has produced only dead children – thereby highlighting the failed character of the fertility of the Ascendancy – but she can, by a second sight, still see these 'angels' (444) so that, though dead they have not disappeared. Silas kills himself, but – especially given the general depiction in Le Fanu's fiction of suicide as a path to spectrality, vampirism, and immortality – this does not necessarily represent the last of him. The very term 'Ascendancy' always had astrological associations with notions of birth and establishment. Thomas Blout's *Glossographia* (1681) defines it this way: 'Ascendant (*ascendens*) or *Horoscope*, is the point of the Ecliptick, arising at some determinate moment of the natural day; in which the Infant is conceived or born…the condition of the whole life is believed to depend on that moment.'[57] If Ascendancy must decline, then perhaps it could also revive. The constant reference to the metaphors of resurrection throughout the narrative suggests death is not the end for these characters.

Swedenborg taught that the universe was composed of 'correspondences', and that for humans true character was not revealed in this mortal body but only when freed and released into the corresponding world of the spirits. Dr Bryerly insists to Maud:

> Remember, that when you fancy yourself alone and wrapt in darkness, you stand, in fact, in the centre of a theatre, as wide as the starry floor of heaven, with an audience, whom no man can number, beholding you under a flood of light … and when the hour comes, and you pass forth unprisoned from the tabernacle of the flesh, although it still has its relations and its rights … You will rejoice. (133)

In a spiritual Ireland, perhaps Protestant Ascendancy power would be restored. The novel as a whole is determined by repetition, so that degeneration will, by circular reasoning, be followed by ascent. This circularity is best demonstrated by the episode when Maud attempts to escape Bartram-Haugh for France, only to find that her journey actually takes her right back to the Big House again. In this world of repetition and cycles, time is obliterated, which means that the extinction of the Anglo-Irish can be perpetually postponed.

Le Fanu's narratives suggest the collapse of faith in authority and retreat to an occult space where a different kind of power can be reconstituted; deciphering the ideological allegiances of Le Fanu's fellow Anglo-Irishman Bram Stoker has been difficult, and has become something of a full-time job for many scholars.

*Dracula* has, of course, provided rich pickings, and it has been read as everything from a novel of liberated sexuality to a conservative crusade against sexual freedom, as both feminist and misogynist, and as a nationalist attack on English notions of superiority, as well as an aggressive defence of imperialism.[58] Much of the ideological ambivalence of Stoker's work is considered to be profoundly unconscious. For most critics, Stoker is best read as a reactionary conservative whose writings (despite his avowed support for Irish Home Rule) should be, as Jeffrey Richards expressed it, 'finally set in a context of belief in and support for the British empire and the Anglo-Saxon race'.[59] Not much regional 'writing back', then. Yet, if we turn to Stoker's last novel, *The Lair of the White Worm* (1911), the ideological gravitation of the author or his fictional output do not become any clearer, though its status as a regional text is obvious. So textually dishevelled is this novel that it has been considered a product of a mind disintegrating due to the onslaught of syphilitic meningitis, but also as an experimental forerunner of the Surrealists.[60] A better explanation for the bizarrely dissipated nature of the novel may simply be that in it Stoker attempted to synthesise and summarise the mythological, folkloric, religious and political themes which run through his other texts, and is simply not up to such a job. The novel, on this account, is extraordinarily ambitious but simply beyond the talents of the writer. In *Dracula*, Stoker managed to successfully synthesise seven years of research on Transylvania and vampire lore to produce a compelling narrative; in *The Lair of the White Worm* he tries to cram a lifetime's worth of study in English and Irish folklore, myth and religious tradition into a relatively short novel, and cannot manage it.

The political implications of this novel are not easy to sort out, either. This is because it is never quite clear what the 'White Worm' of Mercia legend – as embodied by Lady Arabella March – actually represents. Mercia is a region that may be 'at the heart of England', but is also as beyond the borders as Transylvania, in that it straddles at least three different calendrical zones. As Kate Hebblethwaite has usefully pointed out, Mercia means 'the land of the boundary people', and these people are presented with borders representing the complexity of English religious history.[61]

Lady Arabella lives in 'Diana's Grove', a pagan zone of chthonic energies connected to the deep primordial past. The worm comes out from a hole in the ground that clearly seems to be an infected vagina of some kind, reflective of the sordid primeval past in which people worshipped an unwholesome feminine principle: the Worm's hole smells like 'the drainage of war hospitals, of slaughter-houses, the refuse of dissecting rooms ... with, added, the sourness of chemical waste and the poisonous effluvium of the bilge of a water-logged ship whereon a multitude of rats had been drowned' (364).[62] The grove is dotted with many remnants of pagan temples, including 'a Roman temple, possibly founded on a pre-existing Druidical one' (170). Edward Caswall lives in Castra Regis, which also has its roots in paganism, and we are told that 'when the Romans came' there was already a structure there, as it was 'a place of importance in Druid times' (170). In these two zones pagan antiquity maintains its dominance. Mercy Farm, where the heroine Mimi lives, is, in contrast, a zone of Christian energy, and was 'originally a nunnery founded by Queen Bertha' (170), Bertha having been one of the key figures in the introduction of Christianity into England. If in *Dracula* the 'horseshoe of the Carpathians' is where 'every known superstition in the world is gathered' (8), then Mercia is so brimful of English history and legend that it effectively implodes. There is no way to keep control of the multitudes of resonances that are explicated by the antiquarian Nathaniel de Salis, so that the novel becomes inordinately confused in trying to hold them in tension.

At the heart of these places, however, there is a relatively simple ideological struggle going on here, and that is the struggle between pre-Christian forces and the powers of Christianity. For an Irishman like Stoker, of course, the struggle between pagan and Christian energies was not far removed from the struggle between Irish nationalism and English imperialism. After all, Irish nationalism was often represented as both pagan and serpentine in the English press, and the old story of George and the dragon was resurrected in order to give a narrative coherence to the difficulties in which England found its relations with Ireland. In *Judy* magazine, 26 October 1881, the forces of the Land League (a nationalist organisation agitating for agrarian rights) were caricatured as a serpent against which English law and order were fighting. After the Phoenix Park Murders in 1882, nationalist violence was depicted as 'The Irish Sea Serpent' in *Judy*, 17 May 1882.[63]

That atavistic and pagan regional (Irish) violence needs to be roundly defeated by the forces of Christian and cosmopolitan (English) order is not, however, the unambiguous message of *The Lair of the White Worm*. For one thing, the married couple at the end of this novel are not really any simple Glorvina and Horatio. They are, in fact, new constituents of an entirely transformed race. The hero is, after all, called 'Adam', as he is the new man as much as his bride-to-be Mimi Watford is a kind of New Woman. Far from being passive or tepid, Mimi accompanies her husband into battle and is resourceful and intelligent in the struggle with the evil Caswall. Moreover, Mimi is no pure-bred Englishwoman but a hybrid already, the daughter of an English father and a Burmese mother, and 'almost as dark as the darkest of her mother's race' (182). The whiteness of the worm they must defeat illustrates its association with white Anglo-Saxons, while black Mimi is surely as high up on the 'index of nigrescence' as the Irish were considered to be.[64] As in *Jane Eyre*, whiteness is continually defeated in the novel in favour of a more complex kind of Arnoldian hybridity (in which the Saxon retains sexual and political dominance). Indeed, Lilla Watford is linked to Lady Arabella in her colouring, and is described as 'all fair, like the old Saxon stock she is sprung from' (182). If Lady Arabella is the monstrous version of pagan and primitive nationalist energy now threatening England, then Lilla is the embodiment of pure English femininity: both must be wiped out because they are not useful in the new world to come. What is defeated here is a type of English purity, and it is defeated by a version of regional hybridity. In this recreated Garden of Eden, the serpent of temptation is resisted by both Adam and Eve, and a new era can begin. The old dispensation is associated with white English hegemony, and the new age is linked to a genuinely more harmonious relationship between the different constituents of the British Isles. The chaotic forces of anarchic Irish femininity need to be contained, but the solution is not, as Arnold recommended, a complete Saxon biological as well as political hegemony, but rather a truly companionate marriage.

Like the countryside, the past and childhood, the regions are configured in profoundly ambivalent terms in Gothic fiction, both horrifically revolting and fascinatingly desirable. The fiction dealing with the regions desperately examines the relations between these two impulses and consistently fails to choose between them. In the occult the Victorian mind found the ultimate expression of this ideological, sexual and religious ambivalence, because the occult represents such a dichotomy at the metaphysical level.

# 4

# *Ghosting the Gothic and the New Occult*

৯

## *Crisis of Faith?*

This chapter will detail how an interest in the occult developed in Victorian society, and examine the interrelations between the new occult 'sciences' and organisations with the Gothic. I need to first account for the importance of the occult in the nineteenth century in general terms, as the engagement of Gothic literature with occultism will only make sense in this context. The first point to make is that the occult was everywhere in nineteenth-century Britain, and it was far from being a marginal concern. No major Victorian thinker or writer, from the Brontës to the Brownings, from Dickens to Darwin, was unconcerned about the occult. Such pervasiveness requires explanation, and situating the discourse of the occult in the 'crisis of faith' enables this explaining.

Calibrating the 'crisis of faith' is difficult.[1] It involved not a move away from religion per se, but a profound crisis of confidence, by both intellectual and public opinion, in the ability of orthodox Christianity to account for the universe.[2] A number of challenges to orthodox Christianity came to public fruition in this period. Philosophically, the major challenge had come from David Hume's eighteenth-century analysis of the notion of the interventionist God, particularly his undermining of the concept of the 'miraculous',[3] and Deism, a philosophical belief in a distant deity who had started the cosmic process off but now minded his own metaphysical business, had been fashionable among eighteenth-century intellectuals.[4] It had been believed that the problems raised by philosophical Deism had been answered by the Revd William Paley, whose *Natural Theology* (1801) had rebutted scientifically the claims made against traditional Christianity, but Paley's robust use of science to support theology made it appear that religion required scientific evidence in order to be credible.

In the field of biblical studies, the belief in plenary inspiration, the theory that every word of the Bible was literally true because it was the unmediated word of God, was basic to much Protestant theology. It encouraged a forensic approach to the biblical texts themselves, which (ironically) led to a highlighting of inconsistencies and difficulties in a literal reading. What is termed the 'critical-historical' method of Bible hermeneutics began to demonstrate that, far from being a transparently divine text, the Bible was in fact a complex anthology of books which very much reflected the historical moments in which they were written, edited and compiled. From Bishop Colenso rigorously totting up the figures provided in the Book of Leviticus and finding that they did not add up, to Professor William Jowett proclaiming the Bible a book like any other, a 'scientific' approach to Scripture undermined the apparent unassailability of the Bible.[5] The growth, and eventually the separation into different disciplines, of geology, biology and physics further suggested that orthodox Christianity had gotten it factually wrong in a number of crucial areas, primarily in its account of cosmology and cosmogony. Charles Lyell's *Principles of Geology*, Robert Chamber's *Vestiges of Creation* (1844), Charles Darwin's *Origin of Species* (1859) and a host of other scientific texts contradicted biblical Protestantism on a number of levels.[6] Added to this was an all-enveloping growth in strict exterior morality, which enjoined on people the most extensive version of purity and etiquette imaginable. Although much of this morality was religiously inspired, it also highlighted that the God of the Old Testament did not behave in the same way that a good Victorian Christian man believed morally right. Indeed, in the light of Victorian moralism, Yahweh looked like a kind of sociopath to many honest Victorians, especially in his orders to the Israelites to wipe out neighbouring tribes in the Middle East. Hell, to which sinners were sent after death, also seemed intolerable: how could an almighty, omniscient, merciful Deity consign large numbers of his own creations to everlasting torment?[7]

What we witness through the nineteenth century, then, is a shift in intellectual, philosophical, epistemological, moral and social authority, away from the Anglican Church (though we should not exaggerate this). This movement was not towards atheism, but rather towards a proliferating body of institutions and alternative discourses often governed by a vocabulary of naturalism. I think it is best to conceive of this as, in the language of Thomas Kuhn, a 'paradigm shift'. Indeed, the religious paradigm shift is so great that we are still in the moment of transition, and this transition may never be completed (possibly because both the human condition and the nature of ultimate reality are simply not amenable to this transition). Kuhn rejected the notion that science should be understood as a progressive discipline, one that slowly builds up facts and accommodates its theories to better understood realities, offering more truthful explanations; he showed that science is, in fact, a discipline dominated by paradigms or models of reality, into which newly discovered 'facts' are appropriated and placed. The models with which science deals are extraordinarily robust but can change when the anomalies thrown up by experimentation and observation are too great to be accommodated; what happens then is a 'paradigm shift', as a new model, which seems to account better for the anomalies, takes over. The new model is not necessarily more 'true' than the old, it just appears to account better for the anomalies.[8]

In the nineteenth century the model of the universe which took for granted the division between the 'natural' and 'supernatural', and the relations between these 'realms', became difficult to hold together.[9] The notion of the supernatural – with its concomitant idea of a God who had to suspend the laws of nature in order to reveal Himself – came under pressure. To adapt to this pressure, 'religious discourse' began to adopt the newly authoritative discourse of naturalism. Religious concepts were reconfigured rather than abandoned. When people became disillusioned with the supernatural and with orthodox Christianity they did not become irreligious (it would be hard to find a people more fervently and seriously religious as the Victorians), but reformulated their religious convictions. In some cases this manifested itself in a complete rejection of the paradigm shift and a movement towards a much more supernaturalist version of religion.[10] The vast majority, however, accommodated themselves to the new paradigm. God was reconfigured, for example, in the minds of many, as working through the evolutionary process, and therefore not required to 'intervene' or breach natural laws. For others 'God' was reconsidered as a kind of metaphysical morality, à la Matthew Arnold, towards which we should strive, rather than a supernatural figure. Religion was held up to scientific standards and was required to demonstrate its compatibility with cutting-edge research.[11] James R. Moore calls this paradigm shift a change in 'creeds', and I think this is a good way to describe the transformation in knowledge that took place, as it acknowledges that what happened was not some dramatic movement from error into truth, but rather a religious shift to a new mode of belief.[12]

The main problem people had to confront was a deep epistemological chasm concerning where truth was to be sought and how it was to be expressed – and into this chasm the Gothic asserted itself, since the Gothic is concerned with finding a way to articulate 'uncertainty' or Todorovian 'hesitancy' between two vastly different epistemologies and metaphysics. Into the epistemological breach a vast number of often bafflingly complex Gothic-occult 'disciplines' stepped, some of them old and venerable, many of them of a relatively new configuration, as they seemed capable of bridging the gap between science and religion. The baffling varieties of occultism include: mesmerism, electrobiology, phrenology, spiritualism, ghost-hunting, Swedenborgism, alchemy, theosophy, esoteric Buddhism, Brahmism, telepathy, Rosicrucianism.[13] The occult was attractive because it accepted the paradigm shift to naturalism, yet maintained that a spiritual aspect (reconfigured as a special articulation of the natural rather than as supernatural) was central to both the universe and the human personality. In doing this it either provided comfort to those who felt that their faith was undermined – since it tended to agree that survival after death was possible – or addressed the basic human investment in the spiritual. Gross materialism and simple supernaturalism were both side-stepped by the occultists.[14] Annie Besant, for example, described theosophical thinking in this way:

> Whatever forces may be latent in the Universe at large or in man in particular, they are wholly natural ... This repudiation of the super-natural lies at the very threshold of Theosophy: the supersensuous, the superhuman, Yes; the supernatural, No ... the Theosophist ... alleges that matter exists in states other than those at present known to science.[15]

Moreover, for those involved in it, the occult offered forms of power and ways to access this power, especially to those who had previously been denied power, including women in general (who were thought to have a special quality which gave them particular gifts in the occult arena), the working class (since some kinds of occult abilities were not class-specific – especially mediumship and clairvoyance), and foreigners (since occult powers were often believed to be concentrated in exotic bodies, or were believed to have been passed down by Oriental (Theosophy), Celtic (folk-lore) or African elites). The occult, in all its bewildering complexity and variety of manifestations, was both a scientific and a spiritual zone. The (scientific) Society for the Investigation of Psychic Phenomena was matched by the (magical/religious) Hermetic Order of the Golden Dawn:[16] the one appeared to provide a certain scientific validation for occult phenomena, the other was a means to understand, access and (crucially) activate these phenomena.

### Victorian ghosts

Haunting, ghost-seeking/hunting and ghost-story writing were pervasive and interlinked activities throughout the Victorian period. Srdjan Smajic has complained that too many analyses of ghost stories have failed to take notice of the 'significance of cultural and historical context and, instead, emphasize the immutability of certain mythic structures or psychological constants', so I will try to set ghost stories in a cultural context before looking at a couple of them.[17] The cultural anxiety over time, highlighted in chapter 1, is also evident in the ghost story. The ghost, after all, represents a breach in historical progression: in a stark reproach to the Victorian investment in notions of linearity and progress, the ghost is a manifestation of the 'past-in-the-present'. If Ainsworth's historical romances expressed nostalgia for a cultural past of wholeness, the ghost story, too, returns again and again to primal scenes, this time scenes more personal in nature. While Ainsworth tracked a rupture in historical time, ghost stories invariably zone in on ruptures in personal history, telling of personal betrayal, crimes of passion, robbery, treachery and familial strife which need to be settled before cosmic order can be restored.

Some cultural historians have argued that in the face of the traumas of 'deep time' in which the importance of individual identity is lost, Victorians often turned inward to biography, autobiography, diaries – life-writing – in order to reassert the significance of individual agency.[18] The ghost story goes further than this, indicating that personal history can have cosmic effects, that private betrayal can open up a chasm in the cosmic order that requires correction. The ghost represents a primal scene in a deeper sense also, as the past that comes back to haunt the present is almost always a deeply domestic one, involving mothers, fathers, sons and daughters, and personal transgression that has been repressed, shut away in a bottom drawer of the family dressing-table.

This is why the vocabulary of psychoanalysis has been so important and useful to critics and cultural historians who have looked at the ghost story; just like psychoanalysis, the ghost reminds us that the past we refuse to deal with can re-emerge in deeply traumatic and dislocating ways. Psychoanalysis tells the tale of how the personal past that has been repressed haunts the present in odd and disturbing ways, such as bodily or psychological disorders; ghost stories tell us how the sins of the past impact on the present in ways which knock it out of kilter. The notion of the 'uncanny', as delineated by Freud in his 1919 essay on the subject, concerns the means by which that which is most known to us, that which is closest to us, that which means most to us, is estranged, up-ended: the way that the homely and domestic become the unhomely, the strange. Freud argued that 'the uncanny is that class of the frightening which leads back to what is known of old and long familiar', so that 'this uncanny is in reality nothing new or alien, but something which is familiar and old-established … and which has become alienated from it only through the process of repression'.[19] When a ghost appears in the front room it effectively subverts historical time itself: if the Victorians were feeling less at home in the cosmos as it was being re-described by the geologists, biologists and physicists, then this sense of dislocation manifested itself in the domestic and personal world – the domestic space where they felt the safest – as the ghost story.[20] The ghost tells us that that which we believe to be complete and known is, in fact, possessed of gaps and fissures, that reality is undercut by a kind of otherworldly double. Psycho-analyst Hélène Cixous has argued that ghosts undermine realism as a practice, as their weirdness destabilises any attempt to repre-sent the real as unified or whole, and asserts breaches and absences rather than presence or completeness.[21]

Ironically, however, the ghost does not speak of the forces or discourses of materialist modernity that were actually decentring Victorians from confident at-homeness-in-the-universe. If the new versions of the sciences were dislodging homocentrism, the ghost story undermines the very instrument through which some of these new versions of science were articulated, the language of empirical reasoning. After all, ghosts could not exist, according to both Protestant theology and dogmatic naturalism. It is no acci-dent that Christmas became the key point of the year for the publication of ghost stories, because Christmas was precisely that moment when Victorians had to confront the cultural past most directly. Christmas is a disturbing time as it is the point of the year most intensely haunted by the (miraculous) past. Christmas cele-brates the uncanny notion of the Incarnation, in which a domestic space – the human body – becomes possessed by the odd, the weird and the disturbing: Christ is a human body housing (haunted by, possessed by) the divine. Every Christmas this miraculous notion – considered absolutely impossible by Matthew Arnold, who famously opined that there was no such thing as a miracle[22] – returned to challenge the rational discourses of the Victorian mind. As people gathered around the hearth – the most homely of places – to read of uncanny violations of domestic sanctity, the homely and rational Logos of the 'Victorian frame of mind'[23] was also being haunted by the whispers of an older and much more frightening truth. The elevation of Christmas in this world makes perfect sense, as cultures often make a fetish of that which is most fearful and threatening. The fact that the 'nineteenth century up-to-date' made Christmas into the most elaborate of festivals, but also the most private and domestic, tells us something of the struggle between internal and external forms of dislocation: indeed, perhaps the uncanny return of the miraculous past in the form of the ghost was, in part, a means of combating the uncanny arguments coming from the laboratories of Victorian sciences. It may be easier to face the repressed past than the cosmic emptiness of deep time and the Second Law of Thermodynamics. Or, perhaps, the abyss without in the universe was simply being matched by an abyss both within the home and within the self.

The most famous ghost story of Victorian England is, of course, Charles Dickens's *A Christmas Carol* (1843). If Christmas is a disturbing reminder of the questions about existence which haunted the Victorians, since it speaks of a profoundly uncanny invasion of the 'supernatural' into the human body, Scrooge's eventual resolution to 'honour Christmas in my heart, and try to keep it all the year' (83) is in fact a resolution to domesticate this uncanniness.[24] When Marley's Ghost first appears to Scrooge, the everyday and the ordinary are suddenly imbued with extraordinarily disturbing qualities, signified most startlingly when his doorknob transforms (a similar uncanny transformation of an inanimate object can be found in J. Meade Falkner's 'The Lost Stradivarius (1895)). Scrooge's domestic bedroom becomes the site where the past, present and future are worked out in front of him, the site of comfort and retreat transformed into the nexus of time. What Scrooge is forced to do by the end of the narrative is internalise the transformations of time that he has witnessed. Much as the Victorians had to confront the implications of the 'deep' past and the cosmic future, Scrooge declares he will 'live in the Past, the Present, and the Future. The Spirits of all Three shall strive within me. I will not shut out the lessons they will teach' (83). He will effectively re-member the past, present and future, and tame the ontological disturbances caused by the existential questioning happening all around him.

The past overdetermines everything in the plot, to an extent that even Freud himself would have been proud of. Only the Ghost of Christmas Past can explain how Scrooge ended up the way he did. We first see Scrooge alone and abandoned by his father and living as a 'solitary boy' (30). When his sister finally comes to 'take him home' she announces that,

> Father is so much kinder than he used to be, that home's like Heaven! He spoke so gently to me one dear night when I was going to bed, that I was not afraid to ask him once more if you might come home, and he said Yes, you should. (32–3)

Father Time stands over this project, and the Father who abandoned Scrooge morphs into Scrooge himself, so that the protagonist becomes a caricature of the theory that the battered child becomes a battered parent: Scrooge is conditioned by his past, and he must confront his repressed memories and thus overcome them. His present miserliness is a hysterical symptom of a repressed set of memories; like a good patient undergoing psychoanalysis, once he meets these memories head-on he can move beyond them into a more psychologically sound reality. This is perhaps one reason why the story found such an avidly consuming public in the twentieth as much as the nineteenth century: Scrooge's culpability for his behaviour is displaced on to a Father we never get to meet, just as the public internalisation of a crude version of Freudian psychology blames the mother for the ills of the child's grown-up life. In common parlance, Scrooge 'never got over' the treatment meted out to him by his father, and he is willing to abandon everyone else as his Father abandoned him. Once Scrooge has seen his earlier self as an abandoned and solitary boy he regrets his own actions: 'there was a boy singing a Christmas Carol at my door last night. I should like to have given him something' (32).

Nicholas Abraham and Maria Torok, both psychoanalysts, argue that past traumas can be enormously influential on present histories, and use the term 'phantom' to designate the psychological presence within the ego of a deceased predecessor, who is hanging on to ensure that the buried trauma remains buried. The phantom is determined to keep the secrets of the past hidden, to protect the taboos that have been buried, through misdirecting the ego. Ghost stories can thus be understood as a means by which the traumas of the past can be revealed, but only if we are willing to decode them. Like a dream, the manifest content of the ghost story, the apparent message that the ghost comes bearing, is actually a trick to deflect the ego from realising the real issue; the true meaning of the ghost and his message is latent, and must be disinterred through a symbolic interpretation of the manifest content. The theories of Abraham and Torok suggest that the messages that fictional ghosts carry are actually diversion devices, and that we must dig deeper to discover what is really at hand.[25] Esther Rashkin has used these theories very fruitfully in her study *Family Secrets and the Psychoanalysis of Narrative* (1992), where she argues that ghost-texts actually contain secrets of which they are unaware and which it is the job of the critic to uncover.[26] Thus, for instance, the true secret revealed by Scrooge's Ghosts is that he was an abused child rather than merely a bad man, and once this past secret is articulated then he can overcome his past – of course, we encounter here the problem that the Ghost of Christmas Past seems not only fully cognisant of this 'secret' but is, *pace* Abrahams and Torok, eager to reveal it to Scrooge rather than deceive him. Abrahams and Torok's psychoanalytical argument tends to deflect attention from the fact that literary ghosts are not really out to deceive, but are engaged in exposure of the hidden truth.

Of course, the interest in human psychology suggests that there is a containment of the supernaturalist past going on within the ghost story, too. After all, the ghost story usually ends with an 'exorcism', in which the ghost is evicted from the house and the supernatural is evacuated from the natural, re-enthroning Christian Protestant reason. Moreover, as 'supernatural' pheno-mena, Victorian ghosts are bizarrely elemental and empirical: they are not invisible objects but are open to scientific verification, including sight, multiple witness, photography and record. Many protagonists in a typical ghost story start off deeply sceptical about the existence of ghosts and come to believe in them only because the ghost presents itself for quasi-scientific examination. In a reversal of the Christian virtue of believing rather than seeing, these ghosts have to be seen to be believed. It could not be too long, some must have thought, before a ghost would find a way to slip under a microscope for a more thorough examination. These physical manifestations of the 'supernatural' therefore demonstrated the primacy of the physical sciences. Ghosts here cannot be believed in until physical evidence, open to verifica-tion, is presented. If one of the basic elements of scientific verification is the repeatability of the experiment, these ghosts allow for frequent access. One complaint about religious experi-ence has always been that, since it is usually confined to individuals, it cannot operate as public evidence of the truths of religion; Victorian ghosts do not suffer from this problem as they appear to anyone who comes into their orbit. Rather than gesturing towards another mode of being, perhaps these ghosts are simply aspects of the natural world that are not yet under-stood – there is always a possibility that their disturbing otherwordly presence can be dissolved into something much more tangibly of this world.[27]

These uncanny, hesitant, disruptions of time and the domestic can also usefully be spoken about in the terminology of high post-structuralism, which accounts for their attraction for critics like Julian Wolfreys and Nicholas Royle, since the ghostly is where strict dualities break down and opposites are held in perpetual traction.[28] Haunting has been very topical in contem-porary theoretical work, partly due to Jacques Derrida's controversial *Specters of Marx* (1993), in which post-structuralism was configured as a kind of cultural descendant of Marxism. That specific argument need not concern us here, but we need to be cognisant of Derrida's term 'hauntology' as a means by which to attend to the figure of the Ghost. For Derrida the ghost is important precisely because of its category-defying and ontology-bending nature: since the ghost cannot properly be termed dead or alive, indeed cannot be assigned to any category of definition which it does not exceed, it serves to indicate the undecidability lurking within the modes of thinking we currently hold. Since the ghost cannot be contained within them it traces their limits and suggests the possibilities of, not only other ways of thinking, but other ways of being (which is why hauntology is a kind of 'supplement' to ontology, the philosophy of being). Paying attention to hauntology is a means of exposing our own limits and awakening us to the ethical responsibilities we have to Otherness in all its forms. The ghost points us in other ethical directions.[29]

Derrida's argument is useful in thinking about Victorian ghosts as it points up that aspect of the ghost story which distinctly traces the limits of the Real as it had been defined by rational and scientific discourses, and opens a space within the Real in which the Other (whether that Other is defined as the past or the foreigner or the woman, or, more hesitatingly, the 'supernatural') can escape. Derrida's argument has been very influential and, in the field of Gothic studies, it can be seen in the writings of Nicholas Royle, Jodey Castricano and Julian Wolfreys.[30] Derrida's spectrality offers an extraordinary opening-out of things which were considered closed, which is why it is so closely linked by Nicholas Royle to the uncanny. Ghosts simply reveal what is true about all things in general: that they are haunted by that which they are not, and which therefore challenges univocity. For the post-structuralist all texts are haunted by this deconstructive spectrality, so all texts are (potentially) ghost stories – hence the expansiveness of Julian Wolfreys' view of the ghost as the origin of textuality. However, what this approach evades is a direct acceptance of the ghost as a ghost. For Derrida, hauntology certainly does not involve the question of whether the ghost is 'real' or whether the ghost exists: as Fredric Jameson has pointed out, 'all it says, if it can be thought to speak, is that the living present is scarcely as self-sufficient as it claims to be'.[31] Perhaps, however, rather than shifting analysis so quickly away from these ghosts as ghosts, as things that we actually see or, at least, that fictional characters experience, we need to deal with the possibility that they are indeed at least in part, gestures towards the true alterity, the 'wholly other' (to use Rudolf Otto's term),[32] of the divine and its forces.

Vanessa D. Dickerson has argued that, rather than the 'wholly other', Victorian ghost stories are actually about the position of women, and that this explains why a large number of such stories were composed by women writers. For Dickerson, it was the peculiar position of women that attracted them to the ghost story: they were socially 'invisible', despite the fact that they were depended upon by men. Since the Victorian woman was often pressurised to become a kind of ethereal figure in discourses concerning the 'angel-in-the-house', while also maintaining a punishing work-schedule, they found a means of expressing their anger at this invisibility and ethereality through the ghost story. The ghost-in-the-house terrorising the male owner may be a sublimated means by which the 'angel-in-the-house' terrorises her husband.[33] The ghost story may be a means of dealing with and using women's liminality to their own advantage. The clearest representative of this argument may be in Oliver Onion's 'The Beckoning Fair One' (1911), where Paul Oleran, the protagonist, is attacked and possessed by a female ghost who causes him to kill the woman he loves, the story perhaps expressing the male fear of what a domestic goddess could really do to her male 'partner'. However, this is a story written by a man.

Mrs J. H. Riddell was one of the most successful and prolific writers of supernatural stories throughout the Victorian era, although she is now a sadly neglected figure, and she provides a useful test-case for Dickerson's hypothesis. Riddell had more reason to feel dislocated than many other writers. She had been born Charlotte Cowan in Carrickfergus, near Belfast, in 1832, and had come to London at the age of twenty-one after her father's death. He had been a High Sheriff in Antrim but had brought the family from comfortable living to penury, apparently through a nervous breakdown and becoming indebted. Riddell was forced, in straitened circumstances, to back rooms and seedy lodging-houses in London. E. F. Beiler writes that Riddell arrived in London in January 1855, during a winter reported to be unusually severe … [and spent] shivering days when she trod the streets, trying to place her work with editors and publishers, and the colder nights when she wrote for long hours in draughty rooms heated only by a candle.[34]

Her marriage to the civil engineer Joseph Hadley Riddell in 1857 was a serious error of judgement, since he was a disaster in business and they had to depend on her income from writing, and she was further burdened by having to pay for his debts. In response to her father's poverty and her husband's lack of business sense, Riddell was forced into writing novels by the dozens, writing to a kind of schedule that resembles a mass-production factory.

Riddell's *The Uninhabited House* was published in *Routledge's Christmas Annual* of 1875. Its main female character, Miss Blake, seems partly created out of memories of Riddell's own life. She is an aging Irishwoman, near penury, with a single dependant (a niece rather than a husband). Her only asset is a house, left to her by her sister's late husband, which she is desperate to either rent out or sell. Unfortunately the house is haunted and impossible to live in. Being left with a financial burden by men was a familiar story to Riddell, so it is not that difficult to see autobiographical elements in this tale. However, the burden here is a house haunted by a *man* rather than a woman: the ghost may speak of female difficulties, in other words, but does not represent the nature of femininity in Victorian England, rather the compromised nature of masculinity. It is the men in this text who fail to live up to a role that their culture has foisted upon them, and who are dragging their female dependants down with them. The male narrator constantly tells the reader how impossible it is to deal with Miss Blake and how unfair she is to her late brother-in-law, Mr Elmsdale, but the fact is that he has effectively left her in a financial mess because he was a 'bear' in his dealings with other men, torturing and antagonising one so much that he murdered him (leaving his ghost to haunt the now uninhabitable house). His 'clients' report at the inquest into his death that he was a 'thief', a 'scoundrel' and a 'swindling old vagabond' who took pleasure in breaking them (14).[35]

Riddell must have resented those who had made a financial fool of her husband and brought him to ruin, and here such men find their representative in the ghost: far from femininity being imaged in haunting, the ghost represents the kinds of financial and personal pressures that endanger the very existence of women. Miss Blake's position at the edge of poverty is excuse enough for her desperate behaviour with money. Solving the mystery as to why the ghost of her brother-in-law haunts the house is a means by which to end her dependence on him for her financial future and give herself independence; what she finds is that the entire edifice of the male Victorian establishment is against her. She sues one tenant, Colonel Morris, who refuses to pay her the full cost of his agreed rent because of the presence of the ghost, and she loses her court case against him. Only through the endeavours of the narrator, who works for her solicitor, is the original murder revealed and the killer brought to justice to face his crime, resulting in the departure of the ghost and the sale of the house. What the story demonstrates is Riddell's use of the ghost to represent, not female liminality, but male power and its danger to women.

Gender may play an important role in the cultural reception of ghosts and ghost Stories. For example, a common complaint about 'real' Victorian ghosts has been that, as opposed to their literary contemporaries, they are profoundly 'dull', doing very little, pottering around houses, scratching a bit, squeaking a bit, moving the odd item of furniture, but rarely having something as banal as a reason to appear.[36] This was often the case with spirits in general, if spiritualists are to be believed. Theodor Adorno was merely echoing the complaint of generations of sceptics when he pointed to the triviality of the messages spiritualists received from the dead as a reason for the negative effect they had on modern culture.[37] Diana Basham suggests a different reason for male rationalist discomfort, pointing out the prevalence of women in both ghost-story writing and spiritualism, the practice of calling up the spirits of the dead.[38] While what these spirits had to say was often incredibly banal and pointless, the fact of their appearance through a woman may be the crucial issue. There was a double edge to this: women could be considered blessed with particular 'gifts' which enabled them to contact the dead or to channel spirits, but these very gifts could also be a reason for continuing to deny women the right to social, educational and political power. If, for example, the ghosts speaking through mediums had nothing of significance to say, perhaps the women through whom they spoke or appeared had nothing important to add to society either. If women were so odd that they could contact the dead, perhaps it was best to leave them in the darkened drawing rooms where seances were taking place than admit them to the House of Commons.

Alex Owen and Diana Basham have expertly traced the links between occult investigations and feminist agitation, with membership of occult and feminist organisations overlapping.[39] However, many in the emerging discipline of psychology suggested that there was a link between apparent occult powers, even occult investigations, and hysteria, and we know that many women were incarcerated in asylums because of their associations with the occult. What happened to Catherine Crowe, for example, serves to illustrate this. Crowe is famous for her compendium of real-life ghost stories, *The Night Side of Nature*, published in 1848 and never out of print until the end of the century. She started off as a celebrated and at least quasi-scientific researcher of the occult, culminating in her final work *Spiritualism and the Age We Live In* (1859). However, and tragically, Crowe had a nervous breakdown and, in one of the last references to her while she still lived, Charles Dickens reports that she was spotted running through London naked, apparently confirming the link between the occult, femininity and madness.[40]

A writer like Amelia Edwards is a very different matter. Far from going insane, Edwards became an increasingly recognised voice of authority on ancient Egypt, and as well as writing many ghost stories and novels she composed the entry on 'Egyptology' for the ninth edition of the *Encyclopaedia Britannica*, received three honorary degrees from American universities, and was widely consulted for her expertise. Her attraction to the ghost story is, in fact, part of her wider interest in a 'dead' culture like Egypt, as she correctly believed that this culture lived on in new forms in the nineteenth century – a belief also articulated in Bram Stoker's sadly underestimated *The Jewel of the Seven Stars* (1903). If the ghost story is essentially about how the past refuses to go away, Edwards's scholarship demonstrated the fascination of Victorian academic life with the living death of ancient cultures. Most of her best ghost stories date from the 1860s, when she often composed the Christmas story for Dickens's *All the Year Round* or *Household Words*, while her interest in Egyptology can be dated from a trip to Cairo in 1873, but the fact is that her Ghost Stories laid the intellectual ground for an interest in revivifying the dead. There was nothing obviously 'feminist' in Edwards's dual roles, but, as Basham suggests, 'attraction to the form seems to have been directed by its potential for covert meanings and excluded presences'.[41]

'The Phantom Coach' (1864) concerns the adventures of a new bridegroom who leaves his wife for a brief walk on the Yorkshire moors, but who gets lost on his way back. He is forced to seek shelter and help from a reclusive occultist scholar-scientist, whose interest in forbidden knowledge has led to his marginalisation by the scientific community and his isolated experiments and reading in the moors. The narrator then leaves to catch the only coach, the Mail, which could bring him back to his bride before the morning. After catching this mysterious coach he realises that it is in fact the phantom reappearance of a coach which had crashed nine years ago, killing its three occupants. He manages to get out before the coach makes a renewed tumble into the abyss it ended up in previously. What is clear is that the reader is meant to make some link between the marginalised occult interests of the hermetic scientist and the phantom coach which plunged into darkness. The very scientists who deny the existence of ghosts have also banished the hermit because of his investment in occult science. If the phantom coach is a reality, then the gaps in modern science so important to our philosopher-alchemist are perhaps real also. The hermit makes the point that the history of science speaks of the holistic nature of ultimate reality and the means by which to understand it, including the occult, while modern science tries to banish these methodologies to a zone as remote as the Yorkshire Moors. However, like the phantom coach, they have power all the same; ignorance of the ghostly powers of the occult could result in modern science plunging into the precipice. Basham argues that what these spaces and discourses also have in common is their link to femininity and marginality: the narrator needs to reconnect to his 'phantom' bride, left behind on his linear journey into the heart of darkness in his attempt to conquer and control the feminine wilderness. The arts of which the hermit speaks are those which have been rendered feminine by the men of science who associate the occult with old wives' tales and folklore, the zones of women and children. In rehabilitating forbidden spaces and occult knowledge Edwards is also rehabilitating the discourses of women, and warning those who continue to ignore and marginalise these supposedly dead places and languages that their return may have deadly repercussions for the 'mail'/male who ignores them.[42]

## Psychic phenomena and the satanic

Edwards's attempted rehabilitation of the occult for science was basic to occult study in this period. For example, far from proclaiming her subject to be beyond, above or even different from the investigations of scientists, Catherine Crowe was contemptuous of those who refused to recognise the scientific validity of her projects. She conceived of *The Night Side of Nature* as composed of scientific evidence: for her, the sheer amount of material she has gathered together demonstrated that there is something serious to these stories which it is the duty of the scientist to investigate. While she admits that the ghost stories are 'irreducible within the present bounds of science', she is equally hopeful that this will not remain so. Science needs to expand its horizons and take cognisance of the realm of the spirit.[43] This is very much in the same vein as the arguments of those who established the Society for Psychical Research in 1882. Indeed, the point for most occultists was that the mysteries of Nature had not yet been probed deeply enough, and that some scientists had illegitimately and unscientifically called off the search for complexity. In an address in Belfast in 1874, John Tyndall famously issued a ridiculously pompous rallying call for science, informing every

other discipline that it was time for them to graciously accept that
they had become defunct:

> The impregnable position of science may be described in a few
> words. We claim, and we shall wrest from theology, the entire
> domain of cosmological theory. All schemes and systems which
> thus infringe upon the domain of science must, in so far as they do
> this, submit to its control, and relinquish all thought of controlling
> it.[44]

Most investigators who believed that there was something to
hauntings, clairvoyance, telepathy, theosophy, were also sure that
this something was not supernatural but merely a hitherto unex-
plained aspect of nature. Electricity and technological developments often served as useful metaphors for occult phenomena:
perhaps the powers of mediums and clairvoyants were due to a
peculiarity in their physical or mental make-up, investigation of
which would demonstrate what it was; perhaps communication
with the dead would eventually be shown to be no more supernatural than new telecommunications, such as the telegraph (hence
the term telepathy[45]). The members of the Society for Psychical
Research all felt that that they were investigating some of the more
occluded aspects of Nature, but Nature nonetheless, and their
publications all point towards the same conclusion. Many of them
were deeply involved in research into versions of energy invisible
to the human eye, and they saw little difference between psychic
research and laboratory work. William Crookes is probably the
most famous of the syncretists: he refined the design of a piece of
laboratory equipment intended to detect a kind of radiation (for
which he was lauded by the 'scientific world') as well as conducting
a variety of experiments with D. D. Home, perhaps the most
famous medium/psychic of the Victorian period (for which he
received the disapproval of the 'scientific world'). Crookes believed
that 'psychic force' was equivalent to the other invisible forces he
was studying. Ghosts were simply a particularly thin kind of mate-
riality; mesmerism might be due to a particular physical substance
possessed by some; telepathy was down to some kind of mental
wire running between two people.[46]

Marie Corelli's first novel, *A Romance of Two Worlds* (1886), makes a great deal of the relationship between the practices of spiritualism and the strange new tele-technologies, such as the telegraph and the telephone. In the novel the scientist-theologian Heliobas discourses on the 'electrical' connection and communication between the Creator and his creatures, established when Christ ascended into heaven, and claims that each individual is like an electronic device given life through a sudden burst of electricity from God. The reason Christ was sent to earth was, in fact, to set up efficient and new spiritual telegraph-wires, since the old ones – dating from the Creation – had become rather worn by original sin. As Heliobas explain, 'this Earth and God's World were like America and Europe before the Atlantic Cable was laid. Now the messages of goodwill flash under the waves, heedless of storms. So God's Cable is laid between us and His Heaven in the person of Christ' (223).[47]

As an extraordinarily popular woman writer, Corelli was often attracted to versions of extremity and transgression, while simultaneously almost hysterical and paranoid in marginalising them, in part because of her negative experience with male critics. *A Romance of Two Worlds* was derided as the work of a fool, and her subsequent novels were similarly criticised for their vacuity and psychological implausibility. This was partly due to the genres in which she wrote, since in her novels practically anything is possible, including space travel, hypnosis, reincarnation – it is hard to maintain complete authorial integrity when your novels contain scenes as overwrought as the chapter in *The Sorrows of Satan* (1895) where the half-naked Lady Sibyl throws herself on the fascinatingly handsome Prince Lucio who is also the Devil, only to be caught in flagrante delicto by her husband. At the same time that she was being attacked by the established critics, Corelli was also being read by political and social leaders of the highest standing (including Gladstone), and the Queen was said to demand a copy of each new Corelli novel as soon as it appeared. The public were lapping up her work, and the *Sorrows of Satan* sold more copies than any other novel in English ever had, becoming what many consider the first bestseller.

In *The Sorrows of Satan* the depth of Corelli's pain at being criticised is evident in her creation of Mavis Clare, a brilliant writer,
of intellectual and moral purity (clearly meant to represent
herself), but whose genius is dismissed by literary critics and
reviewers, who despise her for her popularity as well as her bril-
liance. Corelli satirises the literary press as packed full of envious
failed authors (such as Geoffrey Tempest, the narrator), motivated
only by jealousy. Tempest has penned a biting attack on the latest
Mavis Clare masterpiece, but only because he knows that her
novel is better than his; when he actually gets to meet Clare he
falls head over heels in love with her. She is unconcerned with
the critics and has named a pack of birds in her back garden after
each of the major ones:

> 'there is the "Speaker"' – and she pointed to a fat fussy fantail – 'He
> struts very well, and fancies he's important, you know, but he isn't.
> Over there is "Public Opinion", that one half-asleep on the wall;
> next to him is "The Spectator"'. (187)[48]

Mavis is associated with the divine, even to the extent that when
her name is uttered 'a sort of hush fell on our party as though an
"Angelus" had rung' (112).

For all the loving authority lavished on Clare, it is in Satan
(Prince Lucio Rimânez) that Corelli is most interested. The novel
attacks supposedly evil writers and thinkers, like the New
Women, Thomas Hardy (who is never directly mentioned, but
against whose *Tess of the d'Urbervilles* this novel is in a Bloomian
struggle of influence), Algernon Swinburne and Henrik Ibsen.
They are blamed for the power of Satan in the late-Victorian
period. Ironically, however, they have not written novels in which
Satan comes across as a most fascinating and interesting figure,
who actually hates evil and desires only God's forgiveness and a
return to heaven. In fact, Satan and his female equivalent, Lady
Sibyl, are the most sympathetic characters in the narrative. He
proclaims that Victorian society is going to the dogs, not least
because it does not appreciate enough the genius of Mavis Clare
(that is, Marie Corelli). Corelli herself said that part of the moti-
vation of the novel was the idea that 'Satan himself might be glad

for men to so reject him, as he then might have the chance of recovering his lost angelic position'.[49] Although the novel appears to be one of complete religious certainty, the only character (besides Clare) who believes in 'God as a very Actual and Positive Being' is the Devil (351). This somewhat undermines the unassailable morality of the text: after all, the last person a completely orthodox Christian would want rooting for her side would be Satan. Adriana Craciun has shown that the satanic had a particular interest for women writers in the nineteenth century, and Sandra Gilbert and Susan Gubar have convincingly demonstrated how, since Milton at least, women have been linked in literary terms with Satan.[50] The association between woman and Satan in male-authored work is rather belaboured in much nineteenth-century literature, ranging from banal serpentine imagery to blatant depictions of the satanic female in art. When women approached satanic imagery it was often to express a (sometimes unconscious) rebellious streak against versions of femininity – especially that of the angel-in-the-house – to which they were expected to conform. Gilbert and Gubar argue that '[satanically] rebellious politics have often been used by women as metaphorical disguises for sexual politics', and while this seems initially unlikely in Corelli's often embarrassingly orthodox tale – which contains multiple attacks on the New Woman – her own subordinate position in relation to the male critical establishment and her over-sympathetic depiction of Satan suggests a rather unhidden subtext of rebellion,[51] understandable since she also felt like an outcast. She was probably illegitimate, and spent her public life creating a shroud of mystery around her origins. As a bastard she might not have been received into polite society, and both she and her melodramatic and generic work have more in common with the authors she attacks in *The Sorrows of Satan* than she cares to admit. She was really Minnie MacKay but renamed herself Signorina Marie Corelli, pretending she was of Venetian descent – as foreign as Prince Rimânez.

## The Occult Mother and Theosophy

Male writers, too, were fascinated by this connection between femininity and the occult, and also terrified, a duality that can be found in the pattern of male romance writers of the late Victorian period. If many writers were convinced that spiritualists and theosophists were on to something, in their insistence that there was more to the universe than could be measured by the narrow-gauge scientism of men like John Tyndall and Thomas Huxley, then they were also afraid of what the women who possessed such knowledge could do to them. This was, after all, the period of the New Woman and the incipient women's movement, where agitation for increased rights went hand in hand with a more assertive and sexual form of femininity. It was also the period when anthropological investigation and speculation led to a belief in a grand matriarchal and goddess-worshipping force in the distant past, before the coming of the patrilinear society and its almighty male God. Friedrich Engels was not the only major intellectual arguing that deep in human prehistory was a gynocentric past, and some were afraid that, given the powerful sexuality and agitation of the New Woman, perhaps a gynocentric future lay in wait. Associated with this was a crisis of masculinity, emerging from the mid century but becoming almost frenzied towards the century's end. This crisis stemmed from the increasing bureaucratisation of men's work, the disappearance of the need for muscular power, the rise of the woman's movement and a growing sense of sexual ambivalence invading the land (which reached its climax in the trial of Oscar Wilde). In an attempt to reclaim authority a movement known as Muscular Christianity emerged (manifested primarily in the celebration of athleticism in the public schools), and imperial bravery became one means of solving the male existential crisis. This Muscular Christianity often set out to confront female power at its most potent.[52] Since Africa was often configured as both a feminine and an occult space, by casting out into this space and conquering it men could reassert their power and authority before returning home to do the same in the domestic sphere.

These confrontations are best seen in the fascinating though disturbing *She* (1886–7), by H. Rider Haggard. The story concerns the journey by three Englishmen, the intellectual Horace Holly, his ward Leo Vincey and their manservant Job, into a region of Zanzibar ruled by Ayesha, a two-thousand-year-old goddess (also known as She Who Must Be Obeyed) who rules the Amahaggar tribe. They are on a quest to discover the truth of a collection of ancient shards left to Leo by his dead father, telling of his family's pre-Christian Egyptian ancestor, Kallikrates, who was killed by Ayesha when he renounced her for another lover, Amenartas. Leo has been enjoined to enact revenge on the still-alive Ayesha for this ancient crime. Instead of taking care of his father's business, however, Leo (who appears to be the reincarnation of Kallikrates) falls deeply in love with Ayesha and is prepared to throw himself into a pillar of fire, which she claims holds the secret of her eternal youth. Prior to his stepping into this fire Ayesha, wanting to renew herself, walks in and immediately suffers the debilities of age, transforming from an awesomely beautiful woman into a horrifically ugly ape-like deformity before turning to dust. Leo and Holly then return to England, pass on the story to another scholar, and set out in a renewed search for Ayesha (since it turns out that She did not die but merely relocated, reappearing in the sequel *Ayesha: The Return of She* (1904)).

While often read as rather simplistically misogynist, *She* is far more complex. It is certainly true that much of the language used about Ayesha in the novel openly associates her with diabolical as well as merely forbidden knowledge. She is seen 'throwing back her head like a snake about to strike' (160), and is not only a murderer but an avatar of evil.[53] The main danger she represents is of a rival power to that of the 'passive' Queen Victoria. Both rule empires of sorts, but Ayesha's is an empire of hidden and esoteric structures. Diana Basham calls her the archetypal 'Occult Mother', in horrific opposition to the Domestic Mother back home in England, embodied by the Empress on the throne.[54] However, they are more alike than they seem. Victoria was not content with ruling domestically and was thrilled to become Empress of India; likewise, Ayesha has plans for England: Holly tells us that,

the terrible She had determined to go to England and it made me shudder to think what would be the result of her arrival there ...

In the end, I had little doubt, she would assume absolute rule over the British Dominions, and probably the whole earth, and, though I was sure that she would speedily make ours the most glorious and prosperous empire that the world had ever seen, it must be at the cost of a terrible sacrifice of life. (255)

These were precisely the colonial ambitions of the British Empire at this moment in her history, and they were indeed accompanied by a terrible waste of human life, as Haggard himself was well aware. He had already expressed disgust at the conduct of empire officials in South Africa, after his arrival there in 1875, but instead of reacting by openly criticising empire-building, he decided to spend his career promoting an enterprise with which he was already disillusioned. In the fears of Holly for what would happen should this female goddess rule the Empire we can find a coded disquiet at what Haggard knew was already happening throughout the female-ruled British Empire.

The Theosophical Movement was emerging contemporaneously with Haggard's *She*, which is extremely appropriate, since it was spearheaded by a woman not unlike Haggard's heroine. The Movement had its first meeting in New York in 1875 and was presided over by Madame Helena Petrovna Blavatsky. It is hard to trace Blavatsky's exact origins as she changed her biography several times during her lifetime. 'Theosophy' means 'divine wisdom', and if Ayesha obtained her knowledge deep in the heart of Egyptian Africa before the coming of Christ, Blavatsky claimed to have learned the secrets of the universe high in the Himalayas from a secret isolated group of Mahatmas, and attempted to set them down in *The Secret Doctrine* (1888), where she reveals the 'hidden' or occult basis of ultimate reality. The basic thesis of this book seems to be that what constitutes the cosmos is a constant and evolutionary movement of spirit and matter, and that the goal of human existence is to become one with this flux through spiritual exercises and shifts of consciousness.[55] Higher faculties need to be developed to enable the individual to move up the evolutionary chain and get closer to becoming one with the Absolute. If Darwin had described the physical evolution of the human race, Blavatsky was to be his spiritual equivalent, and she traces this development through a vast body of forbidden knowledge, incorporating pre-Christian mythology, Eastern religious belief, Western occult traditions, all coalescing in the feminine principle – the 'power of the Mother' (although contrarily she insists that this higher power is actually sexless). Goddess worship is basic to her plan of salvation – although in part this segues into Blavatsky-worship, since she saw herself as an incarnation of the goddess. The new knowledge was to be a synthesis of all forms of knowledge:

> Until recently, Religion and Science had nought to do with the beautiful mythos. Yet, the cold, chaste moon stands in closer relations to Earth than any other sidereal orb. The Sun is the giver of life to the whole planetary system; the Moon is the giver of life to our globe; and the early races understood and knew it, even in their infancy ... She is pre-eminently the deity of the Christians, through the Mosaic and Kabalistic Jews, though the civilized world may have remained ignorant of the fact for long ages; in fact, ever since the last initiated Father of the Church died, carrying with him into the grave the secrets of the pagan temples.[56]

Here, Blavatsky echoes the intuition of Haggard in his depiction of She, since Ayesha is both past and future. The future of the race is found in returning to what our ancestors knew about the unity of knowledge. This was a theme echoed in the more authoritative versions of occult science in this period. Many of the scientific researchers of the Society for Psychic Research suggested that the mediums and clairvoyants manifesting the phenomena they were investigating were in fact presenting elements of an ancient and possibly buried natural ability, common in early man and only now returning to the fore. This development, some felt, could bring mankind to the next stage of the evolutionary ladder. Powers of the past could mark out the future. Blavatsky warned that what was preventing this next evolutionary step was ignorance of the unity of knowledge, an ignorance she set mainly down to Christianity, with its masochistic fetishisation of the male principle. Christianity transformed the female deities of the past into Jehovah and neutralised the feminine principle by consigning it to the Virgin Mary. For Blavatsky, Jehovah is actually a perversion of 'Binah ... the Upper mediating Mother, the Great Sea or Holy Spirit'.[57] Christianity distorts the worship of the feminine principle in Moon worship, and so throws the genders into an everlasting war which can only be solved by recovering the ancient knowledge hidden by Christianity's distortions.

Blavatsky believed that true knowledge was the exclusive property of a small intellectual and spiritual elite, those who had proved themselves to be more spiritually evolved than the majority. It subsisted in esoteric sects like the (fictional) Mahatmas who lived in the Himalayas, or in select societies like the Hermetic Order of the Golden Dawn, populated by worthy intellectuals. The poet W. B. Yeats came into the Order after involving himself with spiritualism, moving through the Dublin Hermetic Society and its London equivalent, the Theosophical Society. He was admitted into Blavatsky's innermost circle, the Esoteric Section of the Theosophical Society, in December 1888, and joined the Golden Dawn in March 1890. For Yeats these theosophical interests had a direct political goal since, like many Irish Protestants, he believed that the sectarian divisions of Irish society could be bridged by linking with a pre-Christian occult wisdom which was still being manifested in the intricacies of peasant folklore. In this way gnostic Protestant Ascendancy members (both socially and intellectually affiliates of inner circles) could connect with the peasants of the west of Ireland – who constituted pure Irishmen – and bypass the petty-minded middle-class bourgeois attitudes of the common run of Catholic nationalists. As Roy Foster points out, 'the superstitiousness of Irish Protestants was famous', many of them being Freemasons, and their interest in the occult can be explained as motivated by political estrangement: as they watched the rise of the Catholic middle class Irish Protestants felt alienated from the political establishment and sought consolation in the occult power offered them in theosophical societies (see chapter 3 for this).[58]

Yeats was thoroughly dedicated to the promotion of folklore – which he believed was a repository of ancient wisdom – in the 1890s, and its influence on him led to the publication of *Fairy and Folktales of the Irish Peasantry* (1888), which he edited, and *The*

*Celtic Twilight* (1893), in which he reworked folk material. He believed that these tales, and the traditions of which they were a part, were fragments of a deep mythological culture, of a pre-modern mentality, which could be found only in some cultural outposts of western Europe (such as County Sligo, where his mother came from and to which his poetic imagination returned again and again), as well as in the Eastern cultures. Although in editing the folk material he collected Yeats constantly resolves it into etiological, psychological and sociological rationalism – demonstrating that these beliefs have practical reasons to exist, and thus linking himself with the work of the great mythographers and anthropologists of religion, Fraser and Evans, who were also working at this time– what is different in Yeats's work is that the practical and the spiritual do not cancel each other out. Yeats insists that people believe in traditions of changelings in order to cope with autistic children, or believe that their dead partners are 'gone with the fairies' in order to assuage the grief of losing them, but insists also that these beliefs are elements of a more hidden belief-system that he has yet to fully penetrate:

> I have not yet lost the belief that some day, in some village lost among the hills or in some island among the western seas, in some place that remembers old ways and has not learned new ways, I will come to understand how this pagan mystery hides and reveals some half-forgotten memory of an ancient knowledge.[59]

In other words, Irish folk belief is an aspect of a deeper gnostic system that has to be brought to the surface, and of which perhaps even the Irish peasants were only half aware. Yeats saw the occult world as a means by which he could confront the Tyndall-shaped scepticism of his father and find a way to become closer to the wellsprings of Ireland's difference:

> I was unlike others of my generation in one thing only. I am very religious, and deprived by Huxley and Tyndall, whom I detested, of the simple-minded religions of my childhood, I had made a new religion, almost an infallible Church of poetic tradition, of a fardel of stories, and of personages, and of emotions, inseparable from

their first expression, passed on from generation to generation by poets and painters with some help from philosophers and theologians.[60]

In his building a 'new religion' Yeats attempted to construct a symbolic system which allowed him access to knowledge impenetrable to the quotidian mind, and which could be reached only through an investment in symbols. Through the texts and institutions of theosophy and the occult, and the occult figures he met – including Blavatsky, but especially her Indian associate, Mohini Chatterjee – and Irish myth and folklore, Yeats built a partly private religious philosophy which would eventually culminate in *A Vision* (1925). The esoteric and arcane nature of this knowledge was crucial to its attraction for Yeats, since he was wedded to a reified and gnostic mentality which divided the world into the adepts and the laity. Like the theosophists, Yeats, despite his declared disgust with scientific method, was constantly attempting to use his occult researches to 'prove' the reality of the spiritual realm, and he hoped to be able to provide a knock-down blow to materialism, considering that 'to prove the action of man's will, man's soul, outside his body would bring down the who[le] thing [materialism] – crash'.[61] He was already involved in another secret society by this time, anyway – the nationalist organisation the Irish Republican Brotherhood, which he may have joined in 1885 – and there is a deep connection between Irish nationalist cabals and the occult ones with which he also associated. He was also a member of the Irish Literary club (later the Irish Literary Society of London), and explicitly linked his increasing 'Celticism' with his occultism (Celticism is a mode of thought which saw the Celt as the opposite of the Saxon, a spiritual, poetic, emotional people as opposed to the materialist, prosaic, rational Saxons). As far as he was concerned, Celticism held at the very least potent fragments of the ancient world religion he wished to penetrate, to the mythologisation of which Yeats contributed *Fairy and Folktales of the Irish Peasantry* in 1888, and he worked assiduously on an edition of the poetry of William Blake, whom he thought to be of Celtic origin. As well, he was reading accounts of the Celtic legends in Standish James O'Grady's *History of Ireland* (1878–80).

Yeats's credo was relatively simple, believing 'that the borders of our mind are ever shifting, and that minds can flow into one another ... and create a single mind', and also that 'the borders of our memories are as shifting, and that our memories are part of one great memory, the memory of Nature herself', and finally that 'this great mind and great memory can be evoked by symbols'.[62] These symbols include the Cross and the Rose. His Gothic short stories attempt to connect the mundane with the eternal through the rhythms of the prose. In this period, too, Yeats wanted to create a Celtic Order of Mysteries in Castle Island, Lough Kee, whose aim would be to introduce through occult rituals and writing suffused with occult symbolism, the ancient religion of the world, and so transform it into a site for a new age, a place where the millennium would be ushered in (a theme which suffuses his prose at this time). It is out of this occult maelstrom that *The Secret Rose* (1897) emerged, a collection in which visionaries (such as Red Hanrahan and Owen Aherne) have to constantly struggle with sceptics and materialists, and are determined to make real the symbols of the occult necessary for transformation. There is terror of, as well as desire for, the revelatory visions of the spiritual geniuses running through the volume, as the people they encounter are very attached to the daily round, the suggestion being that those who are too afraid to encounter this vision in all its uncanniness deserve to be wiped out. As Yeats announced in his dedication of *The Secret Rose* to Æ, these stories represent a 'war of spiritual with natural order', and such a war can be devastating to its combatants (79).[63]

## Secret Societies

The idea of a spiritual elite at war with the mediocre was everywhere in nineteenth-century British culture, as manifested in such organisations as the Golden Dawn. However, these were merely developments of a long tradition of such secret societies and occult brotherhoods. The Freemasons is, perhaps, the archetypal secret society, to which some people have ascribed the sovereignty of the globe, believing its members secretly control world politics. Secret societies act as a focal point for theories of mass conspiracy and a conviction that the running of the world has been given to a select group of people who are behind everything.[64] Many of the people involved in the occult revival were in fact Freemasons, and indeed Freemasons established the Order of the Golden Dawn. However, ideas of secret brotherhoods had other manifestations than the Freemasons, and perhaps the most important of these was the Rosicrucians. 'Knowledge' of this group can be traced to an anonymous pamphlet, *The Universal and General Reformation of the Whole Wide World* (an ambitious title), published in 1614, which claimed that a secret society it called the 'Brotherhood of the Rosy Cross' was behind a project of global transformation. Soon, further anonymous pamphlets followed, claiming that this society had been set up in 1407 by Christian Rosenkreutz, a German monk with knowledge of Arabic magic and medicine, who had established a group of eight to preserve these secrets and gain control of world affairs. They supposedly met in a specially built temple of the Holy Spirit, where Christian was buried and which also contained his occult writings and alchemical texts. It is probable that there was no such group as the Rosicrucians when the manifestos were 'released' in the seventeenth century. Alchemical thinkers and scientists, such as Giordano Bruno, John Dee, Philip Sidney, Francis Bacon and Robert Fludd, all found their names linked to this organisation, and what some historians have called a 'Rosicrucian Enlightenment', promoting alchemy and Arabic magic to transform the world, certainly took place. Real Rosicrucian societies were soon set up, most claiming some spurious connection to the original society, from about the 1620s, and its members were accused by their enemies of having made a bargain with the Devil in exchange for knowledge and power. They also became linked, in membership, symbology and secrecy, to the Freemasons. Yeats's stories in *The Secret Rose* are partly indebted to the iconography of the Rosicrucians, and one of the most important occult Gothic writers of the Victorian period, Edward Bulwer Lytton, was (probably) a member of a Rosicrucian society whose writing should be labelled part of a 'Rosicrucian Gothic'.[65]

Bulwer Lytton has been rather neglected by critical scholarship, and this may be because he represents a strain of Victorian literature – the literature of the secret society – that now appears bizarre. His rate of production was stunning, and his style – which could charitably be termed gratuitous – is difficult to appreciate in the cold light of literary history, but his books sold in their thousands. Moreover, he stands at the very nexus I have been discussing in this chapter, the space where the scientific and the spiritual coalesce and emerge in a new genre. Although *Zanoni* is subtitled *A Rosicrucian Tale* (1842), *A Strange Story: An Alchemical Novel* is a much more interesting and complex text. It first appeared in Dickens's *All the Year Round* between August 1861 and March 1862. Its plot is difficult to summarise, but it involves Doctor Allen Fenwick, a scientist thoroughly committed to an uncompromisingly materialist view of the world which does not allow for unexplainable phenomena. He works in L———, and is determined to write a major treatise to demonstrate the non-existence of the soul and show that everything can be reduced to the actions of material movement and 'common sense' (his favourite phrase). He falls in love with Lilian, a woman more of spirit than matter, and the plot follows his relationship with her and the obstacles they face. The chief obstacle is Margrave, a mysterious and beautiful young man whose travels in the Middle East have provided him with occult knowledge and access to occult powers, by using which he places Lilian under a mesmeric spell which alienates her from Fenwick, and eventually renders her a mental idiot. Through his encounters with Margrave, Fenwick is introduced to powers and 'sciences' which he cannot account for in his ultra-materialist philosophy, including a life-renewing elixir of youth, disembodied spirits, electromagnetism, mesmerism of various kinds, telepathy, alchemy and a terrifying 'race' of invisible creatures. Eventually Fenwick comes to accept the existence of the soul, Lilian is cured, Margrave killed, and the marriage appears to be back on track.

The novel is, in a basic sense, about transformation of mind as well as matter, the alchemy posited in the novel's subtitle a reference to how Fenwick himself is changed through the course of the plot to an acceptance of a faith in the soul and the continued existence of the Self (in some form or another) after death. The interesting thing in the novel is the sheer paraphernalia of the occult employed to change his mind. Fenwick would do Richard Dawkins proud in his stubborn refusal to accept the reality of the occult phenomena he encounters and his obstinate clinging to a strictly rationalist understanding of the cosmos. Every occult encounter is rationalised as an illusion, a hallucination or – at worst – the workings of a material force not yet fully understood. As Grand Patron of the Society of Rosicrucians, Bulwer Lytton was himself committed to the belief in forms of hidden knowledge although not necessarily in anything supernatural. In a letter to John Foster he wrote that,

> In regard to the supernatural … I want to intimate that in their recorded marvels which are attested by hundreds and believed by many thousands, things yet more incredible than those which perplex Fenwick are related … There must be a natural cause for them – if they are not purely imposture.[66]

This letter aptly condenses the mindset of most occult researchers in the nineteenth century, who saw the supernatural as the natural world operating in a way we do not currently understand and which, when understood, will be accepted as normative. What Fenwick has to come to appreciate is that his narrow definition of science is what needs to be altered in order to gain access to the full complexity of material reality. Certainly, the race of invisible creatures that manifests at the close of the novel during Fenwick and Margrave's attempt to extract the elixir of youth from the earthly substance found near gold are material enough in their effects. What Fenwick actually learns is about new *scientific* procedures and instruments, which allow him to access a greater material reality than his five senses reveal. These instruments are the property of those labelled 'magicians', and Fenwick's greatest struggle is to unlearn the training which forced him to dismiss non-Western science from the borders of his common-sense world. Science is simply expanded, not contradicted in this text; the only form of science that is dismissed is the narrow-gauge form found in the work of Thomas Huxley. Through his conversations with his mentor, Dr Julius Faber, Fenwick is shown how most of the scientific thinkers of the past, to whom he looks up, invested in the notion of the spiritual. The Soul is salvaged by the end of the novel, but it is as a kind of electrical spark which jolts the animalistic nature of the human upwards to something more intellectual and spiritual. God here is the great electrician who operates to guide evolutionary development. Faber tells Fenwick:

> If some old cosmogenist asked you to believe ... that the origin of the present system of organized beings ... dispensed with the agency of a creative mind, and could be referred to molecules formed in the water by the power of attraction, till by modifications of cellular tissue in the gradual lapse of ages, one monad became an oyster and another a Man – would you not say this cosmogony could scarcely have misled the human understanding even in the earliest dawn of speculative enquiry? Yet such are the hypotheses to which the desire to philosophize away that simple proposition of a Divine First Cause ... led ... La Place and La Marck (396–7).[67]

The point here is not, I think, to reject the evolutionary hypothesis but to revision it taking place at different levels – in a way that Madame Blavatsky would echo years later. The emergence of an animal with the kind of Mind displayed by Man can be accounted for only by accepting a level of existence some call the spiritual through which intellectual evolution is guided by a 'divine' cause. The non-supernatural origin of this needs to be registered. Darwinian evolution alone is rejected as too mechanical; it is supplemented by a spiritual evolution. The cause of the universe is actually Mind rather than Matter, though this is also entirely 'natural'. Ultimate reality is non-material, though not supernatural; the Newtonian view which configures the universe as the interaction of particles gives way here to the view that it is all the expression of a cosmic Mind, a view incompatible with atomistic materialism (though, again, it does not necessitate a belief in anything supernatural). This is a kind of gnostic science, whereby a hidden reality produces the material reality we experience and measure with 'orthodox scientific' procedures. The underlying reality is 'veiled' or hidden, and can be accessed only through things like alchemy and symbology, the kinds of things invested in by Rosicrucians. There is not, I think, an ambiguity about science here, simply about what Lytton appears to think is the perversion of science into gross materialism.[68]

This is a theme repeated in Lytton's 'The Haunters and the Haunted' (1857), where the main character is assured that, despite the most extraordinary events taking place in a supposedly empty house, nothing 'supernatural' is happening. The plot concerns our rationalist narrator investigating a reputedly haunted house in London by staying there for a night. He certainly confirms that there is something weird happening to the house, so extraordinary that it kills his dog, inflicts a nervous breakdown on his servant, and almost destroys the narrator himself. What he finds is that these events are caused by the existence of a certain extremely powerful, sensitive mind with superior powers of will who – through a type of electrical charge connected to apparatuses left in the house – affect the material make-up of any place on earth. The subtitle to this story explains much of the thesis of the text: 'The House and the Brain'. The issue is the impact of the mind on external objects. The previous owner, Mr Richards, is a mesmerist with shockingly powerful mental powers. Again, the key point is that this does not result in a hardened materialism – which was the desire of many who investigated apparently supernatural phenomena and demonstrated that there was nothing supernatural going on. Instead, it leads to a more complex version of Idealism, in which Mind is the basic constituent of the universe. As Mark Knight explains, Lytton's point is to subject the marvellous to scientific scrutiny and reclaim it for mainstream science and philosophy.[69] The narrator insists that 'Wonderful, therefore, as such phenomena may be (granting them to be truthful), I see much that philosophy may question, nothing that it is incumbent on philosophy to deny – viz. nothing supernatural' (57).[70] The supernatural is explained away, à la Radcliffe, but materialism is also dismissed as an inadequate philosophical position to explain the variety of phenomena in the cosmos. This makes understandable the conclusion that the narrator comes to: 'Now, my theory is that the Supernatural is the Impossible, and that what is called supernatural is only a something in the laws of

nature of which we have been hitherto ignorant' (40) – a brilliantly concise description of what most psychic investigators
thought around this period.

In the occult the Victorians found the best expression of their
Gothic refusal to be either wedded completely to modernity or
completely turned towards the past. As a hybrid discourse it could
articulate the complexities of the kind of modern human the
Victorian wanted to be, without compromising either of the
forces thus expressed. Both scientific and 'pseudo-scientific', religious and heretical, about the past but looking to the future, old
and new, the Occult Gothic propelled the Victorian mind into the
twentieth century.

# Conclusion: Moving to the Gothic Trenches

✒

The Occult Queen herself, Madame Blavatsky, died in London on 8 May, 1891; her real-life counterpart, the Empress of India, Queen Victoria, lasted almost another decade, finally expiring on 22 January 1901. With the end of the Victorian age, a Gothic era begins to draw to a close. The issues raised by Victorian Gothic continued, however, and debates about the city, time, childhood, the regions and the occult did not recede in the Edwardian age. The fear of both internal social and political collapse and invasion from the outside intensified in the first two decades of the twentieth century, particularly as groups demanding social changes, such as anti-vivisectionists, feminists, anarchists and socialists, turned to more violent means of expression. Although G. K. Chesterton's *The Man Who Was Thursday* (1908) satirised the paranoid belief that behind every bush was an anarchist agent, Martin Tropp points out that 'the anarchist scare reached epidemic proportions because it focused familiar fears of the parallel breakdown of self and society' found in novels like *Dr Jekyll and Mr Hyde*. The anarchist was configured as a diseased body as well as a political usurper, and was usually believed to be, if not foreign, at least under the influence of foreign agents and powers.[1] If the anarchists were foreign threats, the fear of the Continental Catholic powers actually declined in this period, and the terror of invasion was shifted towards Germany, as articulated in novels such as William Le Quex's *The Invasion of 1910* (1906). As Tropp outlines, the entire paraphernalia of the Gothic was transposed wholesale to understandings of Germany, and when the First World War broke out many appear to have believed that in fighting for the Empire they would be participating in one glorious imperial Gothic narrative, not unlike that found in H. Rider Haggard's novels. What happened when they arrived in the trenches was that all the props of the Gothic were to be found, but in encountering a non-narrated, non-authorial, almost unmediated version of the stories they had been reading since Walpole's *Castle of Otranto*, excitement and suspense were replaced by absolute, unremitting terror. Although 'horror stories prepared their audience for a universe of darkness and despair dominated by the dead, with the living perpetually underground', the fact that they were now starring in a personal horror story meant that psychological trauma rather than narrative tension dominated the experience.[2] In the Gothic narrative convolutions and editorial interventions, paratextual apparatuses intervene between the reader and the pure articulation of horror so that a kind of sublime distance can be achieved, the kind described by Burke when he spoke of sublime horror as being based in part in a realisation by the observer that she is actually safe from any real physical threat. The 'dreadful pleasure' evoked by both the sublime and the Gothic is dependent on the fact that danger and threat are not too close to the observer/reader.[3] This safety was absolutely destroyed by actual life inside the trenches, and although the soldiers often expressed their experiences in the imagery borrowed from a history of Gothic fiction, this was an expression unable to find relief in the narrative safety-features conventional to the Gothic. As Tropp notes, 'the physical distance between the ideal and actual, between heroic fantasy and what became Gothic reality' was short.[4] After the war writers would constantly return to the imagery of the Gothic in their attempts to describe the experience of a soldier on the Western Front, and, as Terry Phillips has outlined, in novels like Rebecca West's *The Return of the Soldier* (1918), R. H. Mottram's trilogy *The Spanish Farm* (1924), *Sixty Four, Ninety-Four!* (1925) and *The Crime at Vanderlynden's* (1926), May Sinclair's *Tree of Heaven* (1917) and Annie Vivanti Chartres's *Vae Victis* (1917), 'the trenches … are more like the medieval past of original Gothic, in that they constitute a world unknown to most who read about them'.[5]

It turned out, in other words, that death would not be 'an awfully big adventure' as promised by Peter Pan. J. M. Barrie's 1906 play centred in part around the nostalgic belief of the adult that perpetual youth away from the confines of the Victorian home and the control of mother and father would be a paradise of constant play. Horrifically comic versions of the father, like Captain Hook, would still have to be confronted and defeated, but essentially life would be one long lingering escapade. That Peter, the boy who will never grow up, actually speculates on the exciting possibilities of death is partly an acknowledgement by him of the eventual weariness of constant play, and his recognition of the inextricability of youth and death, as pointed out in chapter 2. It is also a realisation of the ultimate fantasy of much Gothic: in a genre where nostalgia and terror meet, a perpetual boy who travels to faraway lands and makes them his own appears like a culmination of all the themes I have outlined in this book. After all, Peter does 'conquer' the Redskins, and the beauty of their subjugation is that it takes place only in 'play', and no one really gets hurt. The imperial Gothic and the Gothic of the child combine with the Gothic fear of time's march: all are defeated in one imperial figure who can run the pirates of seriousness out of Never-Never Land. Poignantly, Barrie wrote the play for one group of boys, George, Peter, Michael and Nico Llewelyn Davies, to whom he became guardian after both their parents died, and these children too had to learn that death was not an adventure. George and Peter both signed up to fight in 1914, but George was to die the following year. If in one sense Peter Pan is already dead, since he cannot grow up, and since many Victorians appear to have believed that the best child was a dead child, since that child would never be corrupted by adult life, it was only logical partly to hope that beautiful young boys would die before they were made impure by sex and marriage.

In his 'The Bugler's First Communion' (1918), Gerard Manley Hopkins is confronted by a young Catholic soldier and is so overcome with the intensity of his beauty that the poet expresses a desire that, rather than grow up, the bugler die during the Crimean War:

Let mé though see no more of him, and not disappointment

Those sweet hopes quell whose least me quickenings lift,
In scarlet or somewhere of some day seeing
    That brow and bead of being,
An our day's God's own Galahad. Though this child's drift

Seems by a divíne doom chánnelled, nor do I cry
Disaster there ...[6]

'Divine doom' is preferable to the 'hell-rook's ranks' that 'sally to molest him', especially if that death be in the defence of the Empire. Gothic threats can be vanquished by the good fight offered by the pure in heart. Likewise, Peter Pan leads a group who refuse to become pirates because they would have to proclaim 'Down with the King!', and instead they sing the National Anthem to prove their allegiance to the Empire. Wendy expresses a hope that they will all die 'like English gentlemen', which seems to be the equivalent to Hopkins's fantasy of death before corruption set in.[7] Neither appears to be aware that death on the battlefield itself constitutes not simply a fight against Gothic foreign forces, but also an implication in Gothic darkness itself; that rather than preserve purity through death, death on the battlefield precisely stains and strains its warriors, compromising their innocence. Though Peter Llewelyn Davies returned from the war, his purity had not been preserved but scarified in the trenches, despite his Military Cross. So debilitated was he by both his wartime experiences and his inability to escape the shadow of Barrie's fictionalised version of him, Peter Pan, that he threw himself under a train in 1960. The pre-eminent historian of 'the real story behind Peter Pan', Andrew Birkin, points out that 'the mass media never allowed Peter Davies to forget his namesake, and it was little wonder that he came to loathe his association with what he once referred to as "that terrible masterpiece"'.[8]

The boys who grew up on a diet of Imperial Gothic adventure stories and Gothic nostalgia fests, such as *Peter Pan*, must have been shocked beyond belief when they found what awaited them in Flanders Fields. As Diane Purkiss points out, many of them configured themselves as fairies and fairy children, desiring to become real-life Pans and Tinkerbells.[9] In Robert Graves's wartime collection, *Fusiliers and Fairies* (1917), such palpable desire is all too evident. The poem 'I'd love to be a Fairy's Child' poignantly speaks of the hopes of the generation brought up before the First World War:

> Children born of fairy stock
> Never need for shirt or frock,
> Never want for food or fire,
> Always get their heart's desire:
> Jingle pockets full of gold,
> Marry when they're seven years old.
> Every fairy child may keep
> Two strong ponies and ten sheep;
> All have houses, each his own,
> Built of brick or granite stone;
> They live on cherries, they run wild—
> I'd love to be a Fairy's child.[10]

Here Graves is expressing the simple enough desire of main-taining childhood wildness and extravagance while escaping from parental control. In part, though, the poem is an ode to something that has been lost by the war experience: before coming on to the Front the growing child could configure himself in fairy-sport, conquering mock savages like Barrie's Redskins for Queen and Country; after an encounter in no man's land, no such childhood apotheosis is possible. On Flanders Fields the soldiers realised that they had, in some respects, been sold a lie, and that Gothic nostalgia would have to be reconsidered. You might 'love to be a Fairy's child' but, with bombs raining down on you rather than fairy dust, it was clear that childhood dreams of Neverland had, perhaps, led you to an awful death in a labyrinthine, mud-filled, rat-infested hell in the trenches. The nostalgia now looked like so much propaganda.

In Graves's 'A Child's Nightmare' the nursery is configured not as a prefiguration of Neverland, but as a preparation for the war and a premonition of horrible, not glorious death:

Through long nursery nights he stood
By my bed unwearying,
Loomed gigantic, formless, queer,
Purring in my haunted ear
That same hideous nightmare thing,
Talking, as he lapped my blood,
In a voice cruel and flat,
Saying for ever, 'Cat! … Cat! … Cat! …'
…

He had faded, he was gone
Years ago with Nursery Land,
When he leapt on me again
From the clank of a night train,
Overpowered me foot and head,
Lapped my blood, while on and on
The old voice cruel and flat
Says for ever, 'Cat! … Cat! … Cat! …'
…

When I'm shot through heart and head,
And there's no choice but to die,
The last word I'll hear, no doubt,
Won't be 'Charge!' or 'Bomb them out!'
Nor the stretcher-bearer's cry,
"Let that body be, he's dead!"
But a voice cruel and flat
Saying for ever, "Cat! … Cat! … Cat!"[11]

Death is now something there is no choice over; the soothing tones of a mother's lullaby have become a monstrous, bestial, death-bearing voice. The voice falls as swiftly as a bullet or a bomb. Gothic would never be the same again. In the stories of George and Peter Llewelyn Davies, and their imbrication in the Gothic nostalgia of *Peter Pan* and the unmediated Gothic horror of the First World War, it is appropriate to end this study of the Victorian version of Gothic.

# Survey of Criticism

ॐ

Reading too much of what Baldick and Mighall call Gothic Criticism may not be bad for your health, but it certainly produces a feeling of vertiginousness and bewilderment akin to that of Dr Watson, as he speeds with Holmes through the streets of London in *The Sign of Four* (1890):

> At first I had some idea as to the direction in which we were driving; but soon, what with our pace, the fog, and my own limited knowledge of London, I lost my bearings and knew nothing save that we seemed to be going a very long way. Sherlock Holmes was never at fault, however, and he muttered the names as the cab rattled through squares and in and out by tortuous by-streets.[1]

Any surveyor of a body of critical work must hope to eventually gain a Holmes-like mastery over her materials, but will more likely end up feeling a Watsonian relief at having arrived at her destination in one piece. Other critical cartographers have articulated a similar feeling of exasperated inadequacy in the face of the sheer scale of the task of mapping an area as vast as Gothic criticism. Donna Heiland suggests that the 'sprawling body of work' that Gothic criticism has generated 'can be either alarming or exciting to contemplate', though it is certainly overwhelming;[2] Aviva Briefel argues that Gothic Criticism has taken on a certain monstrosity, enough to make the critic 'fear that behind every doorway there lurks a spectre'.[3] In the following remarks I will try to articulate what I see as the main trajectories taken by the major critics of Victorian Gothic in the last thirty years or so, without in any sense claiming completeness, and I will argue that, although many useful lines of inquiry are being pursued, there is a dominant interpretative language through which this perusal is taking place, a language of ideological and formal ambivalence.

In almost all critical writing on the Gothic in general, and Victorian Gothic in particular, the Gothic is now configured as a genre operating as a highly ambivalent product in which nothing, whether formally, ideologically or culturally, is ever settled or decided. In the terminology of Victor Sage, the Gothic is a form constituted by 'uncertainty',[4] and when this 'uncertain' form meets an era as uncertain as the Victorian one, an age riven with religious doubt, high levels of migration, political instability and the rise in various fundamentalisms which tried to assuage this uncertainty, ambiguity and anxiety become key terms in analysis. I have consistently argued throughout this study that the Gothic cannot be reduced to either a modernising or a nostalgic ideology as it contains both in an attempt to find a new way to be modern. Critics have been very alert to this pervasive uncertainty – an uncertainty that amounted to panic at times – and have appropriately tried to highlight it in their reading of Victorian Gothic fiction. In practically all studies of the Gothic genre in the Victorian era, it turns out to be both conservative *and* subversive, misogynist *and* (crypto/quasi/proto/explicitly) feminist, conformist *and* transgressive, homophobic *and* homoerotic, racist *and* attracted to foreign exoticism, closed *and* open, religious *and* secular, superstitious *and* enlightened, Catholophobic *and* Catholophilic. In Noel Carroll's study of *The Philosophy of Horror* (1990), he describes monstrosity as a 'category mistake', 'categorically interstitial, categorically contradictory, incomplete or formless'.[5] Monsters, he argues, are both physically and intellectually slippery, and incapable of being shoehorned into any ideological straitjacket:

> our impure monsters [are accounted for by calling them] 'unnatural'. They are un-natural relative to a culture's conceptual

scheme of nature. They do not fit the scheme; they violate it. Thus, monsters are not only physically threatening; they are cognitively threatening. They are threats to common knowledge.[6]

The monster is precisely monstrous to the extent that it cannot be pinned down by the discourses of the cultures that produce it, and it is the polyvalence of the Gothic, the Gothic as ideologically and formally dialogic, as understood by Gothic criticism that renders it a monstrous genre itself. Jacques Derrida famously claimed that it was impossible to stabilise a text through assigning it to a genre, since although 'a text cannot belong to no genre, it cannot be without … a genre', it is also true that 'every text participates in … several genres'.[7] The instability Derrida points to here appears to be inherent in the Gothic genre. If, for Derrida, textual stability is disrupted by the fact that texts can never simply be assigned to one genre and therefore explicated through reference to the meaning of that genre, the Gothic has been read as (almost essentially) about and productive of such ambivalence. Gothic criticism sees the Gothic as a monster defined by ambiguity.

This argument may seem strange since, in their invigorating survey of 'Gothic criticism' (2000), Chris Baldick and Robert Mighall have controversially claimed that most recent critics have actually taken a less than ambiguous line in reading Gothic literature and that, especially in David Punter's magisterial *The Literature of Terror* (1980), Rosemary Jackson's *Fantasy* (1981) and Fred Botting's *Gothic* (1994), the now-canonical critical works, but also more generally, Gothic has been consistently configured as both a formally and ideologically subversive genre. Baldick and Mighall argue that contemporary critics of the Gothic have attempted to associate it with the revolutionary energies involved in the French Revolution and as antagonistic to anything deemed (in these critics' minds) conventional or smelling of orthodoxy, 'mistakenly presenting Gothic literature as a kind of "revolt" against bourgeois rationality, modernity and the Enlightenment', hence associating it with a general tradition of radical theoretical studies coming from the Marxist-inflected Frankfurt School.[8] The clear implication in this argument is that critics have allowed their own political sympathies to cloud their objective judgement. Since, because of their ideological sympathies, they dislike the bourgeoisie so much and the ideology upon which bourgeois hegemonic control rests, so too must the Gothic:

> in this respects, Gothic Criticism is not an eccentric current in modern literary debate. In fact it stands as a central, if more colourfully flagrant, instance of the mainstream modernity, postmodernist, and left-formalist campaign against nineteenth-century literary realism and its alleged ideological backwardness [and, they may have added, their contemporary representatives, the modern forces of conservatism].[9]

In direct opposition to the purveyors of subversion, Baldick and Mighall propose that, in fact, the Gothic is a rather tame version of bourgeois Whiggism promoting precisely the kinds of values associated with middle-class liberals that Punter *et al* seem most impatient with (because they are ultimately not socially and politically radical enough). They argue that the Gothic is a liberal genre, in general promoting a version of bourgeois ideology so hated by its postmodern detractors, and largely in favour of protecting the state and the family from breakdown, 'gratefully endors[ing] Protestant bourgeois values as "kinder" than those of feudal barons'.[10]

However, to depict recent Gothic studies as almost singular in their ideological reading is to ignore that, when it comes to actual textual analysis, almost all these studies have accepted that it is simply impossible to fit Gothic into one critical or ideological box – radical or conservative. Indeed, although Baldick and Mighall complain about the constant focus on 'anxiety' as a central trope of Gothic criticism (anxiety about Victorian masculinity or femininity, or about colonial hegemony, or about middle-class security), it is in tracing such anxieties that the power of recent Gothic criticism comes to the fore, because anxiety opens ideological possibilities rather than closes them. In other words, through focusing on anxieties Gothic criticism has consistently demonstrated the even the most apparently ideologically conservative texts, such as Bram Stoker's *Dracula* or H. Rider

Haggard's *She*, speak of the problems as well as the power of bourgeois ideology. If at times some Gothic criticism strays close to suggesting that there is a simplistic way in which the Gothic is a radically left-wing quasi-Marxist instrument for attacking all that the middle-class holds dear (and I would accept that this is certainly true of some Gothic criticism some of the time), the actual textual readings produced by these critics almost always highlight ideological ambiguity rather than secure closure.

For example, Mighall and Baldick select for particular disapprobation the claims by Stephen Arata in his *Fictions of Loss in the Victorian Fin de Siècle* (1996) and Kelly Hurley in her *The Gothic Body* (1996) that the Gothic 'articulates' and 'negotiates' 'anxieties' – of colonial superiority and masculine hegemony respectively – and contend that it is not the '"business" of Gothic fiction to "articulate" or "negotiate" anxieties … [but] to be scary or sensational'.[11] Personally, I cannot see the reason for their division between making an audience frightened and articulating the anxieties an audience may be experiencing in what the philosopher Alfred Schutz calls the 'monumental' paramount reality of its everyday life:[12] is it not more likely that a text will succeed in being frightening when it focuses on the anxieties of its audience, whatever they may be?[13] Baldick and Mighall seem to be wary of the focus on bourgeois anxiety because they suspect that what the critic really means is that the Gothic always works to undermine bourgeois superiority and thus places it on the side of the Marxist-inflected exegete; that, for example, a text like H. Rider Haggard's *She* might be superficially imperialist, patriarchal, misogynist, classist, but in a close reading it is unable to maintain these strictly conservative lines and breaks down ideologically at a number of crucial moments, so that the ensuing book is rather more radical and subversive than it initially appears. This, however, does not actually promote a strictly subversive version of the Gothic, since Arata and Hurley especially, and Gothic critics more generally, acknowledge that conservative as well as subversive energies inhere in the text.

So, although Baldick and Mighall usefully alert us to a general critical tendency to remake the literature we love in our own ideological image, they are being rather unfair in their depiction of Gothic criticism as insensitive to the conservative (often violently conservative) liberalism of most Gothic writing.[14] A more accurate description of Gothic criticism would acknowledge that a broadly post-structuralist view of textuality has become normative. In a now famous analysis of the textual condition of all novels, Lennard J. Davis argued that ambivalence is the basic condition of fiction itself:

> The novel must always be thought of as inherently ambivalent. It was so at its origins and it continues to be so. One might say that the quality of ambivalence is one which has permitted the novel to survive by refusing to be assigned one particular meaning or function ... In its sense of ambivalence, the novel is beyond the control of even its best practitioners.[15]

This, more or less, is, after all, precisely what Fred Botting means when, in his now basic *Gothic*, he argues that what characterises the Gothic is 'excess'.[16] While Davis is making a claim about all novels, about the novel form itself, what Gothic critics have claimed is that Gothic is a genre particularly afflicted with the inability to make up its ideological or formal mind. Gothic is an extreme case of what Roland Barthes has termed the 'writerly', in that it is constituted by texts which refuse closure and constantly open out into new readings. Rather than a version of the Gothic as ideologically subversive, the dominant critical position is that the Gothic is subversive of all attempts at closure, whether that closure be for left- or right-wing reasons. This is the critical orthodoxy that needs to be grappled with, and it is a much more difficult view to tackle than a simple liberal/radical binary would be.

The evidence for this discourse of ambivalence is everywhere in Gothic criticism. For example, one of Baldick and Mighall's *bêtes noires* is Rosemary Jackson's *Fantasy*, which does on the surface appear to be very dogmatic in designating fantasy (within which the Gothic is located) as 'a literature of subversion'. She writes that 'it exists alongside the "real", on either side of the dominant cultural axis, as a muted presence, a silenced imaginary other. Structurally and semantically, the fantastic aims at dissolution of an order experienced as oppressive and insufficient.'[17] However, when engaged in actual exegesis, Jackson is far more alert to ideological ambivalence than left-wing subversion. Her analysis of the texts of Victorian Gothic acknowledges that 'they manipulate apparently non-political issues into forms which would serve the dominant ideology ... [and] difficult or unpalatable social realities are distorted ... to emerge as melodramatic shapes ... [so that these] troublesome social realities can be destroyed in the name of exorcising the demonic', though insisting that 'the drive of [these] narratives is towards a "fantastic" realm', so that they are ultimately 'contradictory', ideologically speaking.[18] Likewise, in an authoritative study of *The History of Gothic Fiction* (2000), Markman Ellis argues that the Gothic as a genre is split between

> on the one hand ... offer[ing] a critique of the enlightenment construction of history as a linear account of ... the 'progress and varieties of civilisation' ... [and] on the other hand ... propos[ing] a scepticism not only towards supernatural experience and superstitious belief but towards all naïve forms of credulity,[19]

and traces this dialectic of enlightenment and superstition from *The Castle of Otranto* to *I Walked with a Zombie* (directed by Jacques Tourneur, 1943).

The same emphasis on ambivalence can be found everywhere in Gothic criticism. Peter K. Garrett's *Gothic Reflections: Narrative Force in Nineteenth-Century Fiction* (2003) concerns the narrative attempt by Gothic writers to gain 'total mastery' and control over the reader through the standard tropes and narrative patterns basic to the Gothic genre. Achieving such mastery is regarded by Garret as, however, ultimately impossible, so that the genre ends up collapsing into a version of madness, as mastery is attempted and constantly frustrated. Alison Milbank's 'Victorian Gothic in English novels and stories, 1830–1880', in *The Cambridge Companion to Gothic Fiction* (2002), emphasises the vacillation of the genre in the Victorian period between entrapment and liberation of the Gothic heroine, a vacillation reflecting the ambivalences of the age as a whole split between radical politics of escape – 'republican liberation', 'revolutionary education' – and conservative politics of stability – 'social consensus', 'monarchical tyranny', though her terms indicate where Milbank's own political sympathies lie.[20]

Turning to more focused approaches, the recurrence of ambivalence rather than closure is striking. One of the most important growth areas in Gothic Studies has been the treatment of gender and sexuality. Women writers dominated the Gothic genre in the eighteenth century, in terms of volumes produced, sales numbers reached and audience aimed at, facts identified and scrutinised by E. J. Clery in *Women's Gothic* (2000), which examines in detail six female participants in the Gothic: Clara Reeve, Sophia Lee, Ann Radcliffe, Joanna Baillie, Charlotte Dacre and Mary Shelley. The pioneering study that identified gender not simply as an issue of production and reception, but of ideology and aesthetics, however, was Ellen Moers's *Literary Women* (1976), where she coined the term 'female Gothic' to explain not simply the gender of the writer, but Gothic works where 'the central figure is a young woman who is simultaneously persecuted victim and courageous heroine'.[21] This configuration places the question of ideology centre-stage, as it suggests that Gothic is centrally concerned with the dynamics of gender and that 'female Gothic' traces and highlights for its female readers the dangers to women of patriarchal society, although, and conversely, it actually plays a part in the persecution it depicts, by aestheticising female pain and suffering. The Gothic, in this view, is primarily a means for women to explore the terrors involved in eighteenth-century gender theory and the threat to both their physical and psychical well-being that resides in men, but it also constitutes an extension of that threat by sexualising persecution.

While Moers's linking of an analysis of the limitations and dangers of patriarchy to the biological sex of an author has been criticised, especially by E. J. Clery in her essay 'Ann Radcliffe and D. A. F. de Sade: thoughts on heroism' (1994), with some pointing out that 'female Gothic' thus defined has also been produced by male writers (with *The Castle of Otranto* by Horace Walpole easily assigned to the 'female Gothic' role), it did usefully alert critics to the importance of gender and the dynamics of the domestic in

Gothic writing. Moers's analysis is basic to a seminal study like that of Sandra Gilbert and Susan Gubar, whose *The Madwoman in the Attic: The Woman Writer and the Nineteenth-Century Literary Imagination* (1979), although not exclusively concerned with the Gothic, evokes the Gothic figure of the hysterical woman as a means to understand nineteenth-century literary culture. Gilbert and Gubar argue that women writers constantly reproduced images of the monstrous, transgressive woman throughout the period – in figures such as Bertha Mason in *Jane Eyre*, Catherine Earnshaw in *Wuthering Heights*, Lucy Snowe in *Villette* – as a means of both appearing to conform to patriarchal values and simultaneously rebelling against them, by identifying with these apparently 'mad' women. The monstrosity of the uncontrolled woman may be finally exorcised by the end of the text (thus apparently making safe patriarchal bourgeois value-systems), but by this stage the transgressive nature of the monster has radically destabilised traditional, patriarchally controlled spaces. The Gothic acts as a means by which spaces controlled by the dictates of a patriarchal culture are exposed as ideological rather than natural, and allow the woman writer, for a brief period, to destroy that space. The burning by Bertha Mason of Thornfield acts, in this way, both to raze the domestic prison in which she was trapped, and also allows Charlotte Brontë to expose the ideology trapping women in this space, though her death allows the prison to be rebuilt and refurnished for another woman – Jane Eyre.

The notion of the Gothic as a partial exposé of female imprisonment in the domestic realm has been taken up vigorously by subsequent feminist studies. Kate Ferguson Ellis's *The Contested Castle: Gothic Novels and the Subversion of Domestic Ideology* (1989), insists that the genre of the Gothic has the ability to radically undermine the domestic beyond repair, and thus provide intellectual sustenance for 'rebelling' women, but most feminist critics have insisted that while there is indeed, a radical, proto-feminist edge to many Gothic texts, particularly those produced by women, in the end this struggle is abandoned in favour of an uneasy conformity. Ellis's is a text which may seem – from its title – to be straightforward, in its association of Gothic with a radical attack on middle-class hegemony. However, while on one level it does indeed trace in Gothic a female 'resistance to an ideology [of the separate spheres] that imprisons them even as it posits a sphere of safety for them', it finally concludes that 'the Gothic discourse on the home is not univocal' and that 'the family is both a point of departure and a point of return'.[22] Juliann E. Fleenor, the editor of *The Female Gothic* (1983), works with the idea that 'the Gothic and ... female experiences have a common schizophrenia', in that the form and the women both want to undermine patriarchal violence towards women and yet also endorse the patriarchal system which holds women in a place of subordination.[23] Another feminist critic, Nina Auerbach, in *Our Vampires, Our Selves* (1995), is explicit in seeing no central ideological coherence in vampire fictions, and divides them into two groups: the first group, epitomised by Sheridan Le Fanu's *Carmilla*, empowers women, while the second, epitomised by Stoker's *Dracula*, demonises and exorcises these same powerful women. In *City of Dreadful Delight: Narratives of Sexual Danger in Late-Victorian London* (1992), Judith Walkowitz sees the geographical divisions of nineteenth-century London into East End and West End as indicative of a series of binaries working across Victorian culture as a whole, gender, class and colonial divisions. Despite the fact that many Gothic writers were apparently dedicated to upholding these rigid divisions, in their actual writings they constantly transgressed the boundaries separating the two terms, so that their Gothic texts became radically ambivalent.

The Gothic raises questions about gender roles it is unable to settle completely. Diane Long Hoevler, in *Gothic Feminism: The Professionalisation of Gender from Charlotte Smith to the Brontës* (1998), asserts that while there is certainly a thread of what she calls 'victim feminism' running through Gothic texts authored by women, a feminism which imaginatively critiques 'all of those public institutions that have been erected to displace, contain, or commodify women', what is ultimately proposed as an alternative to a masculinist public space in which women are always threatened is 'the confines of the ultimate fantasy home – the female-dominated companionate marriage'.[24] In Alison Milbank's impressive *Daughters of the House: Modes of the Gothic in Victorian Fiction* (1992), she argues that feminist criticism has rather erred on the critical side in examining the fiction of Charles Dickens, Wilkie Collins, and Sheridan Le Fanu and finding it unambiguously misogynist, and she concludes that 'the conservative writer has a more complex agenda than is usually supposed', though what she means by this is that there are both misogynist and feminist strands within the fiction of these men (and one woman – Charlotte Brontë).[25] Its version of Victorian gender-relations is certainly more problematised than the rigidly dichotomised account put forward by Kate Millett in *Sexual Politics* (1970), and argues not only that men were not so rigidly committed to the image of the subordinate woman as has been assumed by many, but also that, in Victorian reality, men and women simply did not fit into the separate spheres, anyway. Although most Gothic writers are rightly considered socially conservative when it comes to gender roles, their fiction – because of the ambivalence of the form itself – forced them into unearthing some of the limitations of the gender roles ascribed to women in the Victorian period. The emphasis on ambivalence in gender identity in the Gothic should not blind the reader to the impassioned fear and disgust that runs through much Gothic writing when it comes to women. Although it concentrates mostly on the visual arts, Bram Dijkstra's *Idols of Perversity: Fantasies of Feminine Evil in Fin-de-Siècle Culture* (1986), demonstrates how ingrained the version of femininity as monstrous and threatening was in Victorian culture as a whole, though even here some fantasies of feminine evil are also articulations of a male desire for powerful women. Sensation fiction has been the locus of many examinations of gender and the Gothic, and in particular Lyn Pykett's *The 'Improper' Feminine: The Women's Sensation Novel and the New Woman Writing* (1992) brilliantly demonstrates that while much sensation fiction is geared towards a critique of 'transgressive' women (including New Women), most of them, including Mary Elizabeth Braddon's *Lady Audley's Secret*, are unable to relinquish their attraction towards these radical women and actually perform a withering attack on the homosocial world of the Victorian male to which the woman was seen as an appendage.

The ambivalence around gender and sexual roles in the Gothic, the inability of the form to repudiate either conservative or radical readings, its attraction to both subversive women and sexually ambiguous men, and its simultaneous revulsion towards these very figures, has led to a productive relationship growing between Queer Studies and the Gothic, helped by the fact that Eve Kosofsky Sedgwick has been a central figure in both critical enterprises. The homosociality of much of British society was outlined in Sedgwick's *Between Men* (1985), which argued that Gothic was a species of 'homosexual panic', where the increasingly interdependent roles of men in the eighteenth and nineteenth centuries were shadowed by a growing focus on the dangers of such close male friendships as signifiers of homosexuality. The Gothic is torn between endorsing, examining and extolling these homosocial bonds – of school, club, political party, work and church, spaces which excluded women – and producing a paranoid critique of them as if always anticipating accusations of homosexual desire: 'The Gothic novel crystallized for English audiences the terms of a dialectic between male homosexuality and homophobia, in which homophobia appeared thematically in paranoid plots.'[26] In this way the Gothic explores possible relationships between men, while being paranoid about these relationships going too far and positively homophobic in punishing any that do stray into ambiguous territory. In *Sexual Anarchy* (1991), Elaine Showalter highlighted the sexual ambiguity of the Gothic male romance of the imperialist adventure writers such as H. Rider Haggard, whose misogynistic rejection of women comes dangerously close to a kind of homosexual desire for the company of beautiful men, and also pointed out that *Dr Jekyll and Mr Hyde* was a novel which promoted exclusively male relationships while also hysterically warning against them.

This 'queering' of the form by reading it through its ideological ambivalences, its bipartisanship, reached something of a zenith in George Haggerty's *Queer Gothic* (2006), which argues that although saturated by conservative politics, the Gothic is ultimately radically subversive, as it continually exposes as ideological and cultural the sexual and gender identities the conservative would like to posit as natural. Haggerty believes that Gothic is a fruitful site, where the limitations of 'normative' versions of sexuality are tested by experimenting with 'unauthorised genders and sexualities, including sodomy, tribadism, romantic friendship (male and female), incest, paedophilia, sadism, masochism, necrophilia, cannibalism, masculinised females, feminised males, miscegenation, and so on'. Yet he also acknowledges that, even while 'trying on' these transgressive versions of gender and sexuality, the Gothic often ends up supporting the normative:

> I attempt to show the ways in which all normative … configurations of human interaction are insistently challenged and in some cases significantly undermined in these fictions. [Yet] I cannot make too broad a claim because these fictions never significantly challenge the 'dominant fiction' of the age.[27]

This argument echoes that concerning Victorian masculinity in Cyndy Hendershot's *The Animal Within* (1998) and Andrew Smith's *Victorian Demons* (2004), both of which trace how the Gothic form subjects cultural notions of normative masculinity to a destructive scrutiny and exposes the aporia and contradictions within such constructions. Smith's study is especially useful as it demonstrates that, far from producing a monological version of masculinity that could only be threatened externally, the middle-class professionals in the medical, legal and journalist establishments themselves produced texts which destabilised normative masculinity and showed how the most 'normal' men could be driven to extremes of transgressive action – such as the fear the medical profession was itself producing monsters in men, who saw the human body in purely objective terms and were capable of committing horrific acts upon that body. The Gothic's 'queerness' is essentially its nature as an ideological octopus: it has fingers in every pie. For Smith, while for some the 'crisis of masculinity' was a terrifyingly threatening event precipitating the loss of a manly ability to take on the world, for others this crisis was 'the opportunity for new forms of expression', so that his reading of the Gothic hesitates between terror and celebration.[28]

If gender and sexuality have been central concerns of Gothic Criticism, so too has tracing the aesthetics of ethnicity, race and colonialism. Again, the dominant argument here has been that while much Gothic produces monstrous and horrific stereotypes of foreignness and consistently identifies the monstrous with different races and ethnicities, ultimately the Gothic actually works to undermine secure notions of ethnic and racial purity to produce a more precariously hybrid version of the race. The Gothic is both an instrument of Orientalism, imperialism and colonial discourse, and a means of exposing the limitations of this same discourse. The most straightforward reading of the Gothic and race has been H. L. Malchow's *Gothic Images of Race in the Nineteenth Century* (1996), which traces the sheer amount of Gothic material that resorts to racialising the Gothic monster. For Malchow, racial discourse and Gothic fiction are imbricated in the nineteenth century, in that both

> manipulate deeply buried anxieties [though, after reading Malchow's book, they do not seem to have been *that* buried], both dwell on the chaos beyond natural and rational boundaries, and massage a deep, often unconscious and sexual, fear of contamination, both present the threatened destruction of the simple and pure by the poisonously exotic, by anarchic forces of passion and appetite, carnal lust and blood lust.[29]

Carol Davison's *Anti-Semitism and British Gothic Literature* (2004) unearths the basic anti-Semitism of the Gothic since its inception. Davison finds anti-Semitism is a basic trope of the Gothic. Although the central figure in her study is Stoker's Dracula, who possesses obviously Semitic physical features, she traces his origins back to the tradition of the 'demonic Wandering Jew' in the eighteenth century, a tradition that she demonstrates manifests itself firstly in Matthew Lewis's *The Monk* (1796). This tradition is, however, unstable and, to a degree, ambivalent, and ranges from benign though patronising through to pathological and hysterical by the end of the nineteenth century as theological anti-Judaism was combined with racial anti-Semitism, where Jews become versioned as monstrous, bestial, pollutants, sexually deviant, satanic and child-killers. For Davison, the Jew was crucial in allowing a national identity to form, as the British projected on to this demon all that they did not wish to acknowledge as intrinsic to the national Self, even she concludes that the anti-semitism of the Gothic works 'to both strengthen and unsettle an idealized vision of Englishness'.[30]

Cannon Schmitt's *Alien Nation: Nineteenth-Century Gothic Fictions and English Nationality* (1997) also insists that the Gothic is an instrument of radically conservative British (and indeed, English) nationalism. Gothic was central in the construction of English nationality in the late eighteenth century through to the end of the nineteenth century, with the genre continually employed to produce the despised foreign Other to the stable English Self. However, Schmitt warns that 'the workings of such a logic could produce unexpected results', including the actual undermining of 'national purity from within by way of … Mother England's nightmarish double'.[31] So, although as a whole Schmitt's book is designed to undermine studies of the Gothic which emphasise its subversive and radical nature by establishing a link between the Gothic and a chauvinistic nationalism, he also demonstrates how destabilised by anxiety this version of nationalism is and how the Gothic traces, rather than simply elides, the borderlands of these anxieties. Even here, then, secure definitions of Englishness and Britishness are undermined rather than simply strengthened. Andrew Smith and William Hughes argue, in their editorial introduction to *Empire and the Gothic* (2003), that the Gothic poses the question of 'what it means to be human', and answers it with: white, Anglo-Saxon, male.[32] This legitimates colonial enterprises as a form of civilising the primitive and the barbaric. However, far from answering the question with any sense of security, the Gothic in fact generates only anxiety over the issue. In Patrick Brantlinger's analysis of what he calls 'imperial Gothic' (the racist, empire-supporting writing of H. Rider Haggard, Rudyard Kipling and Arthur Conan Doyle), fears and anxieties over imperial superiority are revealed. This literature articulates 'anxieties about the ease with which civilisation can revert to barbarism or savagery and thus about the weakening of Britain's imperial hegemony'.[33] Imperial Gothic is anxiety-ridden rather than confidently imperialist, fearing that racial difference may not be absolute, and also fearing that degeneration to a more primitive state is possible. In exploring the outer reaches of the colonial darkness these writers expose the fears of a heart of darkness lurking at home.

Stephen Arata supports this view of colonial ambiguity in *Fictions of Loss in the Victorian Fin de Siècle* (1996), claiming that 'British culture in the 1880s and 1890s was marked by a sense of irretrievable decline', and traces how the perception of an impending loss of imperial hegemony 'was cast into narrative, into archetypal stories which sought to account for the culture's troubles and perhaps assuage its anxieties'.[34] In *Skin Shows: Gothic Horror and the Technology of Monsters* (1995), Judith Halberstam likewise demonstrates that racial monstrosity becomes so overdetermined in Gothic texts that the purity of the Self/Other division begins to break down. Thus, for example, Dracula may be an insignia of racial otherness (shown in his Eastern European origin, his Semitic features, his primitive childlike brain), but so overburdened by Otherness does he become that he begins to disappear entirely – which explains how he finds it easy to pass himself off as Jonathan Harker when he goes on his child-abduction missions. Her study as a whole focuses on how Gothic produces monsters of threatened subjectivity – they are bodies and psyches radically permeable by otherness of many forms, most particularly racial and ethnic otherness. Kelly Hurley's analysis of the 'abhuman' in *The Gothic Body* demonstrates how caught up in the question of delineating the human race into acceptable and beyond the pale the Gothic is, but again and again she also shows how the Self, the human, becomes inflected by and diluted by the Other, the abhuman. Although studies of race in the Gothic have consistently demonstrated the conservative motivations behind the Gothic texts, they have invariably demonstrated that the Gothic cannot maintain these divisions and that Self/Other binaries collapse.

So, ambivalence dominates the field of Gothic Criticism, which is something of a problem. My frustration with the sheer pervasiveness of this ambivalence in Gothic Criticism is not to suggest that I am not in sympathy with this train of thought. Indeed, in my estimation, the only major study which expressly contradicts this view, Robert Mighall's *A Geography of Gothic Fiction: Mapping History's Nightmares* (1999), which argues with admirable consistency that the Gothic is an Enlightenment-promoting, modernising, progressive form whose main function is to exorcise any remnants of the medieval remaining in the nineteenth century, is (grandly) wrong, mainly because it underestimates the degree to which nostalgia for the past is both manifest and latent in much Gothic, a claim I hope I have supported in chapter 1. Mighall's is probably the pre-eminent approach to the Gothic as a mode of writing imminently concerned, not with universal psychological structures or unconscious imagery, but with specific questions of history that arose in the late eighteenth and nineteenth century. Mighall is convinced that much, if not most, criticism of the Gothic is radically mistaken, in that it fails to understand the historical conservatism of the genre, which he sees as a Whiggish mode of writing designed to reassure its readers that monstrosity and evil are aspects of a pre-modern past that the modern era has left behind or is in the process of exorcising from any spaces where it has hidden itself, from urban slums to dark corners of the criminal and deviant mind. He contends that 'psychological, ontological and "symbolic" approaches' pass over the historical problems examined in the form, where things which had been laid to rest by common society have either returned or refused to go away and are menacing us again.[35] However, the dominant writing on Victorian Gothic has insisted on, rather than escaped from, the historical. Indeed, perhaps the main shift in Gothic criticism has been a move away from predominantly psychoanalytical approaches to the Gothic, where the genre was seen as a means by which artists had articulated the universal conflicts of human psychology in a way best deciphered through the work of intrepid researchers such as Sigmund Freud and Jacques Lacan. For many critics, it was the Gothic that had effectively mapped out the psychoanalytical field, and in some of the more general studies, the Gothic was treated as a literature of dreams, the unconscious and an articulation of id fantasies and oedipal desires that simply could not be expressed in a realist style. In the terms of Maggie Kilgour's *The Rise of the Gothic Novel* (1995), the discipline of psychoanalysis is considered as 'itself a gothic, necromantic form, that resurrects our psychic pasts'.[36] This approach is seen at its best in William Patrick Day's *In the Circles of Fear and Desire* (1985) and Anne Williams's *Art of Darkness* (1995), although elements of it can also be found in David Punter's *The Literature of Terror*. In these studies there is little recognisably 'Victorian' about Gothic texts produced in the nineteenth century, as the anxieties they express are basic to the condition of living through modernity, although the version of the Victorian as a figure beset by repression – described in the Introduction – was useful grist to the psychoanalytical mill. Now, however, the best recent work thoroughly implicates the historical with the Gothic.

For example, Martin Tropp's *Images of Fear: How Horror Stories Helped Shape Modern Culture* (1990) brilliantly traces Gothic imagery across a range of literature of the long nineteenth century, including parliamentary reports, museum exhibitions and Gothic literature, to demonstrate, in a highly convincing fashion, the interaction of literature with cultural and political life, right up to the culmination of such images in the trenches of Flanders in the First World War. For Tropp, horror is everywhere. Likewise, Gail Turley Houston's *From Dickens to Dracula: Gothic, Economics and Victorian Fiction* (2005) demonstrates that there is a relation between the Gothic and political economy in the Victorian period: both are modes of panicked reaction to crises in the economic realm. In her readings of a huge variety of different kinds of literature, including letters, political philosophy (particularly Marx's *Das Kapital*), journalism and the Gothic novel, the discourses of economics and terror interact fruitfully to speak of a wider social panic. In Susan J. Navarrette's *The Shape of Fear: Horror and the Fin de Siècle Culture of Degeneration* (1998), anxieties produced by fears of degeneration are explored through her innovative focus on the prose styles of the writers, who are judged to have produced a style as degenerated as the themes they were exploring. Her argument 'stresses the paradoxically corrupted, and corrupting, nature of highly refined, carefully wrought language', such as is found everywhere in Gothic writing.[37] In one of the most innovative and intellectually challenging studies of the Gothic, *Gothic Radicalism: Literature, Philosophy, and Psychoanalysis in the Nineteenth Century* (2000), Andrew Smith reads Gothic as a kind of commentary on the tradition of philosophical idealism, indeed as what he calls 'a meaningfully coherent critique of this idealist tradition'.[38] Smith traces an intellectual tradition, running from Edmund Burke and Immanuel Kant to Sigmund Freud, which placed increasing emphasis on psychological introspection and the mental world, rather than the world outside the mind. This is particularly challenging, as it suggests that the Gothic is, in effect, a kind of philosophical discourse in itself trying to uncover the gaps and aporia running through the idealist tradition, and that in doing so it helps to undermine the 'dominant intellectual culture'.[39] Far from the historical being neglected, therefore, current Gothic criticism is historicist in assumption and analysis.

It is always tempting at the end of a survey to suggest the direction in which criticism should move in the future. Certainly, historicism and formal and ideological ambivalence represent critical orthodoxy at the time of writing, and, it is tempting to say, critical orthodoxy always needs to be challenged. Since my own perspective on Gothic has largely been shaped by this orthodoxy, however, and because I substantially agree with it, I am not all that anxious to see it superseded. Instead, I will suggest two areas of Gothic Studies for further attention. Peter Coveney's *The Image of Childhood* (1957) is the seminal study of the configuration of childhood from the Romantics to the present day, and for specific examinations of children in the Victorian period I would recommend James Kincaid's controversial but brilliant *Child-Loving: The Erotic Child and Victorian Culture* (1992) and the chapter on Victorian childhood in Hugh Cunningham's delightful and erudite *The Invention of Childhood* (2006). For the 'Gothic Child', the best source is the emerging work of Steven Bruhm. Bruhm is currently working on a project which will examine how, since Rousseau, the figure of the child has been located in a liminal zone between perfect innocence and monstrous evil.[40]

The second area of interest I think will yield critical fruit is the link between religion and the Gothic. Sir Walter Scott argued that Ann Radcliffe's novels operated as therapy for the soul in an age when orthodox religion was coming under increasing threat. He likened the reading of a Radcliffe novel to the taking of drugs, 'of most blessed power in those moments of pain and of languor, when the whole head is sore, and the whole heart sick'. As Donna Heiland has persuasively argued, 'the crucial area of gothic and religion' has produced some important studies, but 'relatively little' by comparison with areas such as gender and empire.[41] The Gerald Parsons-edited, five-volume *Religion in Victorian Britain* (1988), which features a wide range of essays on different subjects by experts in the field, is easily the most helpful way into the complexities of Victorian religious life for the first-time student. This should be supplemented with Owen Chadwick's two-volume *The Victorian Church* (1966) and, for the connections between religion and literature, John Maynard's magisterial *Victorian Discourses on Sexuality and Religion* (1993). The best work on religion and the Gothic has, in fact, demonstrated how impossible it is to separate the questions of race and gender from religious problems. George Haggerty's *Queer Gothic* dedicates a chapter to demonstrating how transgressive sexuality, 'queer' subjectivity, and Catholicism are linked in the Gothic and in eighteenth- and nineteenth-century Britain more generally. This helps explain why the Gothic is a specifically Protestant genre, as it is precisely generated by anxieties (there is that word again) within Protestant cultures about Catholicism as a site of holy terror and holy attraction. Victor Sage's *Horror Fiction in the Protestant Tradition* (1988) articulates how a 'theological uncertainty', which has its origin in the Glorious Revolution, haunted British Protestantism and generated the powerfully repulsed and horrifically attractive versions of Catholicism central to the Gothic.

Patrick O'Malley, in *Catholicism, Sexual Deviance and Victorian Culture* (2006), challenges those who consider the Gothic as a mode dealing only with dangers assigned to the cultural past, since he believes that Catholicism is the crucible of the Gothic, a source of both desire and repulsion for nineteenth-century culture. He shows up anti-Catholicism and Catholophilia in surprising places. For example, even for sexologists such as Havelock Ellis, Catholicism was the repository of much information – and many instances – about sexual deviancy.[42] O'Malley claims persuasively that:

> there is a persistent conjunction of tropes of Catholicism with those of non-normative sexual expression or identity in the literary,

185

artistic, and polemical culture of nineteenth-century Britain and Ireland, and, further, that that conjunction reflects an ongoing contest over Britain's sectarian purity as well as its sexual values.[43]

This is especially the case for Protestant Britain since it had originally been a Catholic country, so that involvement with Catholicism was involvement with its own past. Perhaps, in exploring the religious in the Gothic we can come to new understandings of how Gothic functions in culture at large as a means of reviving a supposedly dead discourse, demonstrating that although some may believe God was buried in the nineteenth century, He immediately rose from the grave, with more awesome and terrible powers than before.

# Gothic Chronology[1]

I indicate only the start of serial publication.

1825: Stockton and Darlington Railway opens; Samuel Taylor Coleridge, *Aids to Reflection*; William Hazlitt, *The Spirit of the Age*.

1826: University College London founded; Thomas Crofton Croker, *Fairy Tales and Legends of the South of Ireland*; Benjamin Disraeli, *Vivian Grey*; Mary Shelley, *The Last Man*; Ann Radcliffe, *Gaston de Blondeville*; William Harrison Ainsworth, *Sir John Chiverton*.

1827: Lord Liverpool resigns as Prime Minister after a stroke; Tory/Whig coalition is formed headed by George Canning and, after his death, by Viscount Goderich; death of William Blake; John Clare, *The Shepherd's Calendar*; Thomas Hood, *National Tales*; John Keble, *The Christian Year*.

1828: Duke of Wellington forms Tory government; Thomas Arnold becomes headmaster of Rugby; Test and Corporations Acts repealed.

1829: Catholic Emancipation; Metropolitan police established; James Hogg, *The Shepherd's Calendar*.

1830: George IV dies; William IV accedes; Wellington government falls and is replaced by a government under Grey; Captain Swing riots; Christina Rossetti born; Edward Bulwer Lytton, *Paul*

*Clifford*; Walter Scott, *Letters on Demonology and Witchcraft*; Coleridge, *On the Constitution of the Church and State*; Alfred Tennyson, *Poems*; Auguste Comte, *Cours de philosophie positive*; Charles Lyell, *Principles of Geology*.

1831: Michael Faraday discovers electromagnetic induction; Jamaica slave rebellion; Amelia Edwards born; Hogg, *Songs, by the Ettrick Shepherd*.

1832: Reform Act, extending the vote to include 500,000 more males and redistributing parliamentary seats more fairly; Charlotte Riddell born; Lewis Carroll born; Scott dies; Lytton, *Eugene Aram*; Harriet Martineau, *Illustrations in Political Economy*.

1833: Abolition of slavery in colonies; Factory Act, prohibiting children under the age of nine from working in factories, and reducing the working hours permissible for women and children over nine; beginning of Oxford Movement; Michael Banim, *The Ghost-Hunter and His Family*; Lytton, *Godolphin*; Thomas Carlyle, *Sartor Resartus*; John Henry Newman et al., *Tracts for the Times*.

1834: Grey resigns as Prime Minister, replaced by government of Lord Melbourne, and then of Sir Robert Peel; 'Tolpuddle Martyrs'; Poor Law Act sets up workhouses; founding of Grand National Consolidated Trade Union by Robert Owen; Houses of Parliament burn; Criminal Law Commission established; Jeremy Bentham, *Deontology*; Ainsworth, *Rookwood*.

1835: Melbourne becomes Prime Minister; Municipal Reform Act requires town councillors to be elected by ratepayers; Elizabeth Braddon born; James Hogg dies; Robert Browning, *Paracelsus*; A. W. Pugin, *Gothic Furniture in the Style of the 15th Century*.

1836: First train in London; beginning of Chartists; William Godwin dies; Pugin, *Contrasts*; Charles Dickens, *Pickwick Papers*.

1837: 20 June, Accession of Queen Victoria; Morse invents electric telegraph; Carlyle, *The French Revolution*; Dickens, *Oliver Twist*; Frederick Marryat, *The Phantom Ship*.

1838: Afghan War; Irish Poor Law; Working Men's Association drafts People's Charter; London–Birmingham railway finished;

Sutherland Menzies, 'Hugues, the Wer-Wolf'; Dickens, *Nicholas Nickleby*; Charles Hennell, *An Inquiry Concerning the Origin of Christianity*; Joseph Sheridan Le Fanu, stories which will eventually comprise the Purcell Papers, begin publication.

1839: Opium War with China breaks out; Bedchamber Plot; Birmingham Riots; daguerreotype photography; Ainsworth, *Jack Shepard*.

1840: Queen Victoria marries Prince Albert; postage is reduced to a penny; Houses of Parliament begin to be rebuilt; New Zealand annexed; Thomas Hardy born; Rhoda Broughton born; Ainsworth, *The Tower of London* and *Guy Fawkes*; Coleridge, *Confessions of an Inquiring Spirit*; Dickens, *The Old Curiosity Shop*; Thomas Ingoldsby, 'The Spectre of Tappington'.

1841: Fall of Whig government; Peel becomes Prime Minister; Britain claims sovereignty over Hong Kong; Second Afghan War; Dickens, *Barnaby Rudge*; Newman, *Tract 90*; *Punch* begins publication.

1842: End of wars with China and Afghanistan; Report by the Commission for Inquiry into the Employment and Condition of Children in Mines and Manufactures, followed by Ashley's Act on Women and Children in Mines; Chartist Riots; Hong Kong is ceded to Britain in Treaty of Nanking; Report on the Sanitary Condition of the Labouring Population published; trial and execution of Daniel Good, who murdered, sawed in pieces and buried his mistress; income tax introduced; Detective Department created in the London Police; *London Illustrated News* begins publication; Ainsworth, *Windsor Castle*; Browning, *Dramatic Lyrics*; Lytton, *Zanoni*; Thomas Macaulay, *Lays of Ancient Rome*; Tennyson, *Poems*.

1843: Annexation of Natal and Sind; Rebecca Riots; St George's in Southwark built, designed by Pugin; Henry James born; Robert Southey dies; Wordsworth appointed Poet Laureate; Dickens, *A Christmas Carol* and *Martin Chuzzlewit*; John Stuart Mill, *System of Logic*; John Ruskin, *Modern Painters*.

1844: Factory Acts; Ragged School Union; first co-operative society; Royal Commission on Health in Towns; Gerard Manley

Hopkins born; serialisation of George William MacArthur Reynold's *The Mysteries of London*; Disraeli, *Coningsby*; William Thackeray, *Barry Lyndon*; Dickens, *The Chimes*; Robert Chambers, *Vestiges of Creation*.

1845: Maynooth Grant; beginning of the Great Irish Famine; Newman converts to Catholicism; Regina Maria Roche dies; Friedrich Engels, *The Condition of the Working Class in England*; Newman, *Essay on the Development of Christian Doctrine*; beginning of the serial publication of *Varney the Vampire*; Disraeli, *Sibyl*; Harriet Martineau, *Letters on Mesmerism*.

1846: Lord John Russell becomes Prime Minister, Whigs take power; repeal of the Corn Laws; *Daily News*, which carries commentary as well as reporting, begins publication; protoplasm discovered; Dickens, *Dombey and Son*; Strauss's *Life of Jesus* published in translation by George Eliot; Reynolds, *Wagner, The Wehr-Wolf*; *Poems by Currer, Ellis and Acton Bell*.

1847: Fielden's Factory Act; chloroform first used in operations; Communist League formed; Bram Stoker born; Annie Besant born; Charlotte Brontë, *Jane Eyre*; Emily Brontë, *Wuthering Heights*; Anne Brontë, *Agnes Grey*; Disraeli, *Tancred*; Thackeray, *Vanity Fair*; Tennyson, 'The Princess'.

1848: Chartist activism in London; a series of revolutions take place throughout Europe; cholera epidemics; formation of Pre-Raphaelite Brotherhood; Queen's College for women established; in Hydesville, New York, Katherine and Magaretta Fox claim that the spirit of a dead man has been contacting them through a series of 'rappings'; Emily Brontë dies; Marryat dies; Karl Marx and Engels, *Communist Manifesto*; Ainsworth, *The Lancashire Witches*; Catherine Crowe, *The Night-Side of Nature*; Anne Brontë, *The Tenant of Wildfell Hall*; Elizabeth Gaskell, *Mary Barton*; Charles Kingsley, *Yeast*; Newman, *Loss and Gain*; Dickens, *The Haunted Man*; John Stuart Mill, *Political Economy*.

1849: Christian Socialism preached; Britain annexes Punjab; Anne Brontë dies; tenant farmer James Rush murders his landlord in Norwich; in the Manning case, G. P. Manning and his Swiss-born wife Maria found guilty of poisoning her Irish lover in their

London house and burying him in the basement; telegraph system in operation; gold discovered in California; Henry Mayhew's columns on poverty and criminality start to appear in the *Morning Chronicle*; Charlotte Brontë, *Shirley*; Thomas Macaulay, *History of England from the Accession of James II*; Dickens, *David Copperfield*; John Ruskin, *Seven Lamps of Architecture*.

1850: Factory Act giving sixty-hour week for women and children; re-establishment of Roman Catholic hierarchy; Papal Aggression; Robert Louis Stevenson born; William Wordsworth dies; Tennyson becomes Poet Laureate; *Household Words* begins publication; Kingsley, *Alton Locke*; Tennyson, *In Memoriam A. H. H.*; Wordsworth, *Prelude*.

1851: The Great Exhibition takes place in the Crystal Palace; Mary Shelley dies; Comte, *Système de politique positive*; Mayhew, *London Labour and the London Poor*; Gaskell, *Cranford*; Ruskin, *Stones of Venice*; Joseph Sheridan Le Fanu, *Ghost Stories and Tales of Mystery*; Wilkie Collins, *Mr Wray's Cash Box*.

1852: Derby becomes Conservative Prime Minister; coalition government under Aberdeen established; Second Anglo-Burmese War; New Houses of Parliament open; Drainage and Sewerage of Towns Report; Pugin dies; Dickens, *Bleak House*; Thackeray, *Henry Esmond*; Gaskell, 'The Old Nurse's Story'; Kingsley, *Hypatia*.

1853: Crimean War begins when Turkey declares war on Russia in October; Queen Victoria uses chloroform while giving birth to Prince Leopold; Charlotte Brontë, *Villette*; Gaskell, *Ruth*; Thackeray, *The Newcomes*; Matthew Arnold, *Poems*; Elizabeth Barrett Browning, *Poems*; *The Spirit World*, a spiritualist magazine, begins publication.

1854: Britain declares war on Russia; Immaculate Conception declared; the first Working Man's College is established; Oxford degrees granted to Dissenters; *The Times* sends the first 'Special Correspondent' to cover the war; Oscar Wilde born; Collins, *Hide and Seek*; Gaskell, *North and South*; Coventry Patmore, *The Angel in the House*.

1855: Palmerston becomes Prime Minister; Marie Corelli born; Charlotte Brontë dies; *Daily Telegraph* begins publication; Dickens, *Little Dorrit*; Kingsley, *Westward Ho!*; Thackeray, *The Rose and the Ring*; Anthony Trollope, *The Warden*; Robert Browning, *Men and Women*; Tennyson, *Maud and Other Poems*.

1856: End of Crimean War; Second Chinese War; Anglo-Persian War; first stage appearance of Henry Irving; in Rugeley Poisoning case, surgeon William Palmer found guilty of killing one person, but suspected of murdering at least fourteen – saturation coverage of case in newspapers; Rider Haggard born; Collins, *After Dark*; serialisation of Reynolds's *Mysteries* ends; Elizabeth Barrett Browning, *Aurora Leigh*.

1857: Palmerston returned to power; Indian Mutiny; transatlantic cable laid; Divorce Court established; trial of Madeline Smith for poisoning her French lover (trial ends in 'not proven' verdict); Charlotte Brontë, *The Professor*; David Jardine, *A Narrative of the Gunpowder Plot*; Collins, *Dead Secret*; George Eliot, *Scenes of Clerical Life*; Thomas Hughes, *Tom Brown's Schooldays*; Trollope, *Barchester Towers*; Lytton, 'The Haunted and the Haunters'.

1858: Derby Prime Minister; Chinese war ends; Sinn Fein founded; Jews admitted to Parliament; Conspiracy to Murder Bill; India taken over by Crown from East India Company; E(dith) Nesbit born; George Macdonald, *Phantases*.

1859: Derby's second minority government comes to end; Palmerston heads Liberal government; case against Dr Smethurst for murder of his wife fails, but he is found guilty of bigamy; Arthur Conan Doyle born; Collins, *The Woman in White*; Dickens, *A Tale of Two Cities*; Eliot, *Adam Bede* and *The Lifted Veil*; Mrs Henry Wood, *East Lynne*; Mill, *On Liberty*; Samuel Smiles, *Self-Help*; Charles Darwin, *The Origin of Species*; Tennyson, *Idylls of the King*; Catherine Crowe, *Spiritualism and the Age we Live In*; Gaskell, *Lois the Witch*.

1860: Huxley–Wilberforce debate; population of London reaches 3 million; James Barrie born; Michael Faraday, *Forces of Matter*; *Essays and Reviews*; Eliot, *Mill on the Floss*; Dickens, *Great Expectations*.

---

1861: Death of Prince Albert; American Civil War; Elizabeth Barrett Browning dies; Clough dies; Mrs Beeton, *Household Management*; Mary Elizabeth Braddon, *Lady Audley's Secret*; Lytton, *A Strange Story*; Kingsley, *Ravenshoe*; Le Fanu, *The House by the Churchyard*; Mill, *Utilitarianism*.

1862: M. R. James born; Braddon, *Aurora Floyd*; Collins, *No Name*; Eliot, *Romola*; Kingsley, *Water Babies*; Ruskin, *Unto this Last*; Rossetti, 'Goblin Market'.

1863: London Underground opens; Arthur Machen born; Thackeray dies; Renan, *Vie de Jesus*; Gaskell, *Cousin Phillis* and *Sylvia's Lovers*; Charles Reade, *Hard Cash*; Le Fanu, *Wylder's Hand*.

1864: Clarendon Report on Public Schools; John Clare dies; Collins, *Armadale*; Dickens, *Our Mutual Friend*; Gaskell, *Wives and Daughters*; Trollope, *Can You Forgive Her?*; Le Fanu, *Uncle Silas*; Amelia Edwards, 'The Phantom Coach'; Newman, *Apologia pro Vita Sua*.

1865: American Civil War ends; Lord John Russell becomes Prime Minister again; Women's Suffrage Committee; antiseptic surgery introduced; Rudyard Kipling born; Gaskell dies; W. B. Yeats born; Kingsley, *Hereward the Wake*; Algernon Swinburne, *Atlanta in Calydon*; Sabine Baring-Gould, *Book of Werewolves*; Ruskin, *Sesame and Lilies*; Lewis Carroll, *Alice in Wonderland*.

1866: Derby becomes Conservative Prime Minister again; Hyde Park Riots; H. G. Wells born; Ainsworth, *Old Court*; Eliot, *Felix Holt*; Trollope, *Last Chronicle of Barsetshire*; Swinburne, *Poems and Ballads*; Arnold, *On the Study of Celtic Literature*.

1867: Second Reform Bill further extends the franchise; Canada established as British dominion; Fenian Rising; Karl Marx, *Das Capital*; Trollope, *Phineas Finn*; Charlotte Riddell, 'The Banshee's Warning'.

1868: Disraeli succeeds Derby as Prime Minister but resigns in December; Gladstone becomes Liberal Prime Minister; last public execution; Lord Kelvin's Second Law of Thermodynamics; Le Fanu, *Haunted Lives*; Collins, *The Moonstone*; Trollope, *He Knew He*

*Was Right*; Robert Browning, *The Ring and the Book*; Adah Isaacs Menken, 'Aspiration'.

1869: Disestablishment of Irish Church; Suez Canal opens; Municipal Franchise Act gives limited votes to women; Vatican Council begins; Algernon Blackwood born; Collins, *Man and Wife*; Le Fanu, *Wyvern Mystery*; Arnold, *Culture and Anarchy*; Mill, *On the Subjection of Women*; Le Fanu, 'Green Tea'.

1870: Outbreak of Franco-Prussian War; Irish Land Act; Papal Infallibility; Married Women's Property Act; Dickens dies; Dickens, *Mystery of Edwin Drood*; Disraeli, *Lothair*; Edward Tylor, *Primitive Culture*; Newman, *A Grammar of Ascent*; D. G. Rossetti, *Poems*; George MacDonald, *The Princess and the Goblin*.

1871: Population of London reaches 4 million; trade unions legalised; religious tests abolished in Oxford, Cambridge and Durham; Eliot, *Middlemarch*; Lytton, *The Coming Race*; Darwin, *The Descent of Man*; Thomas Hardy, *Desperate Remedies*; Le Fanu, *The Rose and the Key*; George MacDonald, *At the Back of the North Wind*; Le Fanu, *Carmilla*.

1872: Secret Ballot Act; Braddon, *Robert Ainsleigh*; Le Fanu, *In a Glass Darkly*; Carroll, *Through the Looking Glass*; Hardy, *Under the Greenwood Tree*; Rhoda Broughton, 'Behold it was a Dream'.

1873: Gladstone's government resigns over defeat of the Irish Universities Bill; Ashanti War; C. T. Onions born; Lytton dies; Le Fanu dies; Mill dies; Trollope, *Phineas Redux*; Newman, *Idea of a University*; Walter Pater, *Studies in the Renaissance*.

1874: Disraeli becomes Conservative Prime Minister; Factory Act institutes fifty-six-hour week; Tichborne claimant convicted of perjury; annexation of Fiji Islands; G. K. Chesterton born; Charles Chiniquy, *The Priest, the Woman, and the Confessional*; Hardy, *Far from the Madding Crowd*; Trollope, *The Way we Live Now*.

1875: First meeting of the Theosophical Society held in New York; Kingsley dies; Charlotte Riddell, *The Uninhabited House*; Trollope, *The Prime Minister*.

1876: Turks massacre Bulgarians; Bell patents telephone; Catherine Crowe dies; Eliot, *Daniel Deronda*; Emily Pfeiffer, 'Aspiration'.

1877: Queen Victoria declared Empress of India; Edison invents phonograph.

1878: Electric street-lighting in London; Congress of Berlin; Second Afghan War; Salvation Army founded; Lord Dunsany born; Hardy, *The Return of the Native*; Standish James O'Grady, *History of Ireland*.

1879: Zulu War; Irish National Land League; Britain and France resume control of Egypt; electric bulb invented; Reynolds dies; George Meredith, *The Egoist*; John Everett Millais, *Cherry Ripe*.

1880: Gladstone becomes Prime Minister again; Eliot dies; Charles Bradlaugh, MP, refuses to swear on the Bible; Margaret Oliphant, 'A Beleaguered City'.

1881: Carlyle dies; Disraeli dies; Alfred Sinnett, *The Occult World*; Arnold, 'The Incompatibles'.

1882: Britain occupies Egypt; Married Women's Property Act; Phoenix Park murders; Society for Psychical Research established; Ainsworth dies; Darwin dies; Trollope dies.

1883: Marx dies; Mary Coleridge, 'A Clever Woman'.

1884: British protectorate established in Somaliland; Third Reform Bill; London Society for the Prevention of Cruelty to Children established; Reade dies.

1885: Salisbury becomes Conservative Prime Minister; D. H. Lawrence born; H. Rider Haggard, *King Solomon's Mines*; Richard Jefferies, *After London*.

1886: Gladstone becomes Liberal Prime Minister, government collapses over Irish Home Rule Bill, Salisbury becomes Conservative Prime Minister; Richard von Krafft-Ebing, *Psychopathia Sexualis*; R. L. Stevenson, *The Strange Case of Dr Jekyll and Mr Hyde*; Haggard, *She*; E. Nesbit, 'Under Convoy'; Hardy, *The Mayor of Casterbridge*; Corelli, *A Romance of Two Worlds*.

1887: Queen Victoria's Jubilee; Trafalgar Square Riots; first colonial Conference; Richard Jeffries dies; Mrs Henry Wood dies; Arthur Conan Doyle, *A Study in Scarlet* (first Sherlock Holmes story).

1888: Jack the Ripper murders, 31 August–9 November; T. S. Eliot born; Arnold dies; Madame Helena Petrovna Blavatsky, *The Secret Doctrine*; W. B. Yeats, *Fairy and Folktales of the Irish Peasantry*; Hardy, 'The Withered Hand'.

1889: London docker strikes; Armenian atrocities; first celluloid film; Prevention of Cruelty to Children Act; Collins dies; Browning dies; Gerard Manley Hopkins dies; Amy Levy, 'Oh, Is It Love?'.

1890: Newman dies; Sir James Fraser's *The Golden Bough* begins publication; Machen, *The Great God Pan*; Oscar Wilde, *The Picture of Dorian Gray*; Clemence Housman, *The Werewolf*; Kipling, 'The Mark of the Beast'; Hardy, 'Barbara of the House of Grebe'.

1891: First appearance of Sherlock Holmes in the *Strand*; Hardy, *Tess of the D'Urbervilles*; Kipling, *Life's Handicap*.

1892: Gladstone becomes Liberal Prime Minister again; Tennyson dies; Edwards dies.

1893: Failure of Irish Home Rule Bill in the Lords; cinematograph patented; Nesbit, *Grim Tales*; Yeats, *The Celtic Twilight*.

1894: Lord Rosebery becomes Liberal Prime Minister; Stevenson dies; Christina Rossetti dies; Hardy, *Jude the Obscure*; Wells, *The Time Machine*; Le Fanu, *The Watcher, and Other Weird Stories*.

1895: Salisbury made Prime Minister; burning of Bridget Cleary by her husband, who suspected her of being a changeling; Marconi's 'wireless' telegraphy; Armenian massacre; Lumière brothers invent cinema camera; Oscar Wilde trials; Robert Graves born; Robert W. Chambers, *The King in Yellow*; Wilde, *The Importance of Being Earnest*; Machen, *The Three Impostors*; J. Meade Falkner, *The Lost Stradivarius*; M. R. James, 'Lost Hearts'; Corelli, *The Sorrows of Satan*.

1896: Discovery of radioactivity; first modern Olympic Games; Wells, *The Island of Dr Moreau*; M. P. Shiel, *Shapes in the Fire*; Hardy, 'The Committee-Man of "the Terror"'.

1897: Queen Victoria's Diamond Jubilee; Dennis Wheatley born; Bram Stoker, *Dracula*; Richard Marsh, *The Beetle*; H. G. Wells, *The War of the Worlds*; W. B. Yeats, *The Secret Rose* and 'The Tables of the Law' and 'The Adoration of the Magi'.

1898: Curies discover radium; Carroll dies; Gladstone dies; Henry James, *The Turn of the Screw*.

1899: Boer War; Sigmund Freud, *Interpretation of Dreams*; Joseph Conrad, *Lord Jim*.

1900: Salisbury returned to office; Labour Party formed; Planck develops quantum theory; Ruskin dies; Oscar Wilde dies; Hardy, 'A Changed Man'; Kipling, *Kim*.

1901: 22 January, Death of Queen Victoria; Accession of Edward VII; Australia becomes a dominion; Doyle, *The Hound of the Baskervilles*.

1902: End of the Boer War; Balfour becomes Prime Minister; W. W. Jacobs, 'The Monkey's Paw'; Kipling, *Just So Stories*; Nesbit, *Five Children and It*; Yeats, *Cathleen ní Houlihan*; Conrad, *Typhoon*.

1903: Wright brothers make first flight; Bram Stoker, *The Jewel of the Seven Stars*; Erskine Childers, *The Riddle of the Sands*; George Bernard Shaw, *Man and Superman*; Yeats, *In the Seven Woods*.

1904: Abbey Theatre opens; Conrad, *Nostromo*; Hardy, *The Dynasts*; James, *Ghost Stories of an Antiquary*; Haggard, *Ayesha: The Return of She*; J. M. Barrie, *Peter Pan* performed.

1905: Henry Campbell Bannerman becomes Prime Minister; Macdonald dies; Henry Irving dies; Arnold Bennett, *Tales of the Five Towns*; E. M. Forster, *Where Angels Fear to Tread*; Wells, *Kipps*.

1906: Liberals win election; Riddell dies; Algernon Blackwood, *The Empty House*; Machen, *The House of Souls*; William Le Quex, *The Invasion of 1910*; Barrie, *Peter Pan in Kensington Gardens*; Nesbit, *The Railway Children*.

1907: Daphne du Maurier born; Machen, *The Hill of Dreams*.

1908: Asquith becomes Prime Minister; Blackwood, *John Silence*; William Hope Hodgson, *The House on the Borderland*; G. K. Chesterton, *The Man Who Was Thursday*; Forster, *A Room with a View*.

1910: Death of Edward VII; accession of George V; Hodgson, *Carnacki the Ghost Finder*; Forster, *Howards End*; Yeats, *The Green Helmet*.

1911: Suffragette riots; Bram Stoker, *The Lair of the White Worm*; Oliver Onions, *Widdershins*; Conrad, *Under Western Eyes*; James, *More Ghost Stories of an Antiquary*; Evelyn Underhill, *Mysticism*.

1912: Sinking of the *Titanic*; 'Piltdown Man'; Stoker dies; E. F. Benson, *The Room in the Tower*.

1913: D. H. Lawrence, *Sons and Lovers*; Marie Belloc Lowndes, *The Lodger*; Sax Rohmer, *The Mystery of Dr Fu-Manchu*.

1914: 28 June, assassination of Archduke Franz Ferdinand, heir to the Austro-Hungarian throne, precipitating declaration of war on Serbia by Austro-Hungary; Machen, 'The Bowmen'; William de Morgan, *When Ghost Meets Ghost*; Yeats, *Responsibilities*.

1916: Easter Rising; Lloyd George becomes Prime Minister; Lawrence, *The Rainbow*.

1917: May Sinclair, *Tree of Heaven*; Annie Vivanti Chartres, *Vae Victis*.

1918: Robert Graves, *Fairies and Fusiliers*; Rebecca West, *The Return of the Soldier*.

1919: Sigmund Freud, 'The "Uncanny"'.

1920: Broughton dies.

1924: R. H. Mottram, *The Spanish Farm*; Nesbit dies.

1925: Mottram, *Sixty Four, Ninety-Four!*

1926: Mottram, *The Crime at Vanderlynden's*.

1938: Daphne du Maurier, *Rebecca*.

# Notes

ℒ

## Introduction

1   Maurice Levy, '"Gothic" and the critical idiom', *Gothick Origins and Innovations*, ed. Allan Lloyd Smith and Victor Sage (Amsterdam-Atlanta: Rodopi, 1994), pp. 1–15.
2   Fiona Robertson, *Legitimate Histories: Scott, Gothic, and the Authorities of Fiction* (Oxford: Clarendon, 1994) p. 70.
3   Ibid., pp. 70–1.
4   Robert Mighall, *A Geography of Gothic Fiction: Mapping History's Nightmares* (Oxford: Oxford University Press, 1999), p. xiv.
5   It is a charge repeated in Chris Baldick and Robert Mighall, 'Gothic criticism', *A Companion to the Gothic*, ed. David Punter (Oxford: Blackwell, 2000), pp. 209–28.
6   Clive Bloom, 'Horror fiction: in search of a definition', *A Companion to the Gothic*, ed. David Punter (Oxford: Blackwell, 2000), p. 155.
7   Reprinted in E. J. Clery and Robert Miles (eds), *Gothic Documents* (Manchester: Manchester University Press, 2000), pp. 183–4.
8   Julian Wolfreys, *Victorian Hauntings: Spectrality, Gothic, the Uncanny and Literature* (London: Palgrave, 2002), p. 9.
9   Mighall, *Geography*, pp. 1–26.
10  Wolfreys, *Victorian Hauntings*, p. 25.
11  Matthew Sweet, *Inventing the Victorians* (London: Faber and Faber, 2001), p. xix.
12  Ibid., p. xiv.
13  Michel Foucault, *The History of Sexuality*, vol. 1 (London: Penguin, 1990), pp. 1–49.
14  Sweet, *Inventing*, p. xxi.
15  Virginia Woolf, *Moments of Being*, ed. Jeanne Schulkind (New York: Harcourt, 1985), p. 195.

16   Michael Mason, *The Making of Victorian Sexuality* (Oxford: Oxford University Press, 1977), p. 1.

17   Catherine Belsey, *Critical Practice* (London: Routledge, 1994), p. 128.

18   Colin MacCabe, *James Joyce and the Revolution of the Word* (London: Macmillan, 1979).

19   Roland Barthes, *S/Z*, trans. Richard Miller (Oxford: Blackwell, 1990).

20   Quoted in Martin Pugh, *State and Society: A Social and Political History of Britain, 1870–1997* (London: Hodder Arnold, 1999), p. 63.

21   Darryl Jones, *Jane Austen* (London: Palgrave, 2004), p. 3.

22   Raphael Samuel, 'Mrs Thatcher's return to Victorian values', *Victorian Values: Joint Symposium of the Royal Society of Edinburgh and the British Academy, December 1990*, ed. T. C. Smout (Oxford: Oxford University Press, 1992), pp. 9–29.

23   Alice Jenkins and Juliet Jon, 'Introduction', *Rereading Victorian Fiction*, ed. Alice Jenkins and Juliet Jon (London: Macmillan, 2000), p. 6.

24   Ibid., p. 6.

25   Baldick and Mighall, 'Gothic criticism', p. 210.

26   David Punter, *The Literature of Terror: A History of Gothic Fictions from 1765 to the Present Day* (London-New York: Longman, 1996), 2 vols; Rosemary Jackson, *Fantasy: The Literature of Subversion* (London: Routledge, 1981); Fred Botting, *Gothic* (London: Routledge, 1996).

27   Tzvetan Todorov, *The Fantastic: A Structural Approach to a Literary Genre*, trans. Richard Howard (Ithaca, New York: Cornell University Press, 1975), p. 31.

28   Victor Turner and Edith Turner, *Image and Pilgrimage in Christian Culture* (Oxford, 1978), pp. 91–4.

29   Leonore Davidoff and Catherine Hall, *Family Fortunes: Men and Women of the English Middle Class, 1780–1850* (London: Routledge, 2002), p. 26.

30   Victor Turner, *Schism and Continuity in an African Society: A Study of Ndembu Village Life* (Manchester: Manchester University Press, 1978), p. 249.

31   Julian Wolfreys, *Writing London: The Trace of the Urban Text from Blake to Dickens* (London: Macmillan, 1998), p. 102.

32   Richard Lehan (1998). *The City in Literature: An Intellectual and Cultural History* (London: University of California Press), p. 5.

33   Mighall, *Geography*, p. 26.

34   Ibid., pp. 30ff.

35   Ibid., p. 47.

36   Ibid., p. 55.

37   G. W. M. Reynolds, *The Mysteries of London*, ed. Trefor Thomas (Keele, Staffordshire: Keele University Press, 1996). Quotations placed in parenthesis in the main text.

38   Louis Wirth, 'Urbanism as a way of life', *American Journal of Sociology*, XLIV, 1 (1938), 1–24.

39   Trefor Thomas, 'Rereading G. M. Reynolds's *The Mysteries of London*', *Rereading Victorian Fiction*, ed. Alice Jenkins and Juliet Jon (London: Macmillan, 2000), p. 66.

# Notes

40  M. Christine Boyer, *The City of Collective Memory: Its Historical Imagery and Architectural Entertainments* (Cambridge, MA: MIT Press, 1994).

41  Franco Moretti argues that novel-writing was part of a wider mapping of the metropolis, so that in literary analyses of the margins and peripheries of the known city (the middle-class districts), we can see a process analogous to that of the cartographer trying to make visible previously unknown and unexplored areas of the world. *Atlas of the European Novel, 1800–1900* (London: Verso, 1998), p. 83.

42  Alan Pritchard, 'The urban Gothic of *Bleak House*', *Nineteenth-Century Fiction*, 45 (1991), 432–52.

43  Eve Kosofsky Sedgwick, *The Coherence of Gothic Conventions* (London: Methuen, 1986), p. 13.

44  'The distance [Dickens] establishes is between the characteristics (moral and architectural) of the respectable and outcast districts of the same city. Certain parts of London, despite their distance from the castles and monasteries of the Radcliffean landscape, are rendered as strange and remote in their own way as these traditional Gothic locales'. Mighall, *Geography*, p. 43.

45  Charles Dickens, *Bleak House*, ed. Nicola Bradbury (London: Penguin, 1996). All quotations placed in parenthesis in the main text.

46  Martin Tropp, *Images of Fear: How Horror Stories Helped Shape Modern Culture. 1818–1918* (Jefferson, North Carolina and London: McFarland and Company, 1990), pp. 68–9.

47  Wolfreys, *Writing London*, p. 141.

48  Tropp, *Images*, p. 71.

49  Jenny Bourne Taylor, *In the Secret Theatre of the Home* (New York: Routledge, 1998), p. 7.

50  See Kevin Williams, *Get Me a Murder a Day! A History of Mass Communications in Britain* (London: Edward Arnold, 1998).

51  Quoted in Sally Mitchell, 'Introduction', Mrs Henry Wood, *East Lynne* (Rutgers University Press, 1984), p. xii.

52  Quoted in John Murray, 'Sensation novels', *Quarterly Review* 113 (1863), 255.

53  See Nicholas Daly, 'Railway novels: sensation fiction and the modernization of the senses', *English Literary History*, 66, 2 (1999), 461–87.

54  Mary Elizabeth Braddon, *Lady Audley's Secret*, ed. Jenny Bourne Taylor (London: Penguin, 1998). All quotations placed in parenthesis in the main text.

55  Quoted in Daly, 'Railway novels', 469.

56  Anthea Trodd, *Domestic Crime in the Victorian Novel* (London: Palgrave, 1989), p. 96.

57  Elaine Showalter, *A Literature of Their Own* (Princeton: Princeton University Press, 1977), p. 167.

58  See Lyn Pykett, *The 'Improper' Feminine: The Women's Sensation Novel and the New Woman Writing* (London: Routledge, 1994).

59  Eve Kosofsky Sedgwick, *Between Men: English Literature and Male Homosocial Desire* (New York: Columbia University Press, 1985), p. 3.

60  Eve Kosofsky Sedgwick, *Epistemology of the Closet* (Berkeley: University of California Press, 1990), p. 17.

61  For this theme see Richard Nemesvari, 'Robert Audley's secret: male homosocial desire in *Lady Audley's Secret*', *Studies in the Novel*, 27, 4 (1995), 515–17.


## Chapter 1

1   Mark Madoff, 'The useful myth of Gothic ancestry', *Studies in Eighteenth-Century Culture*, 8 (1979), 337–50.

2   Georg Lukács, *The Historical Novel*. trans. Hannah and Stanley Mitchell (London: Merlin, 1962), p. 19.

3   Robertson, *Legitimate Histories*, pp. 6, 7–8.

4   Michael De Certeau, *The Writing of History*, trans. Tom Conley (New York: Columbia University Press, 1988), p. 2.

5   Raymond D. Tumbleson, *Catholicism in the English Protestant Imagination: Nationalism, Religion, and Literature, 1660–1745* (Cambridge: Cambridge University Press, 1998), pp. 98–103; see also Peter Lake, 'Anti-popery: the structure of a prejudice', *Conflict in Early Stuart England: Studies in Religion and Politics, 1603–1642* (London: Longman, 1989), pp. 72–106.

6   Jerome H. Buckley, *The Triumph of Time: A Study of the Victorian Concepts of Time, History, Progress and Decadence* (Cambridge, MA: Belknap Press of Harvard University Press, 1966), p. 41.

7   Quoted in Buckley, *Triumph*, p. 34.

8   Baldick and Mighall, 'Gothic criticism', p. 220.

9   Ibid., p. 219.

10  Mighall, *Geography*, p. xviii.

11  Buckley, *Triumph*, pp. 1–2.

12  Max Weber, 'Religious rejections of the world and their directions', *From Max Weber: Essays in Sociology*, ed. Gerth and Mills (Oxford, 1946), pp. 350–1.

13  Peter Berger, *The Sacred Canopy: Elements of a Sociological Theory of Religion* (Garden City, NY: Anchor, 1969), pp. 111–13.

14  Peter Berger, *The Heretical Imperative: Contemporary Possibilities of Religious Affirmation* (Garden City, NY: Anchor, 1979), p. 20.

15  Émile Durkheim, *The Division of Labour in Society*, trans. G. Simpson (New York, The Free Press, 1933), p. 431n.

16  Robert Miles, *Ann Radcliffe: The Great Enchantress* (Manchester: Manchester University Press, 1995), p. 87.

17  Jackson, *Fantasy*, p. 14.

18  Cited in Edward Said, *Orientalism: Western Conceptions of the Orient* (London: Penguin, 1991), p. 52.

19  Said, *Orientalism*, p. 103.

20  Quoted in John Miller, *Popery and Politics in England, 1660–1688* (London: Cambridge University Press, 1973), p. 75.

21  J. M. S. Tompkins, *The Popular Novel in England, 1770–1800* (Lincoln: University of Nebraska Press, 1961), p. 274.

22  Ian Watt, 'Time and family in the Gothic novel: *The Castle of Otranto*', *Eighteenth-Century Life* 10, 3 (1986), 158.

23  Colin Haydon, *Anti-Catholicism in Eighteenth-Century England, c.1714–80: A Political and Social Study* (Manchester: Manchester University Press, 1993), pp. 164–78.

24  Stephen James Carver, *The Life and Works of the Lancashire Novelist William Harrison Ainsworth, 1805–1882* (Lewiston, Queenston, Lampeter: Edwin Mellen Press, 2003), *passim*.

25  Punter, *Literature*, vol. 1, p. 143.

26  Mark Goldie, 'Ideology', *Political Innovation and Conceptual Change*, ed. Terence Ball, James Farr and Russell L. Hanson (Cambridge: Cambridge University Press, 1989), pp. 266–91.

27  All quotations taken from William Harrison Ainsworth, *The Lancashire Witches: A Romance of Pendle Forest* (Salford: Printwise Publications Limited, 1992). Quotations placed in parenthesis in the main text.

28  Carver, *Life and Works*, p. 252.

29  W. L. Arnstein, *Protestant Versus Catholic in Mid-Victorian England* (Columbia, MO: University of Missouri Press, 1982).

30  Carver, *Life and Works*, p. 60.

31  Ibid., p. 79.

32  Linda Colley, *Britons: Forging the Nation, 1707–1837* (London: Pimlico, 2003), p. 18.

33  David Cressy, *Bonfires and Bells: National Memory and the Protestant Calendar in Elizabethan and Stuart England* (Stroud: Sutton, 2004).

34  William Harrison Ainsworth, *The Tower of London* (Routledge: London, 1897). Quotations placed in parenthesis in the main text.

35  Quoted in Markman Ellis (2000), *The History of Gothic Fiction* (Edinburgh: Edinburgh University Press), p. 26.

36  Ibid., p. 24–7.

37  Carver, *Life and Works*, p. 235.

38  Ibid., p. 238.

39  Ibid., p. 255.

40  Ibid., p. 256.

41  Sedgwick, *Epistemology*, *passim*.

42  Charles Chinquy, *The Priest, the Woman, and the Confessional* (Chino, California, 1979), p. 57.

43  William Harrison Ainsworth, *Guy Fawkes: or, The Gunpowder Treason* (London: The Londoner Press, n.d.). Quotations placed in parenthesis in the main text.

44  Quoted in Antonia Fraser, *The Gunpowder Plot: Terror and Faith in 1605* (London: Phoenix, 1997), p. 349.

45   Ibid., p. 359.
46   Sally Shuttleworth, 'Introduction', *The Lifted Veil and Brother Jacob* (London: Penguin, 2001), p. xiii.
47   Ibid., p. xx.
48   George Eliot, *The Lifted Veil* and *Brother Jacob*, ed. Sally Shuttleworth (London: Penguin, 2001). Quotations placed in parenthesis in the main text.
49   Quoted in Kate Flint (1997), 'Blood, bodies, and *The Lifted Veil*', *Nineteenth-Century Literature*, 51, 4, 459.
50   Quoted in Gustav Krüger, 'David Friedrich Strauss', *American Journal of Theology*, 4, 3 (1990), 525.
51   Quoted in Buckley, *Triumph*, p. 46.
52   Henry George, *Progress and Poverty* (London, 1879), p. 6.
53   Richard Jefferies, *After London; or, Wild England* (London, 1885), p. 69.
54   Mark R. Hillegas, *The Future as Nightmare: H. G. Wells and the Anti-Utopians* (Oxford: Oxford University Press, 1967).
55   H. G. Wells, *The Time Machine*, ed. Patrick Parrinder (London: Penguin, 2005). Quotations placed in parenthesis in the main text.
56   For consumption in Wells, see Peter Kemp, *H. G. Wells and the Culminating Ape: Biological Imperatives and Imaginative Obsessions* (Basingstoke: Macmillan).

## Chapter 2

1    LuAnn Walther. 'The invention of childhood in Victorian autobiography', *Approaches to Victorian Autobiography*, ed. George P. Landon (Athens, OH: Ohio University Press, 1979), p. 64.
2    Philippe Ariès, *Centuries of Childhood* (London: Penguin, 1986), p. 125.
3    Hugh Cunningham, *Children and Childhood in Western Society since 1500* (London: Longman, 1995), pp. 41–78.
4    Ibid., p. 78.
5    Ellen Moers, *Literary Women* (London: The Women's Press, 1986); E. J. Clery, 'Ann Radcliffe and D. A. F. de Sade: thoughts on heroinism', 'Female Gothic', ed. Robert Miles, *Women's Writing*, 1, 2 (1994), 203–14.
6    Claudia Nelson, *Boys will be Girls: The Feminine Ethic and British Children's Fiction, 1857–1917* (New Brunswick and London: Rutgers University Press, 1991).
7    Quoted in John Forster, *The Life of Charles Dickens* (London: Cecil Palmer, 1872–4), p. 26.
8    Alison Lurie, *Boys and Girls Forever: Reflections on Children's Classics* (London: Chatto and Windus, 2003).
9    Quoted in Peter Coveney, *The Image of Childhood* (London: Penguin, 1967), p. 119.
10   Charles Dickens, *Oliver Twist*, ed. Peter Fairclough (London: Penguin, 1966). Quotations placed in parenthesis in the main text.

11  I owe some of the argument of this paragraph to the observations of my student Paul Morrissey.

12  See Carol Margaret Davison, *Anti-Semitism and British Gothic Fiction* (London: Palgrave, 2004).

13  Harry Stone, 'Dickens and the Jews', *Victorian Studies*, 2, 3 (1959), 223–53.

14  Harry Stone, *Dickens and the Invisible World: Fairy Tales, Fantasy, and Novel-Making* (Bloomington and London: Indiana University Press 1979), pp. 99–100.

15  Susan Meyer, 'Antisemitism and social critique in Dickens' *Oliver Twist*', *Victorian Literature and Culture*, 33 (2005), 239–52.

16  Stone, *Dickens and the Invisible World*, p. 99.

17  Ibid., pp. 105–6.

18  Richard Kearney, *Strangers, Gods and Monsters: Interpreting Otherness* (London and New York: Routledge, 2003), pp. 23–45, 63–81; Mary Douglas, *Purity and Danger: An Analysis of the Concept of Pollution and Taboo* (London: Routledge, 2002); see also Timothy Beal, *Religion and its Monsters* (London: Routledge, 2002); Noel Carroll, *The Philosophy of Horror, or Paradoxes of the Heart* (London: Routledge, 1990).

19  Malcolm Andrews, *Dickens and the Grown-Up Child* (London: Macmillan, 1994), p. 179.

20  Charles Dickens, *Great Expectations*, ed. Angus Calder (London: Penguin, 1964). Quotations placed in parenthesis in the main text.

21  Andrews, *Dickens and the Grown-up Child*, p. 94; Stone, *Dickens and the Invisible World*, pp. 314–15.

22  Stone, *Dickens and the Invisible World*, p. 108.

23  Charles Dickens, *The Old Curiosity Shop*, ed. Norman Page (London: Penguin, 2000). Quotations placed in parenthesis in the main text.

24  For Quilp as quasi-supernatural, see Stone, *Dickens and the Invisible World*, pp. 109–10.

25  Charles Dickens, *Dombey and Son*, ed. Alan Horsman (Oxford: Oxford World's Classics, 2001). Quotations placed in parenthesis in the main text.

26  James Kincaid, *Child-Loving: The Erotic Child and Victorian Culture* (New York and London: Routledge, 1992), pp. 236–7.

27  Hugh Cunningham, *The Invention of Childhood* (London: BBC Books, 2006), p. 140.

28  Quoted in Robert Pattison, *The Child Figure in English Literature* (Athens: University of Georgia Press, 1978), p. 13.

29  Lawrence Stone, *The Family, Sex and Marriage in England, 1500–1800* (London: Faber and Faber, 1977), p. 174.

30  Chris Jenks, *Childhood* (London: Routledge), p. 71.

31  Wolfreys, *Victorian Hauntings*, p. 26.

32  Kincaid, *Child-Loving*, p. 237.

33  Carole G. Silver, *Strange and Secret Peoples: Fairies and Victorian Consciousness* (Oxford: Oxford University Press, 1999), pp. 74–8.

34  Ibid., pp. 60, 70.

35  Thomas Hardy, *Jude the Obscure*, ed. C. H. Sisson (New York: Penguin, 1978).

Quotations placed in parenthesis in the main text. Stone also notes this connection, *Dickens and the Invisible World*, p. 161.

36  Richard Dellamora, 'Pure Oliver: or, representation without agency', John Schad (ed.), *Dickens Refigured: Bodies, Desires, and other Histories* (Manchester: Manchester University Press, 1996), p. 62.

37  See Andrews, *Dickens and the Grown-Up Child, passim.*

38  Dennis Grunes, 'The demonic child in *The Turn of the Screw*', *Psychocultural Review*, 2 (1978), 221–39; Since this story will be discussed in detail in volume IV (*American Gothic*) of this series I will not dwell on it now.

39  Kincaid, *Child-Loving*, pp. 246ff.

40  Silver, *Strange*, pp. 117–46.

41  Irving Buchen, 'Emily Brontë and the metaphysics of love and childhood', *Nineteenth-Century Fiction*, 22, 1 (1967), 66–7.

42  Robin De Rosa, '"To save the life of the novel": sadomasochism and representation in *Wuthering Heights*', *Rocky Mountain Review of Language and Literature*, 52, 1 (1998), 30.

43  Emily Brontë, *Wuthering Heights*, ed. David Daiches (London: Penguin, 1965). Quotations placed in parenthesis in the main text.

44  This was pointed out to me by my student Paula Keatley.

45  For Cathy as a Satanic sympathiser, see Sandra Gilbert and Susan Gubar, *The Madwoman in the Attic: The Woman Writer and the Nineteenth-Century Literary Imagination* (New Haven: Yale University Press, 1978), pp. 248–308.

46  Marianne Thormählen, 'The lunatic and the Devil's disciple: the "lovers" in *Wuthering Heights*', *Review of English Studies*, 48 (1997), 191–2.

47  Matthew Beaumont, 'Heathcliff's great hunger: the cannibal Other in *Wuthering Heights*', *Journal of Victorian Culture*, 9, 2 (2004), 137–64; George Boas, *The Cult of Childhood* (Dallas, TX: Spring Publications, 1966).

48  See Stevie Davies, *Emily Brontë: Heretic* (London: The Women's Press, 1994), p. 18.

49  Beaumont, 'Heathcliff's great hunger', p. 155.

50  David Cecil, *Early Victorian Novelists* (New York, 1935), pp. 168, 175.

51  For a reading of the novel as thoroughly sadomasochistic, see De Rosa, '"To save the life of the novel"'.

52  See Davies, *Emily Brontë, passim*, for neo-paganism in the novel.

53  See Toni Reed, *Demon-Lovers and their Victims in British Fiction* (Lexington, KY: University of Kentucky Press, 1988), pp. 70–1.

54  Kincaid, *Child-Loving, passim.*

55  Germaine Greer, *The Boy* (London: Thames and Hudson, 2003), p. 13.

56  Richard A. Kaye, '"Determined raptures": St Sebastian and the Victorian discourse of decadence', *Victorian Literature and Culture*, 27 (1999), 272.

57  Brian Pronger, *The Arena of Masculinity: Sports, Homosexuality and the Meaning of Sex* (London: GMP, 1990), pp. 128–9.

58  Quoted in Michael Anton Budd, *The Sculpture Machine: Physical Culture in the Age of Empire* (London: Macmillan, 1997), p. 37.

59    See Anne McClintock, *Imperial Leather: Race, Gender and Sexuality in the Colonial Contest* (London: Routledge, 1995).

60    See Curtis Marez, 'The other addict: reflections on colonialism and Oscar Wilde's opium smoke-screen', *English Literary History*, 64 (1997), 257–87, for an astute discussion of these images.

61    See Elizabeth Butler Cullingford, *Gender and History in Yeats' Love Poetry* (Cambridge: Cambridge University Press, 1993), for an analysis of Yeats's problematic relationship with gender.

62    Oscar Wilde, *The Picture of Dorian Gray*, ed. Joseph Bristow (Oxford: Oxford University Press, 2006). Quotations placed in parenthesis in the main text.

63    Jacob Korg, 'The rage of Caliban', *University of Toronto Quarterly*, 37, 1 (1967), 75–89.

64    For Nature in this novel see John J. Pappas, 'The flower and the beast: a study of Oscar Wilde's antithetical attitudes toward nature and man in *The Picture of Dorian Gray*', *English Literature in Transition* 15, 1 (1972), pp. 37–48; Mary C. King, 'Digging for Darwin: Bitter Wisdom in *The Picture of Dorian Gray* and "The Critic as Artist"', *Irish Studies Review*, 12, 3 (2004), 315–27.

65    Robert Louis Stevenson, *The Strange Case of Dr Jekyll and Mr Hyde*, ed. Robert Mighall (London: Penguin, 2002). Quotations placed in parenthesis in the main text.

66    Quoted in James B. Twitchell, *'Dreadful Pleasures': An Anatomy of Modern Horror* (New York: Oxford University Press, 1988), p. 234.

67    Ibid., pp. 240ff.

68    Nelson, *Boys*, p. 31.

69    Quoted in Nelson, *Boys*, p. 35.

70    William Veeder, 'Children of the night: Stevenson and patriarchy', William Veeder and Gordon Hirsch (eds), *Dr Jekyll and Mr Hyde after One Hundred Years* (Chicago: University of Chicago Press, 1988), p. 113.

71    Ibid.

72    J. Hillis Miller, *The Disappearance of God: Five Nineteenth Century Writers* (Harvard: Harvard University Press, 1975).

73    Bram Stoker, *Dracula*, ed. Maurice Hindle (London: Penguin, 2003). Quotations placed in parenthesis in the main text.

74    For the feminine Dracula see Cannon Schmitt, *Alien Nation: Nineteenth-Century Gothic Fictions and English Nationality* (Philadelphia: University of Pennsylvania Press, 1997), pp. 135–55; for images of Christ as a mother feeding her children see Caroline Walker Bynum, *Holy Feast and Holy Fast: The Religious Significance of Food to Medieval Women* (Berkeley: University of California Press, 1987).

75    Christopher Herbert, 'Vampire religion', *Representations*, 79 (2002), 100–21.

76    For some interesting comments on Catholicism in the novel see D. Bruno Starrs, '"Keeping the faith": Catholicism in "*Dracula*" and its adaptations', *Journal of Dracula Studies*, 6 (2004).

*Chapter 3*

[1]  Quoted in Alfred E. Longuel, 'The word "Gothic" in eighteenth-century criticism', *Modern Language Notes*, 38 (1923), 455.

[2]  Judith Halberstam, *Skin Shows: Gothic Horror and the Technology of Monsters* (Durham, NC: Duke University Press, 1995), p. 6.

[3]  Edward Tylor, *Primitive Culture: Researches into the Development of Mythology, Philosophy, Religion, Art and Custom*, 2 vols (London: John Murray, 1871), vol. 1, pp. 5–6; see also Mighall, *Geography*, p. 134. As Robert Mighall writes of this development, 'it is the premise that not all cultures have "progressed" at the same rate that enables the anthropologist to fill in the gaps of the prehistocial record, and thus establish the law of progressive and successive universal development with modern European culture as its goal' (p. 135).

[4]  There is a vigorous ongoing debate about whether the Celtic 'fringes' can be termed colonies at all, which I do not have space to examine here, although my use of the term 'colonial' throughout this chapter indicates by which side of the argument I am most persuaded.

[5]  Peggy Phelan, *Unmarked* (London: Routledge, 1993), p. 13.

[6]  Darryl Jones, *Horror: A Thematic History in Fiction and Film* (London: Arnold, 2003), p. 8.

[7]  Ibid., p. 9.

[8]  William Patrick Day, *In the Circles of Fear and Desire: A Study of Gothic Fantasy* (Chicago: University of Chicago Press, 1985), p. 6.

[9]  Kate Trumpener, *Bardic Nationalism: The Romantic Novel and the British Empire* (Princeton: Princeton University Press, 1997).

[10]  See Terence Brown, 'Saxon and Celt: the stereotypes', *Ireland's Literature: Selected Essays* (London: Rowman and Littlefield Publishers, 1989), pp. 3–13.

[11]  For Ireland the popularity of this marriage-as-national-union strategy was even given its own name – the 'Glorvina' solution – after the heroine of Sydney Owenson's blockbusting *The Wild Irish Girl* (1806), which saw the English Horatio Mortimer marrying the learned and very Celtic Glorvina as a way of easing the tensions between the two countries.

[12]  This is, of course, a seriously simplified version of an extremely complicated and drawn-out tendency in eighteenth and nineteenth-century writing. For serious studies of this tradition, see Trumpeter, *Bardic Nationalism*; Claire Connelly, 'Writing the Union', Dáire Keogh and Kevin Whelan (eds), *Acts of Union: The Causes, Contexts, and Consequences of the Act of Union* (Dublin: Four Courts Press, 2001), pp. 171–86; Ina Ferris, *The Romantic National Tale and the Question of Ireland* (Cambridge: Cambridge University Press, 2002).

[13]  Elizabeth Napier, *The Failure of Gothic: Problems of Disjunction in an Eighteenth-Century Literary Form* (Oxford: Clarendon Press, 1987); Day, *In the Circles*, p. 6.

[14]  Cannon Schmitt, *Alien Nation: Nineteenth-Century Gothic Fictions and English Nationality* (Philadelphia: University of Pennsylvania Press, 1997).

[15]  James F. Scott, 'Thomas Hardy's use of the Gothic: an examination of five representative works', *Nineteenth-Century Fiction*, 17 (1963), 370–1.

16  David Cecil, *Hardy: The Novelist* (London: Constable, 1978), pp. 17–18.

17  For Hardy and the Gothic, see Brigitte Hervoche-Bertho, 'Seminal Gothic dissemination in Hardy's writings', *Victorian Literature and Culture*, 29 (2001), 451–67; Jamil Mustafa, '"A good horror has its place in art": Hardy's Gothic strategy in *Tess of the d'Urbervilles*', *Studies in the Humanities*, 32, 2 (2005), 93–115; Robert Carballo, 'Seeing through a glass darkly: Thomas Hardy's poetic gothicism', *Cahiers victoriens et édouardiens*, 53 (2001), 29–39.

18  Charlotte Brontë, *Jane Eyre*, ed. Michael Mason (London: Penguin, 2003). Quotations placed in parenthesis in the main text.

19  For folklore in this novel, see Jacqueline Simpson, 'The function of folklore in *Jane Eyre* and *Wuthering Heights*', *Folklore*, 85 (1974), 47–61.

20  For the classic reading of Bertha as Jane's double, see Gilbert and Gubar, *Madwoman*, pp. 336–71.

21  Cora Kaplan, '"A heterogeneous thing": female childhood and the rise of racial thinking in Victorian Britain', Diana Fuss (ed.), *Human, All Too Human* (London: Routledge, 1996), p. 186.

22  Elsie Michie, 'From simianized Irish to oriental despots: Heathcliff, Rochester and racial difference', *Novel*, 25, 2 (1992), 130–1.

23  Ibid., p. 135.

24  Jenny Sharpe, *Allegories of Empire: The Figure of Woman in the Colonial Text* (Minneapolis: Minneapolis University Press, 1993), p. 29.

25  H. G. Wells, *The War of the Worlds*, ed. Patrick Parrinder (London: Penguin, 2005). Quotations placed in parenthesis in the main text.

26  Stephen D. Arata, 'The Occidental tourist: *Dracula* and the anxiety of reverse colonization', *Victorian Studies*, 33, 4 (1990), 621–45.

27  Glennis Byron, 'Gothic in the 1890s', David Punter (ed.), *A Companion to the Gothic* (London: Blackwell, 2000), p. 140.

28  Paul Kennedy, 'Continuity and discontinuity in British imperialism, 1815–1914,' C. C. Eldridge (ed.), *British Imperialism in the Nineteenth Century* (Hong Kong: Macmillan, 1984), p. 34.

29  Quoted in Ronald Hyam, *Britain's Imperial Century, 1815–1914: A Study of Empire and Expansion* (London: B. T. Batsford, 1976), p. 93; see also Paul Kennedy, *The Realities Behind Diplomacy: Background Influences on British External Policy, 1865–1980* (London: Fontana, 1981); Muriel Chamberlain, *Pax Britannica? British Foreign Policy, 1789–1914* (London: Longman, 1988); C. J. Bartlett, *Defence and Diplomacy: Britain and the Great Powers, 1815–1914* (Manchester: Manchester University Press, 1993).

30  Quoted in Brian Aldiss, 'Introduction', H. G. Wells, *The War of the Worlds* (London: Penguin, 2005), p. xvii.

31  Patrick Brantlinger, *'Rule of Darkness': British Literature and Imperialism, 1830–1914* (London: Routledge, 1994); Elaine Showalter, *Sexual Anarchy: Gender and Culture at the 'Fin de Siècle'* (London: Bloomsbury, 1991).

32  H. G. Wells, *The Island of Doctor Moreau*, ed. Patrick Parrinder (London: Penguin, 2005). Quotations placed in parenthesis in the main text.

33  A similar experiment to tame the beast is tried on zombies in George Romero's *The Day of the Dead* (1985). It, too, fails miserably.

34  See Lucy Bending, *The Representation of Bodily Pain in Late Nineteenth-Century English Culture* (Oxford: Clarendon Press, 2000), pp. 167–76.

35  See Timothy Christensen, 'The bestial mark of race in *The Island of Doctor Moreau*', *Criticism*, 46, 4 (2004), 575–95.

36  Charlotte Riddell, 'The banshee's warning', Susan Williams (ed.), *The Lifted Veil: The Book of Fantastic Literature by Women* (New York: Carroll and Graf Publishers, 1992), pp. 306–24. Quotations placed in parenthesis in the main text.

37  See Bending, *Representation*, pp. 123–8.

38  Homi K. Bhabha, 'Of mimicry and man', *The Location of Culture* (London: Routledge, 1994), pp. 87–8.

39  Arthur Machen, *The Great God Pan*, in *The Three Impostors and Other Stories*, ed. S. T. Joshi (Hayward, CA: Chaosium, 2007), pp. 1–51. Quotations placed in parenthesis in the main text.

40  Botting, *Gothic*, p. 143.

41  W. J. McCormack, 'Irish Gothic and after, 1820–1945', Seamus Deane (ed.), *The Field Day Anthology of Irish Writing*, vol. 2 (Derry: Field Day Publications, 1991), pp. 831–949; for a challenge to the whole notion of an Irish Gothic 'tradition' see Richard Haslam, 'Irish Gothic', Catherine Spooner and Emma McEvoy (eds), *The Routledge Companion to Gothic* (London: Routledge, 2007), pp. 83–94.

42  For this long drawn-out process of identity formation, see especially Nicholas Canny, 'Identity formation in Ireland: the emergence of the Anglo-Irish', Nicholas Canny and Anthony Pagden (eds), *Colonial Identity in the Atlantic World, 1500–1800* (Princeton, NJ: Princeton University Press, 1987), pp. 159–212.

43  Julian Moynahan, 'The politics of Anglo-Irish Gothic: Charles Robert Maturin, Sheridan LeFanu, and the return of the repressed', *Anglo-Irish: The Literary Imagination of a Hyphenated Culture* (Princeton, NJ: Princeton University Press, 1994), pp. 109–35; see also Jarlath Killeen, *Gothic Ireland: Horror and the Irish Anglican Imagination in the Long Eighteenth Century* (Dublin: Four Courts, 2005).

44  Christina Morin, '"Completing the Union": Charles Robert Maturin and the (Ir)reconciliation of romantic national fiction' (unpublished Ph.D. thesis, Trinity College Dublin, 2007), p. 54.

45  C. L. Innes, *Woman and Nation in Irish Literature and Society, 1880–1935* (London: Harvester Wheatsheaf, 1993); Connolly, 'Union', p. 181.

46  Trumpeter, *Bardic Nationalism*, p. 146.

47  L. P. Curtis, *Apes and Angels: The Irishman in Victorian Caricature* (Washington and London: Smithsonian Institution Press, 1997).

48  Sheridan Le Fanu, 'Green Tea', *In a Glass Darkly*, ed. Robert Tracy (Oxford: Oxford World's Classics, 1993), pp. 5–40. Quotations placed in parenthesis in the main text.

49  Helen Stoddart, '"The precautions of nervous people are infectious": Sheridan Le Fanu's symptomatic Gothic', Fred Botting and Dale Townshend

(eds), *Gothic: Critical Concepts in Literary and Cultural Studies*, vol. 3, *Nineteenth-Century Gothic: At Home with the Vampire* (London and New York: Routledge, 2004), pp. 100–5.

50  Elaine Showalter, *The Female Malady: Women, Madness and English Culture, 1830–1980* (London: Virago, 1985).

51  Roy Foster, 'Protestant magic', *Paddy and Mr Punch: Connections in Irish and English History* (London: Penguin, 1995), pp. 212–32.

52  Elizabeth Bowen, 'Introduction', Sheridan Le Fanu, *Uncle Silas: A Tale of Bartram-Haugh* (London: Cresset, 1947), pp. 7–23; W. J. McCormack, *Sheridan Le Fanu* (Gloucestershire: Sutton Publishing, 1997), p. 140.

53  Ibid., p. 162.

54  Sheridan Le Fanu, *Uncle Silas*, ed. Victor Sage (London: Penguin, 2000). Quotations placed in parenthesis in the main text.

55  McCormack, *Sheridan Le Fanu*, p. 168.

56  Bowen, 'Introduction', p. 8.

57  Quoted in W. J. McCormack, *The Dublin Paper War of 1786–1788: A Bibliographical and Critical Inquiry* (Blackrock, Co. Dublin : Irish Academic Press, 1993), p. 98.

58  David Glover, '"Dark enough fur any man": Bram Stoker's sexual ethnology and the question of Irish nationalism', Roman de la Campa, E. Ann Kaplan, Michael Sprinkler (eds), *Late Imperial Culture* (London: Verso, 1995), pp. 53–71; Carol A. Snef, '*Dracula*: Stoker's response to the New Woman', *Victorian Studies*, 26 (1982), 33–9; Richard Haslam, '"Ever under some unnatural condition": Bram Stoker and the colonial fantastic', Brian Cosgrove (ed.), *Literature and the Supernatural* (Dublin: Columba Press, 1995), pp. 95–119.

59  Jeffrey Richards, 'Gender, race and sexuality in Bram Stoker's other novels', Christopher Parker (ed.), *Gender, Roles, and Sexuality in Victorian Literature* (New York: Scholar Press, 1995), p. 143.

60  Daniel Farson, *The Man Who Wrote Dracula: A Biography of Bram Stoker* (London: Joseph, 1975), p. 223; Kate Hebblethwaite, 'Introduction', Bram Stoker, *Dracula's Guest and Other Weird Stories* (London: Penguin, 2006), pp. xxix–xxx.

61  Hebblethwaite, 'Introduction', p. xxviii.

62  Bram Stoker, *The Lair of the White Worm*, *Dracula's Guest and Other Weird Stories*, ed. Kate Hebblethwaite (London: Penguin, 2006), pp. 151–369. Quotations placed in parenthesis in the main text.

63  I owe these references to my student Valeria Angela Cavalli.

64  See David Glover, '"Why white?": on worms and skin in Bram Stoker's later fiction', *Gothic Studies*, 2, 3 (2000), 346–60; The 'index of nigrescence' was used by the race theorist John Beddoe in his influential *The Races of Britain* (1885), in which he argued that, due to a greater concentration of melanin, the average Irishman was 'darker' than the average Englishman. See L. P. Curtis, *Anglo-Saxons and Celts: A Study of Anti-Irish Prejudice in Victorian England* (Bridgeport, CT: University of Bridgeport Press, 1968), p. 72.

Chapter 4

[1]  Bernard M. G. Reardon, *Religious Thought in the Victorian Age: A Survey from Coleridge to Gore* (London and New York: Longman, 1995).

[2]  Even the term 'orthodox Christianity' in the previous sentence needs to be problematised, as what I mean by this term is (generally speaking) Anglicanism, the official religion of Britain.

[3]  David Hume, *An Enquiry Concerning Human Understanding*, ed. L. A. Selby Bigge (Oxford: Clarendon Press, 1902), pp. 114–16.

[4]  James A. Herrick, *The Radical Rhetoric of the English Deists: The Discourse of Scepticism, 1680–1750* (University of South Carolina Press, 1997).

[5]  M. A. Crowther, *Church Embattled: Religious Controversy in Mid-Victorian England* (Newton Abbot: David and Charles, 1970); John Rogerson, *Old Testament Criticism in the Nineteenth Century: England and Germany* (London: S.P.C.K., 1984).

[6]  Frank Miller Turner, *Between Science and Religion: The Reaction to Scientific Naturalism in Late Victorian England* (New Haven; London: Yale University Press, 1974); C. C. Gillespie, *Genesis and Geology* (New York: Harper and Row, 1959).

[7]  H. Murphy, 'The ethical revolt against Christian orthodoxy', *American History Review*, 9 (1955), 800–17.

[8]  Thomas Kuhn, *The Structure of Scientific Revolutions* (Chicago and London: University of Chicago Press, 1996). The shift from Ptolemaic to Newtonian cosmology is the best example of this scientific shift.

[9]  What must be made clear is that this is a profoundly Western problem, and is based on the tradition of thinking about the world in dualist terms, whereas non-Western religious traditions tend to work with completely different understandings of the universe and find much of this talk bizarre.

[10]  In the twentieth century the great German theologian Karl Bath was the major proponent of this view, uttering his famous '*Nein!*' to all attempts to reconcile theology with other disciplines in which the other disciplines were always given the position of normalcy.

[11]  In the early twenty-first century, for example, the proponents of Creation Science and Intelligent Design both appear to adopt something of this position which effectively holds God hostage to science.

[12]  James R. Moore, 'Free thought, secularism, gnosticism: the case of Charles Darwin', *Religion in Victorian Britain*, vol. 1, *Traditions*, ed. Gerald Parsons (Manchester: Manchester University Press, 1988), pp. 276–9.

[13]  Even incorporating some of these 'movements' under the general term 'occult' is controversial and would not be accepted by all experts in the field.

[14]  Alex Owen, *The Place of Enchantment: British Occultism and the Culture of the Modern* (Chicago: University of Chicago Press, 2003), p. 13.

[15]  Anne Besant, *Why I Became a Theosophist* (New York: 'The Path' Office, 1891), pp. 17, 32.

[16]  I have categorised the Order of the Golden Dawn as a magical *and* a reli-

gious order so as to reflect the views of its contemporaries and also more recent academic argument. In the late nineteenth and early twentieth centuries it was felt that there was a clear distinction between religion and magic, a view held by those involved in the Order of the Golden Dawn and which passed into academic study, due to the influence of James Frazer's tripartite distinction between science, religion and magic in *The Golden Bough*, where magic was differentiated from religion in being (in theory) both verifiable and instrumentalist and manipulative. However, Frazer's argument has been very substantially undermined, and many anthropologists would now argue that the division between all three terms in Frazer's study depends on highly questionable ethnocentric biases, and also fails to take into account how magic has been used in different cultures. As Morton Klass puts it: 'for me ... magic simply refers to techniques employed by those who believe that in specific circumstances persons, powers, beings, or even events are subject to control or coercion. Magic, in other words, is a strategy in religion as are prayer ... and sacrifice. Given the particular belief system, some clerics will offer prayers, some will perform sacrifices, and others will engage in magic.' *Ordered Universes: Approaches to the Anthropology of Religion* (Oxford: Westview Press, 1995), p. 89. See also W. J. Goode, 'Magic and religion: a continuum', *Ethnos*, 14 (1949), 172–82; J. van Baal, 'Magic as a religious phenomenon', *Higher Education and Research in the Netherlands*, 7 (1973), 10–21; W. E. A. van Beek, 'The religion of everyday life: an investigation into the concepts of religion and magic', W. E. A. van Beek and J. H. Scherer (eds), *Explorations in the Anthropology of Religion* (The Hague, 1975), pp. 55–69.

17   Srdjan Smajic, 'The trouble with ghost-seeing: vision, ideology, and genre in the Victorian ghost story', *English Literary History*, 70 (2003), 1107–8.

18   David Amigoni (ed.), *Life Writing and Victorian Culture* (Aldershot: Ashgate, 2006).

19   Sigmund Freud, 'The "Uncanny"', *Writings on Art and Literature* (Stanford, CA: Stanford University Press, 1997), pp. 195, 217.

20   See Wolfreys, *Victorian Hauntings*, p. 5.

21   Hélène Cixous, 'Fiction and its phantoms: a reading of Freud's *Das Unheimliche. The "Uncanny"'*, *New Literary History*, 7 (1976), 525–48.

22   Matthew Arnold, *Literature and Dogma: An Essay towards a Better Appreciation of the Bible, The Complete Prose Works of Matthew Arnold*, vol. 6, *Dissent and Dogma*, ed. R. H. Super (Ann Arbor: University of Michigan Press, 1986), p. 146.

23   Walter E. Houghton, *The Victorian Frame of Mind, 1830–1870* (New Haven: Yale University Press, 1963).

24   Charles Dickens, *A Christmas Carol, Christmas Books*, ed. Ruth Glancy (Oxford: Oxford University Press, 1988). Quotations placed in parenthesis in the main text.

25   Nicholas Abraham and Maria Torok, *The Shell and the Kernel*, vol. 1. ed., trans. and intro. Nicholas T. Rand (Chicago: University of Chicago Press, 1994).

26    Esther Rashkin, *Family Secrets and the Psychoanalysis of Narrative* (Princeton: Princeton University Press, 1992), pp. 161–2.

27    Smajic, 'The trouble with ghost-seeing', 1112. This has long been a conundrum to the Christian mind, since in a strictly Christian cosmos matter and spirit are not precisely separate objects (since the Christian is not a dualist in theological terms) – we are embodied souls, not ghosts in a machine; Christ is God and man simultaneously not a fleshy funnel for divinity, as some gnostics seemed to imagine.

28    Wolfreys, *Victorian Hauntings*; Nicholas Royle, *The Uncanny* (Manchester: Manchester University Press, 2003).

29    Jacques Derrida, *Spectres of Marx*, trans. Peggy Kamuf (New York: Routledge, 1994), pp. 118, 51, 11.

30    Royle, *The Uncanny*; Jodey Castricano, *Cryptomimesis: The Gothic and Jacques Derrida's Ghost Writing* (Montreal: McGill-Queen's University Press, 2001); Wolfreys, *Victorian Hauntings*.

31    Fredric Jameson, 'Marx's Purloined Letter,' Michael Sprinkler (ed.), *Ghostly Demarcations: A Symposium on Jacques Derrida's 'Specters of Marx'* (London: Verso, 2000), p. 39.

32    Rudolf Otto, *The Idea of the Holy: An Inquiry into the Non-Rational Factors in the Idea of the Divine and Its Relation to the Rational*, trans. John W. Harvey (London, 1959).

33    Vanessa D. Dickerson, *Victorian Ghosts in the Noontide: Women Writers and the Supernatural* (Columbia and London: University of Missouri Press, 1996), p. 4.

34    E. F. Beiler, 'Mrs Riddell, mid-Victorian ghosts, and Christmas annuals', *The Collected Ghost Stories of Mrs J. H. Riddell* (New York: Dover, 1977), p. vi.

35    Mrs. J. H. Riddell, *The Uninhabited House, Five Victorian Ghost Novels*, ed. E. F. Beiler (New York: Dover Publications, 1971), pp. 1–112. Quotations placed in parenthesis in the main text.

36    R. C. Finucane, *Appearances of the Dead: A Cultural History of Ghosts* (London: Junction Books, 1982), pp. 196–7.

37    Theodor W. Adorno, 'Theses against occultism', *Minima Moralia*, trans. E. F. N. Jephcott (London: Verso, 1978), pp. 238–44.

38    Diana Basham, *The Trial of Woman: Feminism and the Occult Sciences in Victorian Literature and Society* (London: Macmillan, 1992), *passim*.

39    Alex Owen, *The Darkened Room: Women, Power and Spiritualism in Late-Victorian England* (Chicago: University of Chicago Press, 1985).

40    Basham, *Trial*, p. 154.

41    Ibid., p. 158.

42    Amelia B. Edwards, 'The Phantom Coach', *The Lifted Veil: The Book of Fantastic Literature by Women*, ed. Susan Williams (New York: Carroll and Graf Publishers, 1992), pp. 110–22. Quotations placed in parenthesis in the main text.

43    Catherine Crowe, *The Night Side of Nature, or Ghosts and Ghost Seers* (London: Wordsworth, 2000), p. 17.

44  John Tyndal, *Fragments of Science 1–3* (New York: P. F. Collier and Son, 1901), p. 210. Tyndal's place is now occupied by the rather foolish Peter Atkins, who has preached extensively on the 'Limitless Power of Science', and has advised poets, philosophers and theologians to give up the ghost and get down to the unemployment office.

45  See Roger Luckhurst, *The Invention of Telepathy* (Oxford: Oxford University Press, 2002).

46  Pamela Thurschwell, *Literature, Technology and Magical Thinking, 1880–1920* (Cambridge: Cambridge University Press, 2001), p. 3.

47  Marie Corelli, *A Romance of Two Worlds* (Alhambra: Borden, 1986). Quotations placed in parenthesis in the main text.

48  Marie Corelli, *The Sorrows of Satan*, ed. Peter Keating (Oxford: Oxford World's Classics, 1994). Quotations placed in parenthesis in the main text.

49  Quoted in Peter Keating, 'Introduction', Marie Corelli, *The Sorrows of Satan* (Oxford: Oxford World Classics, 1998), p. xvii.

50  Adriana Craciun, 'Romantic Satanism and the rise of nineteenth-century women's poetry', *New Literary History*, 34, 4 (2003), 699–721; Gilbert and Gubar, *Madwoman*, p. 196.

51  Gilbert and Gubar, *Madwoman*, p. 205.

52  Ruth Y. Jenkins, *Reclaiming Myths of Power: Women Writers and the Victorian Spiritual Crisis* (Lewisburg: Bucknell University Press; London–Toronto: Associated University Presses, 1995).

53  H. Rider Haggard, *She*, ed. Patrick Brantlinger (London: Penguin, 2001). Quotations placed in parenthesis in the main text.

54  Basham, *Trial*, p. 189.

55  I am hesitant to assert an understanding of this text since I find it rather baffling.

56  Helena Petrovna Blavatsky, *The Secret Doctrine* (London: The Theosophical Publishing Company, 1888), pp. 386–7.

57  Ibid., p. 392.

58  Foster, 'Protestant magic', p. 220.

59  W. B. Yeats, *Writings on Irish Folklore, Legend and Myth*, ed. Robert Welch (London: Penguin, 1993), p. 317.

60  W. B. Yeats, *Autobiographies* (London: Macmillan, 1955), pp. 115–16.

61  Letter to Katherine Tynan, W. B. Yeats, *The Collected Letters of W. B. Yeats*, vol. 1, 1865–1895, ed. John Kelly, associate ed. Eric Domville (Oxford: Clarendon Press, 1986), p. 212.

62  Quoted in Terence Brown, *The Life of W. B. Yeats* (Oxford: Blackwell, 1999), p. 73.

63  W. B. Yeats, *Short Fiction*, ed. G. J. Watson (London: Penguin, 1995). Quotations placed in parenthesis in the main text.

64  The Bilderberg Group operates as a well-known contemporary focus of conspiracy theories.

65  See Marie Mulvey Roberts, *Gothic Immortals: The Fiction of the Brotherhood of the Rosy Cross* (Routledge: London, 1990), p. 157.

66   Quoted in Joseph I. Fradin, '"The absorbing tyranny of every-day life": Bulwer-Lytton's *A Strange Story*', *Nineteenth-Century Fiction*, 16, 1 (1961), 5, n.6.

67   Edward Bulwer Lytton, *A Strange Story: An Alchemical Novel* (Berkeley and London: Shambala, 1973). Quotations placed in parenthesis in the main text.

68   Fradin, '"The absorbing tyranny"', p. 12.

69   Mark Knight, '"The Haunted and the Haunters": Bulwer-Lytton's philosophical ghost story', *Nineteenth-Century Contexts*, 28, 3 (2006), 245–55.

70   Edward Bulwer Lytton, *The Haunted and the Haunters* (London: Marshall and Kent, 1925). Quotations placed in parenthesis in the main text.

## Chapter 5

1   Tropp, *Images of Fear*, p. 174.

2   Ibid., p. 178.

3   Edmund Burke, *A Philosophical Enquiry into the Origins of Our Ideas of the Sublime and the Beautiful*, ed. Adam Phillips (Oxford: Oxford World's Classics, 1990), p. 35.

4   Tropp, *Images of Fear*, p. 179.

5   Terry Phillips, 'The rules of war: Gothic transgressions in First World War fiction', *Gothic Studies*, 2, 2 (2000), 233.

6   Gerard Manley Hopkins, *The Poems of Gerard Manley Hopkins*, ed. W. H. Gardner and N. H. Mackenzie (Oxford: Oxford University Press, 1970), pp. 82–3.

7   J. M. Barrie, *Peter Pan* (London: Puffin, 1994), pp. 190–1.

8   Andrew Birkin, *J. M. Barrie and the Lost Boys: The Real Story of Peter Pan* (New Haven and London: Yale University Press, 2003), pp. 5–6.

9   Diane Purkiss, *Troublesome Things: A History of Fairies and Fairy Stories* (London: Penguin, 2001), pp. 278–83.

10   Robert Graves, *Fusiliers and Fairies* (New York: A. A. Knopf, 1918), p. 28.

11   Ibid., p. 35.

## Chapter 6

1   Arthur Conan Doyle, *The Sign of Four*, ed. Ed Gilnet (London: Penguin, 2001), p. 22.

2   Donna Heiland, 'Gothic and the generation of ideas', *Literature Compass*, 4, 1 (2007), 48.

3   Aviva Briefel, 'The Victorian literature of fear', *Literature Compass*, 4, 2 (2007), 508.

4   Victor Sage, *Horror Fiction in the Protestant Tradition* (New York: St Martin's Press, 1988), p. xvii.

5   Carroll, *Philosophy*, pp. 31–2.
6   Ibid., p. 34.
7   Jacques Derrida, 'The law of genre', trans. Avital Ronell, *Critical Inquiry*, 7, 1 (1980), 61.
8   Baldick and Mighall, 'Gothic criticism', pp. 209–10.
9   Ibid., p. 210.
10  Ibid, p. 214.
11  Ibid., p. 221.
12  Alfred Schutz, 'On multiple realities', *Collected Papers* (The Hague: Nijhoff, 1962), vol. 1, pp. 207–59.
13  For a brilliant analysis of the 'discourses of affect' in Horror Criticism, see Matt Hillis, *The Pleasures of Horror* (London: Continuum, 2005).
14  Darryl Jones persuasively argues that many critical studies of Jane Austen fall foul of precisely this temptation, precisely because of the love many critics feel for Austen's novels (*Jane Austen*, pp. 2–5).
15  Lennard J. Davis, *Resisting Novels: Ideology and Fiction* (London: Methuen, 1987), p. 225.
16  Botting, *Gothic*, p. 1.
17  Jackson, *Fantasy*, p. 180.
18  Ibid., pp. 121–2.
19  Ellis, *History*, p. 14.
20  Alison Milbank, 'Victorian Gothic in English novels and stories, 1830– 1880', Jerrold E. Hogle (ed.), *The Cambridge Companion to Gothic Fiction* (Cambridge: Cambridge University Press, 2002), pp. 149–50.
21  Moers, *Literary Women*, p. 91.
22  G. K. Ellis, *The Contested Castle: Gothic Novels and the Subversion of Domestic Ideology* (Urbana and California: University of Illinois Press, 1989), pp. x, 220.
23  Juliann E. Fleenor (ed.), *The Female Gothic* (Montreal: Eden Press, 1983), p. 28.
24  Diane Long Hoevler, *Gothic Feminism: The Professionalization of Gender from Charlotte Smith to the Brontës* (University Park: Pennsylvania State University Press, 1998), pp. xii–xiii, xii–xiv.
25  Alison Milbank, *Daughters of the House: Modes of the Gothic in Victorian Fiction* (New York: St Martin's Press, 1992), p. 1.
26  Sedgwick, *Between Men*, p. 92.
27  George E. Haggerty, *Queer Gothic* (Urbana: University of Illinois Press, 2006), pp. 2–3.
28  Andrew Smith, *Victorian Demons: Medicine, Masculinity, and the Gothic at the Fin-de-Siècle* (New York: Manchester University Press, 2004), p. 177.
29  H. L. Malchow, *Gothic Images of Race in Nineteenth-Century Britain* (Stanford: Stanford University Press, 1996), p. 5.
30  Davison, *Anti-Semitism*, p. 8.
31  Schmitt, *Alien Nation*, p. 3.
32  Andrew Smith and William Hughes (eds), *Empire and the Gothic: The Politics of Genre* (Basingstoke: Palgrave Macmillan, 2003), p. 2.

33    Brantlinger, *Rule of Darkness*, p. 229.
34    Stephen D. Arata, *Fictions of Loss in the Victorian Fin de Siècle* (Cambridge: Cambridge University Press, 1996), p. i.
35    Mighall, *Geography*, p. xix.
36    Maggie Kilgour, *The Rise of the Gothic Novel* (London: Routledge, 1995), p. 220.
37    Susan J. Navarette, *The Shape of Fear: Horror and the Fin de Siècle Culture of Decadence* (Lexington: University Press of Kentucky, 1998), p. 214.
38    Andrew Smith, *Gothic Radicalism: Literature, Philosophy and Psychoanalysis in the Nineteenth Century* (New York: St Martin's Press, 2000), p. 1.
39    Ibid., p. 10.
40    For a description of Bruhm's project see his website: *http://faculty.msvu.ca/sbruhm/gothchild.htm*. See also Steven Bruhm, 'Nightmare on Sesame Street: or, the self-possessed child', *Gothic Studies*, 8, 2 (2006), 98–113.
41    Heiland, 'Gothic', p. 57.
42    Patrick O'Malley, *Catholicism, Sexual Deviance and Victorian Gothic Culture* (Cambridge: Cambridge University Press, 2006), p. 22.
43    Ibid., p. 3.

## Chronology

1    I am indebted to a number of sources for this chronology, particularly Michael Cox, *The Concise Oxford Chronology of English Literature* (Oxford: Oxford University Press, 2004); Alan Horsman, *The Victorian Novel* (Oxford: Clarendon, 1990), especially pp. 419–47; Thomas Boyle, *Black Swine in the Sewers of Hampstead: Beneath the Surface of Victorian Sensationalism* (London: Hodder and Stoughton, 1990), especially pp. 231–3; and the anonymous reader for the University of Wales Press, who wisely berated my original chronology for its 'half-heartedness' and suggested a number of ways it could be improved.

# Bibliography

Abraham, Nicolas, and Maria Torok (1994). *The Shell and the Kernel*, vol. 1, ed., trans. and intro. Nicholas T. Rand (Chicago: University of Chicago Press).

Adorno, Theodor W. (1978). 'Theses against occultism', *Minima Moralia*, trans. E. F. N. Jephcott (London: Verso), pp. 238–44.

Ainsworth, William Harrison (1897). *The Tower of London* (Routledge: London).

Ainsworth, William Harrison (1992). *The Lancashire Witches: A Romance of Pendle Forest* (Salford: Printwise Publications Limited).

Ainsworth, William Harrison (n.d.). *Guy Fawkes: or, The Gunpowder Treason* (London: The Londoner Press).

Aldiss, Brian, 'Introduction' (2005). H. G. Wells, *The War of the Worlds* (London: Penguin), pp. xiii–xxxvi.

Amigoni, David (ed.) (2006). *Life Writing and Victorian Culture* (Aldershot: Ashgate).

Andrews, Malcolm (1994). *Dickens and the Grown-Up Child* (London: Macmillan).

Anolik, Ruth Bienstock and Douglas L. Howard (2004). *The Gothic Other: Racial and Social Constructions in the Literary Imagination* (Jefferson, NC: McFarland).

Arata, Stephen D. (1990). 'The Occidental tourist: *Dracula* and the anxiety of reverse colonization', *Victorian Studies*, 33, 4, 621–45.

Arata, Stephen D. (1996). *Fictions of Loss in the Victorian Fin de Siècle* (Cambridge: Cambridge University Press).

Ariès, Philippe (1986). *Centuries of Childhood* (London: Penguin).

Arnold, Matthew (1986). *Literature and Dogma: An Essay towards a Better Appreciation of the Bible*, *The Complete Prose Works of Matthew Arnold*, vol. 6, *Dissent and Dogma*, ed. R. H. Super (Ann Arbor: University of Michigan Press).

Arnstein, W. L. (1982). *Protestant Versus Catholic in Mid-Victorian England* (Columbia, MO: University of Missouri Press).

Auerbach, Nina (1995). *Our Vampires, Ourselves* (Chicago: Chicago University Press).

Bakus, Margot Gayle (1999). *The Gothic Family Romance: Heterosexuality, Child Sacrifice, and the Anglo-Irish Colonial Order* (Durham: Duke University Press).

Baldick, Chris (1987). *In Frankenstein's Shadow: Myth, Monstrosity and Nineteenth-Century Writing* (Oxford: Oxford University Press).

Baldick, Chris, and Robert Mighall (2000). 'Gothic criticism', *A Companion to the Gothic*, ed. David Punter (Oxford: Blackwell), pp. 209–28.

Barker, Juliet (1994). *The Brontës* (New York: St Martin's Griffin).

Barrie, J. M. (1994). *Peter Pan* (London: Puffin).

Barthes, Roland (1990). *S/Z*, trans. Richard Miller (Oxford: Blackwell).

Bartlett, C. J. (1993). *Defence and Diplomacy: Britain and the Great Powers, 1815–1914* (Manchester: Manchester University Press).

Basham, Diana (1992). *The Trial of Woman: Feminism and the Occult Sciences in Victorian Literature and Society* (London: Macmillan).

Beal, Timothy (2002). *Religion and its Monsters* (London: Routledge).

Beaumont, Matthew (2004). 'Heathcliff's great hunger: the cannibal Other in *Wuthering Heights*', *Journal of Victorian Culture*, 9, 2, 137–64.

Beiler, E. F. (1977). 'Mrs Riddell, mid-Victorian ghosts, and Christmas annuals', *The Collected Ghost Stories of Mrs J. H. Riddell* (New York: Dover).

Belford, Barbara (1996). *Bram Stoker: A Biography of the Author of Dracula* (New York: Alfred Knopf).

Belsey, Catherine (1994). *Critical Practice* (London: Routledge).

Bending, Lucy (2000). *The Representation of Bodily Pain in Late Nineteenth-Century English Culture* (Oxford: Clarendon Press).

Berger, Peter (1969). *The Sacred Canopy: Elements of a Sociological Theory of Religion* (Garden City, NY: Anchor).

Berger, Peter (1979). *The Heretical Imperative: Contemporary Possibilities of Religious Affirmation* (Garden City, NY: Anchor).

Besant, Anne (1891). *Why I Became a Theosophist* (New York: 'The Path' Office).

Bhabha, Homi K. (1994). 'Of mimicry and man', *The Location of Culture* (London: Routledge).

Birkin, Andrew (2003). *J. M. Barrie and the Lost Boys: The Real Story of Peter Pan* (New Haven and London: Yale University Press).

Blavatsky, Helena Petrovna (1888). *The Secret Doctrine* (London: The Theosophical Publishing Company).

# Bibliography

Block, Ed, Jr. (1982). 'James Sully, evolutionary psychology and late Victorian Gothic fiction', *Victorian Studies*, 25, 443–67.

Bloom, Clive (2000). 'Horror fiction: in search of a definition', *A Companion to the Gothic*, ed. David Punter (Oxford: Blackwell), pp. 155–66.

Blum, Deborah (2007). *Ghost Hunters: The Victorians and the Hunt for Proof of Life After Death* (London: Century).

Boas, George (1966). *The Cult of Childhood* (Dallas, TX: Spring Publications).

Botting, Fred (1996). *Gothic* (London: Routledge).

Bowen, Elizabeth (1947). 'Introduction', Sheridan Le Fanu, *Uncle Silas: A Tale of Bartram-Haugh* (London: Cresset), pp. 7–23.

Boyer, M. Christine (1994). *The City of Collective Memory: Its Historical Imagery and Architectural Entertainments* (Cambridge, MA: MIT Press).

Boyle, Thomas (1990). *Black Swine in the Sewers of Hampstead: Beneath the Surface of Victorian Sensationalism* (London: Hodder and Stoughton).

Braddon, Mary Elizabeth (1998). *Lady Audley's Secret*, ed. Jenny Bourne Taylor (London: Penguin).

Brantlinger, Patrick (1982). 'What is "sensational" about the "Sensation Novel"?', *Nineteenth-Century Fiction*, 37, 1–28.

Brantlinger, Patrick (1994). *'Rule of Darkness': British Literature and Imperialism, 1830–1914* (London: Routledge).

Briefel, Aviva (2007). 'The Victorian literature of fear', *Literature Compass*, 4, 2, 508–23.

Bronfen, Elizabeth (1992). *Over Her Dead Body: Death, Femininity, and the Aesthetic* (New York: Routledge).

Brontë, Charlotte (2003). *Jane Eyre*, ed. Michael Mason (London: Penguin).

Brontë, Emily (1965). *Wuthering Heights*, ed. David Daiches (London: Penguin).

Brooks, Chris (1999). *The Gothic Revival* (London: Phaidon Press).

Broughton, Rhoda (1992). 'Behold it was a dream', *The Lifted Veil: The Book of Fantastic Literature by Women*, ed. A. Susan Williams (New York: Carroll and Graf Publishers), pp. 211–26.

Brown, Terence (1989). 'Saxon and Celt: the stereotypes', *Ireland's Literature: Selected Essays* (London: Rowman and Littlefield Publishers), pp. 3–13.

Brown, Terence (1999). *The Life of W. B. Yeats* (Oxford: Blackwell).

Bruhm, Steven (2006). 'Nightmare on Sesame Street: or, the self-possessed child', *Gothic Studies*, 8, 2, 98–113.

Buchen, Irving (1967). 'Emily Brontë and the metaphysics of love and childhood', *Nineteenth-Century Fiction*, 22, 1, 63–70.

Buckley, Jerome H. (1966). *The Triumph of Time: A Study of the Victorian*

*Concepts of Time, History, Progress and Decadence* (Cambridge, Massachusetts: Belknap Press of Harvard University Press).

Buckley, Matthew (2002). 'Sensations of celebrity: *Jack Sheppard* and the mass audience', *Victorian Studies*, 44, 3, 423–63.

Budd, Michael Anton (1997). *The Sculpture Machine: Physical Culture in the Age of Empire* (London: Macmillan).

Burke, Edmund (1990). *A Philosophical Enquiry into the Origins of Our Ideas of the Sublime and the Beautiful*, ed. Adam Phillips (Oxford: Oxford World's Classics).

Bynum, Caroline Walker (1987). *Holy Feast and Holy Fast: The Religious Significance of Food to Medieval Women* (Berkeley: University of California Press).

Byron, Glennis (2000). 'Gothic in the 1890s', David Punter (ed.), *A Companion to the Gothic* (London: Blackwell), pp. 132–41.

Canny, Nicholas (1987). 'Identity formation in Ireland: the emergence of the Anglo-Irish', Nicholas Canny and Anthony Pagden (eds), *Colonial Identity in the Atlantic World, 1500–1800* (Princeton, NJ: Princeton University Press), pp. 159–212.

Carballo, Robert (2001). 'Seeing through a glass darkly: Thomas Hardy's poetic gothicism', *Cahiers victoriens et édouardiens*, 53, 29–39.

Carroll, Noel (1990). *The Philosophy of Horror, or Paradoxes of the Heart* (London: Routledge).

Carter, Margaret L. (ed.) (1988). *Dracula: The Vampire and the Critics*. Ann Arbor and London: UMI Research Press.

Carver, Stephen James (2003). *The Life and Works of the Lancashire Novelist William Harrison Ainsworth, 1805–1882* (Lewiston, Queenston, Lampeter: Edwin Mellen Press).

Casey, Janet Galligani (1992). 'Marie Corelli and *fin de siècle* feminism', *English Literature in Transition*, 35, 2, 163–78.

Castricano, Jodey (2001). *Cryptomimesis: The Gothic and Jacques Derrida's Ghost Writing* (Montreal: McGill-Queen's University Press).

Cecil, David (1935). *Early Victorian Novelists* (New York).

Cecil, David (1978). *Hardy: The Novelist* (London: Constable).

Chadwick, Owen (1972). *The Victorian Church* (London: SCM Press), 2 vols.

Chamberlain, Muriel (1988). *Pax Britannica? British Foreign Policy, 1789–1914* (London: Longman).

Chinquy, Charles (1979). *The Priest, the Woman, and the Confessional* (Chino, California).

Christensen, Timothy (2004). 'The bestial mark of race in *The Island of Doctor Moreau*', *Criticism*, 46, 4, 575–95.

Cixous, Hélène (1976). 'Fiction and its phantoms: a reading of Freud's *Das Unheimliche*. The "*Uncanny*"', *New Literary History*, 7, 525–48.

Clarke, William M. (1996). *The Secret Life of Wilkie Collins* (Stroud: Sutton Publishing).

Clery, E. J. (1994). 'Ann Radcliffe and D. A. F. de Sade: Thoughts on Heroinism', 'Female Gothic', Robert Miles (ed.), *Women's Writing*, 1, 2, 203–14.

Clery, E. J. and Robert Miles (eds) (2000). *Gothic Documents* (Manchester: Manchester University Press).

Cohen, Ed (1990). *Talk on the Wilde Side: Towards a Genealogy of a Discourse on Male Sexualities* (New York: Routledge).

Cohen, Morton N. (1960). *Rider Haggard: His Life and Works* (New York: Walker).

Colley, Linda (2003). *Britons: Forging the Nation, 1707–1837* (London: Pimlico).

Connelly, Claire (2001). 'Writing the Union', Dáire Keogh and Kevin Whelan (eds), *Acts of Union: The Causes, Contexts, and Consequences of the Act of Union* (Dublin: Four Courts Press), pp. 171–86.

Connelly, Claire (forthcoming). *The Romantic Novel in Ireland*.

Corelli, Marie (1986). *A Romance of Two Worlds* (Alhambra: Borden).

Corelli, Marie (1998). *The Sorrows of Satan*, ed. Peter Keating (Oxford: Oxford World's Classics).

Coveney, Peter (1967). *The Image of Childhood* (London: Penguin).

Cox, Michael (2004). *The Concise Oxford Chronology of English Literature* (Oxford: Oxford University Press).

Craciun, Adriana (2003). 'Romantic Satanism and the rise of nineteenth-century women's poetry', *New Literary History*, 34, 4, 699–721.

Craft, Christopher (1984). '"Kiss me with those red lips": gender and inversion in Bram Stoker's *Dracula*', *Representations*, 8, 107–33.

Cressy, David (2004). *Bonfires and Bells: National Memory and the Protestant Calendar in Elizabethan and Stuart England* (Stroud: Sutton).

Crowe, Catherine (2000). *The Night Side of Nature, or Ghosts and Ghost Seers* (London: Wordsworth).

Crowther, M. A. (1970). *Church Embattled: Religious Controversy in Mid-Victorian England* (Newton Abbot: David and Charles).

Cullingford, Elizabeth Butler (1993). *Gender and History in Yeats' Love Poetry* (Cambridge: Cambridge University Press).

Cunningham, Hugh (1995). *Children and Childhood in Western Society since 1500* (London: Longman).

Cunningham, Hugh (2006). *The Invention of Childhood* (London: BBC Books).

Curtis, L. P. (1968). *Anglo-Saxons and Celts: A Study of Anti-Irish Prejudice in Victorian England* (Bridgeport, CT: University of Bridgeport Press).

Curtis, L. P. (1997). *Apes and Angels: The Irishman in Victorian Caricature* (Washington and London: Smithsonian Institution Press).

Curtis, L. P. (2001). *Jack the Ripper and the London Press* (New Haven, CT: Yale University Press).

Daly, Nicholas (1999). 'Railway novels: sensation fiction and the modernization of the senses', *English Literary History*, 66, 2, 461–87.

Davenport-Hines, Richard (1998). *Gothic: Four Hundred Years of Excess, Horror, Evil, and Ruin* (New York: North Point Press).

Davidoff, Leonore, and Catherine Hall (2002). *Family Fortunes: Men and Women of the English Middle Class, 1780–1850* (London: Routledge).

Davies, Stevie (1994). *Emily Brontë: Heretic* (London: The Women's Press).

Davis, Lennard J. (1987). *Resisting Novels: Ideology and Fiction* (London: Methuen).

Davison, Carol Margaret (2004). *Anti-Semitism and British Gothic Fiction* (London: Palgrave).

Davison, Carol Margaret (ed.) (1997). *Bram Stoker's Dracula: Sucking Through the Century, 1897–1997* (Toronto and Oxford: Dundurn Press).

Day, William Patrick (1985). *In the Circles of Fear and Desire: A Study of Gothic Fantasy* (Chicago: University of Chicago Press).

De Certeau, Michael (1988). *The Writing of History*, trans. Tom Conley (New York: Columbia University Press).

De Rosa, Robin (1998). '"To save the life of the novel": sadomasochism and representation in *Wuthering Heights*', *Rocky Mountain Review of Language and Literature*, 52, 1, 27–43.

DeLamotte, Eugenia C. (1990). *Perils of the Night: A Feminist Study of Nineteenth-Century Gothic* (New York: Oxford University Press).

Dellamora, Richard (1996). 'Pure Oliver: or, representation without agency', John Schad (ed.), *Dickens Refigured: Bodies, Desires, and other Histories* (Manchester: Manchester University Press), pp. 55–79.

Dellamora, Richard (1998). 'Representation and homophobia in *The Picture of Dorian Gray*'. *Victorian Newsletter*, 73, 28–31.

Derrida, Jacques (1980). 'The law of genre', trans. Avital Ronell, *Critical Inquiry*, 7, 1, 55–81.

Derrida, Jacques (1994) *Specters of Marx*, trans. Peggy Kamuf (New York: Routledge).

Dickens, Charles (1965). *Great Expectations*, ed. Angus Calder (London: Penguin).

Dickens, Charles (1966). *Oliver Twist*, ed. Peter Fairclough (London: Penguin).

Dickens, Charles (1988). *A Christmas Carol, Christmas Books*, ed. Ruth Glancy (Oxford: Oxford University Press).

Dickens, Charles (1996). *Bleak House*, ed. Nicola Bradbury (London: Penguin).

Dickens, Charles (2000). *The Old Curiosity Shop*, ed. Norman Page (London: Penguin).

Dickens, Charles (2001). *Dombey and Son*, ed. Alan Horsman (Oxford: Oxford World's Classics).

Dickerson, Vanessa D. (1996). *Victorian Ghosts in the Noontide: Women Writers and the Supernatural* (Columbia and London: University of Missouri Press).

Dijkstra, Bram (1986). *Idols of Perversity: Fantasies of Feminine Evil in Fin-de-Siècle Culture* (New York: Oxford University Press).

Douglas, Mary (2002). *Purity and Danger: An Analysis of the Concept of Pollution and Taboo* (London: Routledge).

Doyle, Arthur Conan (2001). *The Sign of Four*, ed. Ed Gilnet (London: Penguin).

Dryden, Linda (2003). *The Modern Gothic and Literary Doubles: Stevenson, Wilde and Wells* (London: Palgrave Macmillan).

Duncan, Ian (1992). *Modern Romance and Transformations of the Novel: The Gothic, Scott, Dickens* (Cambridge: Cambridge University Press).

Durkheim, Émile (1933). *The Division of Labour in Society*, trans. G. Simpson (New York, The Free Press).

Dyos, H. J., and Michael Wolff (eds) (1999). *The Victorian City: Images and Realities* (London: Routledge), 2 vols.

Eagleton, Terry (1998). *Heathcliff and the Great Hunger: Essays on Irish Culture* (London: Verso).

Edwards, Amelia B. (1992). 'The Phantom Coach', *The Lifted Veil: The Book of Fantastic Literature by Women*, ed. Susan Williams (New York: Carroll and Graf Publishers), pp. 110–22.

Eliot, George (2001). *The Lifted Veil* and *Brother Jacob*, ed. Sally Shuttleworth (London: Penguin).

Ellis, G. K. (1989). *The Contested Castle: Gothic Novels and the Subversion of Domestic Ideology* (Urbana and California: University of Illinois Press).

Ellis, Markman (2000). *The History of Gothic Fiction* (Edinburgh: Edinburgh University Press).

Farson, Daniel (1975). *The Man Who Wrote Dracula: A Biography of Bram Stoker* (London: Joseph).

Ferris, Ina (2002). *The Romantic National Tale and the Question of Ireland* (Cambridge: Cambridge University Press).

Finucane, R. C. (1982). *Appearances of the Dead: A Cultural History of Ghosts* (London: Junction Books).

Fleenor, Juliann E. (ed.) (1983). *The Female Gothic* (Montreal: Eden Press).

Flint, Kate (1997). 'Blood, bodies, and *The Lifted Veil*', *Nineteenth-Century Literature*, 51, 4, 455–73.

Forster, John (1872–4). *The Life of Charles Dickens* (London: Cecil Palmer).

Foster, Roy (1995). 'Protestant magic', *Paddy and Mr Punch: Connections in Irish and English History* (London: Penguin), pp. 212–32.

Foucault, Michel (1990). *The History of Sexuality*, vol. 1 (London: Penguin).

Fradin, Joseph I. (1961). '"The absorbing tyranny of every-day Life": Bulwer-Lytton's *A Strange Story*', *Nineteenth-Century Fiction*, 16, 1, 1–16.

Fraser, Antonia (1997). *The Gunpowder Plot: Terror and Faith in 1605* (London: Phoenix).

Frederico, Annette R. (2000). *Idol of Suburbia: Marie Corelli and Late-Victorian Literary Culture* (Charlottesville: University Press of Virginia).

Freud, Sigmund (1997). 'The "Uncanny"', *Writings on Art and Literature* (Stanford, CA: Stanford University Press).

Frye, Lowell T. (1998). 'The ghost story and the subjection of women: the example of Amelia Edwards, M. E. Braddon, and E. Nesbit', *Victorians Institute Journal*, 26, 167–209.

Galvan, Jill (2003). 'Christians, infidels, and women's channeling in the writings of Marie Corelli', *Victorian Literature and Culture*, 31, 1, 83–97.

Garrett, Peter K. (2003). *Gothic Reflections: Narrative Force in Nineteenth-Century Fiction* (Ithaca: Cornell University Press).

George, Henry (1879). *Progress and Poverty* (London).

Gelder, Ken (1994). *Reading the Vampire* (New York: Routledge).

Gilbert, Sandra, and Susan Gubar (1978). *The Madwoman in the Attic: The Woman Writer and the Nineteenth-Century Literary Imagination* (New Haven: Yale University Press).

Gillespie, C. C. (1959). *Genesis and Geology* (New York: Harper and Row).

Glover, David (1995). '"Dark enough fur any man": Bram Stoker's sexual ethnology and the question of Irish Nationalism', Roman de la Campa, E. Ann Kaplan, Michael Sprinkler (eds), *Late Imperial Culture* (London: Verso), pp. 53–71.

Glover, David (1996). *Vampires, Liberals and Mummies: Bram Stoker and the Politics of Popular Fiction* (Durham: Duke University Press).

Glover, David (2000). '"Why white?": on worms and skin in Bram Stoker's later fiction', *Gothic Studies*, 2, 3, 346–60.

Goldie, Mark (1989). 'Ideology', *Political Innovation and Conceptual Change*, ed. Terence Ball, James Farr and Russell L. Hanson (Cambridge: Cambridge University Press).

Goode, W. J. (1949). 'Magic and religion: a continuum', *Ethnos*, 14, 172–82.

Graves, Robert (1918). *Fusiliers and Fairies* (New York: A. A. Knopf).

Greer, Germaine (2003). *The Boy* (London: Thames and Hudson).

Grunes, Dennis (1978). 'The demonic child in *The Turn of the Screw*', *Psychocultural Review*, 2, 221–39.

Guinness, Selina (2003). '"Protestant magic" reappraised: evangelicalism, dissent, and theosophy', *Irish University Review*, 33, 1, 14–27.

Haggard, H. Rider (2001). *She*, ed. Patrick Brantlinger (London: Penguin).

Haggerty, George E. (1989). *Gothic Fiction / Gothic Form* (University Park: Pennsylvania State University Press).

Haggerty, George E. (2006). *Queer Gothic* (Urbana: University of Illinois Press).

Halberstam, Judith (1995). *Skin Shows: Gothic Horror and the Technology of Monsters* (Durham, NC: Duke University Press).

Hardy, Thomas (1978). *Jude the Obscure*, ed. C. H. Sisson (New York: Penguin).

Hardy, Thomas (1993). *Tess of the d'Urbervilles*, ed. James Gibson (London: Everyman).

Harrison, Frederic (1907). 'A few words about the nineteenth century', *The Choice of Books* (London: Macmillan).

Hartnell, Elaine M. (2006). 'Morals and metaphysics: Marie Corelli, religion and the gothic', *Women's Writing*, 13, 2, 284–303.

Haslam, Richard (1995). '"Ever under some unnatural condition": Bram Stoker and the colonial fantastic', Brian Cosgrove (ed.), *Literature and the Supernatural* (Dublin: Columba Press), pp. 95–119.

Haslam, Richard (2007). 'Irish Gothic', *The Routledge Companion to Gothic*, ed. Catherine Spooner and Emma McEvoy (London: Routledge).

Haydon, Colin (1993). *Anti-Catholicism in Eighteenth-Century England, c.1714–80: A Political and Social Study* (Manchester: Manchester University Press).

Haywood, Ian (2002). 'George W. M. Reynolds and "the Trafalgar Square Revolution": radicalism, the carnivalesque and popular culture in mid-Victorian England', *Journal of Victorian Culture*, 7, 1, 23–59.

Heath, Stephen (1986). 'Psychopathia sexualis: Stevenson's strange case', *Critical Quarterly*, 28, 93–108.

Hebblethwaite, Kate (2006). 'Introduction', Bram Stoker, *Dracula's Guest and Other Weird Stories* (London: Penguin), pp. xi–xxxix.

Heiland, Donna (2004). *Gothic and Gender: An Introduction* (Malden, MA: Blackwell).

Heiland, Donna (2007). 'Gothic and the generation of ideas', *Literature Compass*, 4, 1, 48–65.

Heller, Tamar (1992). *Dead Secrets: Wilkie Collins and the Female Gothic* (New Haven: Yale University Press).

Hendershot, Cyndy (1984). *The Animal Within: Masculinity and the Gothic* (Ann Arbor: University of Michigan Press).

Herbert, Christopher (1984). 'The occult in *Bleak House*', *NOVEL: A Forum on Fiction*, 17, 2, 101–15.

Herbert, Christopher (2002). 'Vampire religion', *Representations*, 79, 100–21.

Herrick, James A. (1997). *The Radical Rhetoric of the English Deists: The Discourse of Scepticism, 1680–1750* (University of South Carolina Press).

Hervoche-Bertho, Brigitte (2001). 'Seminal Gothic dissemination in Hardy's Writings', *Victorian Literature and Culture*, 451–67.

Hillegas, Mark R. (1967). *The Future as Nightmare: H. G. Wells and the Anti-Utopians* (Oxford: Oxford University Press).

Hillis, Matt (2005). *The Pleasures of Horror* (London: Continuum).

Hirsch, Gordon and William Veeder (eds) (1986). *Dr Jekyll and Mr Hyde After One Hundred Years* (Chicago: University of Chicago Press).

Hoevler, Diane Long (1998). *Gothic Feminism: The Professionalization of Gender from Charlotte Smith to the Brontës* (University Park: Pennsylvania State University Press).

Hogle, Jerrold E. (ed.) (2002). *The Cambridge Companion to Gothic Fiction* (Cambridge: Cambridge University Press).

Hopkins, Gerard Manley (1970). *The Poems of Gerard Manley Hopkins*, ed. W. H. Gardner and N. H. Mackenzie (Oxford: Oxford University Press).

Horner, Avril and Sue Zlosnik (eds) (2005). *Gothic and the Comic Turn* (New York: Palgrave).

Horsman, Alan (1990). *The Victorian Novel* (Oxford: Clarendon).

Houghton, Walter E. (1963). *The Victorian Frame of Mind, 1830–1870* (New Haven: Yale University Press).

Houston, Gail Turley (2005). *From Dickens to Dracula: Gothic, Economics and Victorian Fiction* (Cambridge: Cambridge University Press).

Hughes, William (2000). *Beyond Dracula: Bram Stoker's Fiction and Its Cultural Context* (London: Palgrave Macmillan).

Hughes, William and Andrew Smith (eds) (1998). *Bram Stoker: History, Psychoanalysis, and the Gothic* (London: Macmillan).

Hughes, Winnifred (1980). *The Maniac in the Cellar: Sensation Novels of the 1860s* (Princeton, NJ: Princeton University Press).

Hume, David (1902). *An Enquiry Concerning Human Understanding*, ed. L. A. Selby Bigge (Oxford: Clarendon Press).

Humpherys, Anne (1983). 'G. W. M. Reynolds: popular literature and popular politics', *Victorian Periodicals Review*, 16, 79–89.

Humpherys, Anne (1983). 'The geometry of the modern city: G. W. M. Reynolds and "*The Mysteries of London*"', *Browning Institute Studies*, 11.

Humpherys, Anne (1991). 'Generic strands and urban twists: the Victorian mysteries novel', *Victorian Studies*, 34, 4, 455–72.

Hurley, Kelly (1996). *The Gothic Body: Sexuality, Materialism, and Degeneration at the 'Fin de Siècle'* (Cambridge: Cambridge University Press).

Hyam, Ronald (1976). *Britain's Imperial Century, 1815–1914: A Study of Empire and Expansion* (London: B. T. Batsford).

Innes, C. L. (1993). *Woman and Nation in Irish Literature and Society, 1880–1935* (London: Harvester Wheatsheaf).

Jackson, Rosemary (1981). *Fantasy: The Literature of Subversion* (London: Routledge).

James, Sara (2005). 'Eugène Sue, G. W. M. Reynolds, and the representation of the city as "mystery"', *Babylon or New Jerusalem? Perceptions of the City in Literature*, ed. Valeria Tinkler-Villani (Amsterdam, Netherlands: DQR: Studies in Literature), pp. 247–58.

Jameson, Fredric (2000). 'Marx's purloined letter', Michael Sprinkler (ed.), *Ghostly Demarcations: A Symposium on Jacques Derrida's 'Specters of Marx'* (London: Verso), pp. 26–67.

Jefferies, Richard (1885). *After London; or, Wild England* (London).

Jenkins, Alice, and Juliet Jon (2000). 'Introduction', *Rereading Victorian Fiction*, ed. Alice Jenkins and Juliet Jon (London: Macmillan), pp. 1–12.

Jenkins, Ruth Y. (1995). *Reclaiming Myths of Power: Women Writers and the Victorian Spiritual Crisis* (Lewisburg: Bucknell University Press; London–Toronto: Associated University Presses).

Jenks, Chris (1996). *Childhood* (London: Routledge).

Jones, Darryl (2002). *Horror: A Thematic History in Fiction and Film* (London: Arnold).

Jones, Darryl (2004). *Jane Austen* (London: Palgrave).

Kaplan, Cora (1996). '"A heterogeneous thing": female childhood and the rise of racial thinking in Victorian Britain', Diana Fuss (ed.), *Human, All Too Human* (London: Routledge), pp. 169–202.

Katz, Wendy R. (1987). *Rider Haggard and the Fiction of Empire: A Critical Study of British Imperial Fiction* (Cambridge: Cambridge University Press).

Kaye, Richard A. (1999). '"Determined raptures": St Sebastian and the Victorian discourse of decadence', *Victorian Literature and Culture*, 27, 269–303.

Kearney, Richard (2003). *Strangers, Gods and Monsters: Interpreting Otherness* (London and New York: Routledge).

Keating, Peter (1998). 'Introduction', Marie Corelli, *The Sorrows of Satan* (Oxford: Oxford World Classics), pp. vii–xx.

Kemp, Peter, *H. G. Wells and the Culminating Ape: Biological Imperatives and Imaginative Obsessions* (Basingstoke: Macmillan).

Kennedy, Paul (1981). *The Realities Behind Diplomacy: Background Influences on British External Policy, 1865–1980* (London: Fontana).

Kennedy, Paul (1984). 'Continuity and discontinuity in British imperialism, 1815–1914', C. C. Eldridge (ed.), *British Imperialism in the Nineteenth Century* (Hong Kong: Macmillan).

Kershner, R. Brandon (1994). 'Modernism's mirror: the sorrows of Marie Corelli', *Transforming Genres: New Approaches to British Fiction of the 1890s*, ed. Nikki Lee Manos and Meri-Jane Rochelson, pp. 67–86.

Kilgour, Maggie (1995). *The Rise of the Gothic Novel* (London: Routledge).

Killeen, Jarlath (2005). *Gothic Ireland: Horror and the Irish Anglican Imagination in the Long Eighteenth Century* (Dublin: Four Courts).

Kinahan, Frank (1988). *Yeats, Folklore and Occultism: Contexts of the Early Work and Thought* (Boston; London: Unwin Hyman).

Kincaid, James (1992). *Child-Loving: The Erotic Child and Victorian Culture* (New York and London: Routledge).

King, Mary C. (2004). 'Digging for Darwin: bitter wisdom in *The Picture of Dorian Gray* and "The Critic as Artist"', *Irish Studies Review*, 12, 3, 315–27.

Klass, Morton (1995). *Ordered Universes: Approaches to the Anthropology of Religion* (Oxford: Westview Press).

Klaus, Robert James (1987). *The Pope, the Protestants, and the Irish: Papal Aggression and Anti-Catholicism in Mid-Nineteenth Century England* (New York: Garland Publishing Incorporated).

Knelman, Judith (1997). *Twisting in the Wind: The Murderess and the English Press* (Toronto: University of Toronto Press).

Knight, Mark (2006). '"The Haunted and the Haunters": Bulwer-Lytton's philosophical ghost story', *Nineteenth-Century Contexts*, 28, 3, 245–55.

Korg, Jacob (1967). 'The rage of Caliban', *University of Toronto Quarterly*, 37, 1, 75–89.

Krüger, Gustav (1990). 'David Friedrich Strauss', *American Journal of Theology*, 4, 3, 514–35.

Kuhn, Thomas (1996). *The Structure of Scientific Revolutions* (Chicago and London: University of Chicago Press).

Lake, Peter (1989). 'Anti-popery: the structure of a prejudice', *Conflict in Early Stuart England: Studies in Religion and Politics, 1603–1642* (London: Longman), pp. 72–106.

Le Fanu, Joseph Sheridan (1993). *In a Glass Darkly*, ed. Robert Tracy (Oxford: Oxford World's Classics).

Le Fanu, Joseph Sheridan (2000). *Uncle Silas*, ed. Victor Sage (London: Penguin).

Lehan, Richard (1998). *The City in Literature: An Intellectual and Cultural History* (London: University of California Press).

Levy, Maurice (1994). '"Gothic" and the critical idiom', *Gothick Origins and Innovations*, ed. Allan Lloyd Smith and Victor Sage (Amsterdam-Atlanta: Rodopi), pp. 1–15.

Longuel, Alfred E. (1923). 'The word "Gothic" in eighteenth-century criticism', *Modern Language Notes*, 38, 453–60.

Luckhurst, Roger (2002). *The Invention of Telepathy* (Oxford: Oxford University Press).

Lukács, Georg (1962). *The Historical Novel*, trans. Hannah and Stanley Mitchell (London: Merlin).

Lurie, Alison (2003). *Boys and Girls Forever: Reflections on Children's Classics* (London: Chatto and Windus).

Lytton, Edward Bulwer (1925). *The Haunted and the Haunters* (London: Marshall and Kent).

Lytton, Edward Bulwer (1973). *A Strange Story: An Alchemical Novel* (Berkeley and London: Shambala).

MacAndrew, Elizabeth (1979). *The Gothic Tradition in Fiction* (New York: Columbia University Press).

MacCabe, Colin (1979). *James Joyce and the Revolution of the Word* (London: Macmillan).

Machen, Arthur (2007). *The Great God Pan*, in *The Three Impostors and Other Stories*, ed. S. T. Joshi (Hayward, CA: Chaosium), pp. 1–51.

Mackenzie, Norman and Jeanne (1987). *The Time Traveller* (London: Hogarth Press).

McClintock, Anne (1995). *Imperial Leather: Race, Gender and Sexuality in the Colonial Contest* (London: Routledge).

McCormack, W. J. (1991). 'Irish Gothic and after. 1820–1945', Seamus Deane (ed.), *The Field Day Anthology of Irish Writing*, vol. 2 (Derry: Field Day Publications), pp. 831–949.

McCormack, W. J. (1993). *Dissolute Characters: Irish Literary History Through Balzac, Sheridan Le Fanu, Yeats and Bowen* (Manchester: Manchester University Press).

McCormack, W. J. (1993). *The Dublin Paper War of 1786–1788: A Bibliographical and Critical Inquiry* (Blackrock, Co. Dublin: Irish Academic Press).

McCormack, W. J. (1997). *Sheridan Le Fanu* (Gloucestershire: Sutton Publishing).

Madoff, Mark (1979). 'The useful myth of Gothic ancestry', *Studies in Eighteenth-Century Culture*, 9, 337–50.

Malchow, H. L. (1996). *Gothic Images of Race in Nineteenth-Century Britain* (Stanford: Stanford University Press).

Marez, Curtis (1997). 'The other addict: reflections on colonialism and Oscar Wilde's opium smoke screen', *English Literary History*, 64, 257–87.

Mason, Michael (1977). *The Making of Victorian Sexuality* (Oxford: Oxford University Press).

Maxwell, Richard (1977). 'G. M. Reynolds, Dickens, and the mysteries of London', *Nineteenth-Century Fiction*, 32, 188–213.

Maxwell, Richard (1992). *The Mysteries of Paris and London* (Virginia: Virginia University Press).

Maynard, John (1993). *Victorian Discourses on Sexuality and Religion* (Cambridge: Cambridge University Press).

Meyer, Susan (2005). 'Antisemitism and social critique in Dickens' *Oliver Twist*', *Victorian Literature and Culture*, 33, 239–52.

Michie, Elsie (1992). 'From simianized Irish to oriental despots: Heathcliff, Rochester and racial difference', *Novel*, 25, 2, 125–40.

Mighall, Robert (1999). *A Geography of Gothic Fiction: Mapping History's Nightmares* (Oxford: Oxford University Press).

Milbank, Alison (1992). *Daughters of the House: Modes of the Gothic in Victorian Fiction* (New York: St Martin's Press).

Milbank, Alison (2002). 'Victorian Gothic in English novels and stories, 1830–1880', Jerrold E. Hogle (ed.), *The Cambridge Companion to Gothic Fiction* (Cambridge: Cambridge University Press), pp. 145–66.

Miles, Robert (1993). *Gothic Writing, 1750–1820: A Genealogy* (London-New York: Routledge).

Miles, Robert (1995). *Ann Radcliffe: The Great Enchantress* (Manchester: Manchester University Press).

Miller, J. Hillis (1975). *The Disappearance of God: Five Nineteenth Century Writers* (Harvard: Harvard University Press).

Miller, John (1973). *Popery and Politics in England, 1660–1688* (London: Cambridge University Press).

Miller, Melissa Lee (2002). *White Women in Racialized Spaces: Imaginative Transformation and Ethical Action in Literature*, ed. Samina Najmi and Rajini Srikath (Albany: New York State University Press), pp. 227–41.

Mitchell, Leslie (2003). *Bulwer Lytton: The Rise and Fall of a Victorian Man of Letters* (London and New York: Hambledon and London).

Mitchell, Sally (1984). 'Introduction', Mrs Henry Wood, *East Lynne* (Rutgers University Press).

Moers, Ellen (1986). *Literary Women* (London: Women's Press).

Moon, Brenda (2006). *More Usefully Employed: Amelia B. Edwards, Writer, Traveller and Campaigner for Ancient Egypt* (London: Egypt Exploration Society).

Moore, James R. (1988). 'Free thought, secularism, gnosticism: the case of Charles Darwin', *Religion in Victorian Britain*, vol. 1, *Traditions*, ed. Gerald Parsons (Manchester: Manchester University Press), pp. 274–319.

Moretti, Franco (1983). 'Dialectic of fear', *Signs Taken for Wonders: Essays in the Sociology of Literary Forms*, trans. Susan Fischer, David Forgacs and David Miller (London: Verso), pp. 83–108.

Moretti, Franco (1998). *Atlas of the European Novel, 1800–1900* (London:Verso).

Morin, Christina (2007). '"Completing the Union": Charles Robert Maturin and the (Ir)reconciliation of Romantic National Fiction' (unpublished Ph.D. thesis,Trinity College Dublin).

Moynahan, Julian (1994). 'The politics of Anglo-Irish Gothic: Charles Robert Maturin, Sheridan LeFanu, and the return of the repressed', *Anglo-Irish:The Literary Imagination of a Hyphenated Culture* (Princeton, NJ: Princeton University Press), pp. 109–35.

Murphy, H. (1955). 'The ethical revolt against Christian orthodoxy', *American History Review*, 9, 800–17.

Murphy, Patricia (1999), 'The gendering of history in *She*', *Studies in English Literature 1500–1900*, 39, 4, 747–72.

Murray, Brian (1990). *H. G. Wells* (New York: Continuum).

Murray, John (1863). 'Sensation novels', *Quarterly Review*, 113, 252–68.

Murray, Paul (2004). *From the Shadow of Dracula: A Life of Bram Stoker* (London: Jonathan Cape).

Mustafa, Jamil (2005). '"A good horror has its place in art": Hardy's Gothic strategy in *Tess of the d'Urbervilles*', *Studies in the Humanities*, 32, 2, 93–115.

Napier, Elizabeth (1987). *The Failure of Gothic: Problems of Disjunction in an Eighteenth-Century Literary Form* (Oxford: Clarendon Press).

Navarette, Susan J. (1998). *The Shape of Fear: Horror and the Fin de Siècle Culture of Decadence* (Lexington: University Press of Kentucky).

Nelson, Claudia (1991). *Boys will be Girls: The Feminine Ethic and British Children's Fiction, 1857–1917* (New Brunswick and London: Rutgers University Press).

Nemesvari, Richard (1995). 'Robert Audley's secret: male homosocial desire in *Lady Audley's Secret*', *Studies in the Novel*, 27, 4, 515–28.

O'Malley, Patrick (2006). *Catholicism, Sexual Deviance and Victorian Gothic Culture* (Cambridge: Cambridge University Press).

Oppenheim, Janet (1985). *The Other World: Spiritualism and Psychical Research in England, 1850–1914* (Cambridge: Cambridge University Press).

Otto, Rudolf (1959). *The Idea of the Holy: An Inquiry into the Non-Rational Factors in the Idea of the Divine and Its Relation to the Rational*, trans. John W. Harvey (London).

Owen, Alex (1985). *The Darkened Room: Women, Power and Spiritualism in Late-Victorian England* (Chicago: University of Chicago Press).

Owen, Alex (2003). *The Place of Enchantment: British Occultism and the Culture of the Modern* (Chicago: University of Chicago Press).

Pappas, John J. (1972). 'The flower and the beast: a study of Oscar Wilde's antithetical attitudes toward nature and man in *The Picture of Dorian Gray*', *English Literature in Transition*, 15, 1, 37–48.

Parrinder, Patrick (1995). *Shadows of the Future: H. G. Wells, Science Fiction and Prophecy* (Liverpool: Liverpool University Press).

Parsons, Gerald (ed.) (1988). *Religion in Victorian Britain* (Manchester: Manchester University Press), 4 vols.

Pattison, Robert (1978). *The Child Figure in English Literature* (Athens: University of Georgia Press).

Pearsall, Ronald (2004). *The Table-Rappers: The Victorians and the Occult* (Gloucestershire: Stutton).

Peters, Laura (2000). *Orphan Texts: Victorian Orphans, Culture and Empire* (Manchester: Manchester University Press).

Phelan, Peggy (1993). *Unmarked* (London: Routledge).

Phillips, Terry (2000). 'The rules of war: Gothic transgressions in First World War fiction', *Gothic Studies*, 2, 2, 232–44.

Plunkett, John (2004). 'Regicide and reginamania: G. W. M. Reynolds and the mysteries of London', *Victorian Crime, Madness and Sensation*, ed. Andrew Maunder and Grace Moore (Aldershot, England: Ashgate), pp. 15–30.

Poole, Robert (ed.) (2002). *The Lancashire Witches: Histories and Stories* (Manchester: Manchester University Press).

Poston, Lawrence (1998). 'Beyond the occult: the Godwinian nexus of Bulwer's *Zanoni*', *Studies in Romanticism*, 37, 2, 131–61.

Pritchard, Alan (1991). 'The urban Gothic of *Bleak House*', *Nineteenth-Century Fiction*, 45, 432–52.

Pronger, Brian (1990). *The Arena of Masculinity: Sports, Homosexuality and the Meaning of Sex* (London: GMP).

Pugh, Martin (1999). *State and Society: A Social and Political History of Britain, 1870–1997* (London: Hodder Arnold).

Punter, David (1996). *The Literature of Terror: A History of Gothic Fictions from 1765 to the Present Day* (London-New York: Longman), 2 vols.

Purkiss, Diane (2001). *Troublesome Things: A History of Fairies and Fairy Stories* (London: Penguin).

Pykett, Lyn (1994). *The 'Improper' Feminine: The Women's Sensation Novel and the New Woman Writing* (London: Routledge).

Pykett, Lyn (1994). *The Sensation Novel from* The Woman in White *to* The Moonstone (Plymouth: British Council/Northcote House).

Pykett, Lyn (1998). *Wilkie Collins* (London: Macmillan).

Ransom, Teresa (1999). *The Mysterious Miss Marie Corelli: Queen of Victorian Bestsellers* (Phoenix Mill and New York: Sutton Publishing).

Rashkin, Esther (1992). *Family Secrets and the Psychoanalysis of Narrative* (Princeton: Princeton University Press).

Reardon, Bernard M. G. (1995). *Religious Thought in the Victorian Age: A Survey from Coleridge to Gore* (London and New York: Longman).

Reed, Toni (1988). *Demon-Lovers and their Victims in British Fiction* (Lexington, KY: University of Kentucky Press).

Reynolds, G. W. M. (1996). *The Mysteries of London*, ed. Trefor Thomas (Keele, Staffordshire: Keele University Press).

Richards, Jeffrey (1995). 'Gender, race and sexuality in Bram Stoker's other novels', Christopher Parker (ed.), *Gender, Roles, and Sexuality in Victorian Literature* (New York: Scholar Press), pp. 143–71.

Riddell, Charlotte (1992). 'The banshee's warning', A. Susan Williams (ed.), *The Lifted Veil: The Book of Fantastic Literature by Women* (New York: Carroll and Graf Publishers), pp. 306–24.

Riddell, Mrs J. H. (1971). *The Uninhabited House, Five Victorian Ghost Novels*, ed. E. F. Beiler (New York: Dover Publications), pp. 1–112.

Riquelme, John Paul (2000). 'Oscar Wilde's aesthetic Gothic: Walter Pater, dark enlightenment, and *The Picture Of Dorian Gray*', *Modern Fiction Studies*, 46, 3, 609–631.

Robbins, Ruth and Julian Wolfreys (eds) (2000). *Victorian Gothic: Literary and Cultural Manifestations in the Nineteenth Century* (New York: Palgrave).

Roberts, Marie Mulvey (1990). *Gothic Immortals: The Fiction of the Brotherhood of the Rosy Cross* (Routledge: London).

Robertson, Fiona (1994). *Legitimate Histories: Scott, Gothic, and the Authorities of Fiction* (Oxford: Clarendon).

Rogerson, John (1984). *Old Testament Criticism in the Nineteenth Century: England and Germany* (London: S.P.C.K.).

Rosenman, Ellen Bayuk (1996). 'Spectacular women: *The Mysteries of London* and the female body', *Victorian Studies*, 40, 1, 31–64.

Roth, Phyllis Roth (1977). 'Suddenly sexual women in Bram Stoker's *Dracula*', *Literature and Psychology*, 27, 115–27.

Royle, Nicholas (2003). *The Uncanny* (Manchester: Manchester University Press).

Sage, Victor (1988). *Horror Fiction in the Protestant Tradition* (New York: St Martin's Press).

Sage, Victor (2004). *Le Fanu's Gothic: The Rhetoric of Darkness* (London: Palgrave).

Said, Edward (1991). *Orientalism: Western Conceptions of the Orient* (London: Penguin).

Samuel, Raphael (1992). 'Mrs Thatcher's return to Victorian values', *Victorian Values: Joint Symposium of the Royal Society of Edinburgh and the British Academy, December 1990*, ed. T. C. Smout (Oxford: Oxford University Press), pp. 9–29.

Sayer, Karen and Rosemary Mitchell (eds) (2003), *Victorian Gothic* (Leeds: Leeds Centre for Victorian Studies).

Schmitt, Cannon (1997). *Alien Nation: Nineteenth-Century Gothic Fictions and English Nationality* (Philadelphia: University of Pennsylvania Press).

Schutz, Alfred (1962). 'On multiple realities', *Collected Papers* (The Hague: Nijhoff), vol. 1, pp. 207–59.

Scott, James F. (1963). 'Thomas Hardy's use of the Gothic: an examination of five representative works', *Nineteenth-Century Fiction*, 17, 363–80.

Scott, Sir Walter (1968). 'Ann Radcliffe', *On Novelists and Fiction*, ed. Ioan Williams (London: Routledge).

Seagrott, Heather (2002). 'Hard science, soft psychology, and amorphous art in *The Picture of Dorian Gray*', *Studies in English Literature, 1500–1900*, 38, 741–59.

Sedgwick, Eve Kosofsky (1985). *Between Men: English Literature and Male Homosocial Desire* (New York: Columbia University Press).

Sedgwick, Eve Kosofsky (1986). *The Coherence of Gothic Conventions* (London: Methuen).

Sedgwick, Eve Kosofsky (1990). *Epistemology of the Closet* (Berkeley: Univ. of California Press).

Sharpe, Jenny (1993). *Allegories of Empire: The Figure of Woman in the Colonial Text* (Minneapolis: Minneapolis University Press).

Showalter, Elaine (1977). *A Literature of Their Own* (Princeton: Princeton University Press).

Showalter, Elaine (1985). *The Female Malady: Women, Madness and English Culture, 1830–1980* (London: Virago).

Showalter, Elaine (1986). 'Syphilis, sexuality, and the fiction of the Fin de Siècle', Ruth Bernard Yeazel (ed.), *Sex, Politics, and Science in the Nineteenth-Century Novel* (New York), pp. 88–116.

Showalter, Elaine (1991). *Sexual Anarchy: Gender and Culture at the 'Fin de Siècle'* (London: Bloomsbury).

Shuttleworth, Sally (2001). 'Introduction', *The Lifted Veil and Brother Jacob* (London: Penguin), xi–l.

Silver, Carole G. (1999). *Strange and Secret Peoples: Fairies and Victorian Consciousness* (Oxford: Oxford University Press).

Simpson, Jacqueline (1974). 'The function of folklore in *Jane Eyre* and *Wuthering Heights*', *Folklore*, 85, 47–61.

Skal, David J. and Nina Auerbach (eds) (1997). *Dracula* (London: Norton).

Smajic, Srdjan (2003). 'The trouble with ghost-seeing: vision, ideology, and genre in the Victorian ghost story', *English Literary History*, 70, 983–1002.

Smith, Andrew (2000). *Gothic Radicalism: Literature, Philosophy and Psychoanalysis in the Nineteenth Century* (New York: St Martin's Press).

Smith, Andrew (2004). *Victorian Demons: Medicine, Masculinity, and the Gothic at the Fin-de-Siècle* (New York: Manchester University Press).

Smith, Andrew, and William Hughes (eds) (2003). *Empire and the Gothic: The Politics of Genre* (Basingstoke: Palgrave Macmillan).

Smith, Elton E. and Robert Haas (eds) (1999). *The Haunted Mind: The Supernatural in Victorian Literature* (Lanham, MD: Scarecrow Press).

Snef, Carol A. (1982). '*Dracula*: Stoker's response to the New Woman', *Victorian Studies*, 26, 33–9.

Snef, Carol A. (1998). *Dracula: Between Tradition and Modernism* (New York: Twayne).

Sparks, Tabitha (2002). 'Medical Gothic and the return of the contagious diseases acts in Stoker and Machen', *Nineteenth-Century Feminisms*, 6, 87–102.

Starrs, D. Bruno (2004). '"Keeping the faith": Catholicism in "*Dracula*" and its adaptations', *Journal of Dracula Studies*, 6.

Stevenson, Robert Louis (2002). *The Strange Case of Dr Jekyll and Mr Hyde*, ed. Robert Mighall (London: Penguin).

Stoddart, Helen (2004). '"The precautions of nervous people are infectious": Sheridan Le Fanu's symptomatic Gothic', Fred Botting and Dale Townshend (eds), *Gothic: Critical Concepts in Literary and Cultural Studies*, vol. 3, *Nineteenth-Century Gothic: At Home with the Vampire* (London and New York: Routledge), pp. 97–116.

Stoker, Bram (2003). *Dracula*, ed. Maurice Hindle (London: Penguin).

Stoker, Bram (2006). *The Lair of the White Worm, Dracula's Guest and Other Weird Stories*, ed. Kate Hebblethwaite (London: Penguin), pp. 151–369.

Stone, Harry (1959). 'Dickens and the Jews', *Victorian Studies*, 2, 3, 223–53.

Stone, Harry (1979). *Dickens and the Invisible World: Fairy Tales, Fantasy, and Novel-Making* (Bloomington and London: Indiana University Press).

Stone, Harry (1994). *The Night Side of Dickens: Cannibalism, Passion, Necessity* (Columbus: Ohio State University Press).

Stone, Lawrence (1977). *The Family, Sex and Marriage in England, 1500–1800* (London: Faber and Faber).

Sweet, Matthew (2001). *Inventing the Victorians* (London: Faber and Faber).

Taylor, Jenny Bourne (1998). *In the Secret Theatre of the Home* (New York: Routledge).

Thomas, Trefor (2000). 'Rereading G. M. Reynolds's *The Mysteries of London*', *Rereading Victorian Fiction*, ed. Alice Jenkins and Juliet Jon (London: Macmillan), pp. 59–80.

Thormahlen, Marianne (1997). 'The lunatic and the Devil's disciple: The "lovers" in *Wuthering Heights*', *Review of English Studies*, 48, 183–97.

Thuente, Mary Helen (1980). *W. B. Yeats and Irish Folklore* (Dublin: Gill and Macmillan).

Thurschwell, Pamela (2001). *Literature, Technology and Magical Thinking, 1880–1920* (Cambridge: Cambridge University Press).

Todorov, Tzvetan (1975). *The Fantastic: A Structural Approach to a Literary Genre*, trans. Richard Howard (Ithaca, New York: Cornell University Press).

Tompkins, J. M. S. (1961). *The Popular Novel in England, 1770–1800* (Lincoln: University of Nebraska Press).

Trodd, Anthea (1989). *Domestic Crime in the Victorian Novel* (London: Palgrave).

Tropp, Martin (1990). *Images of Fear: How Horror Stories Helped Shape Modern Culture. 1818–1918* (Jefferson, North Carolina and London: McFarland and Company).

Trumpener, Kate (1997). *Bardic Nationalism: The Romantic Novel and the British Empire* (Princeton: Princeton University Press).

Tumbleson, Raymond D. (1998). *Catholicism in the English Protestant Imagination: Nationalism, Religion, and Literature, 1660–1745* (Cambridge: Cambridge University Press).

Turner, Frank Miller (1974). *Between Science and Religion: The Reaction to Scientific Naturalism in Late Victorian England* (New Haven; London: Yale University Press).

Turner, Victor (1978). *Schism and Continuity in an African Society: A Study of Ndembu Village Life* (Manchester: Manchester University Press).

Turner, Victor and Edith (1978). *Image and Pilgrimage in Christian Culture* (Oxford).

Twitchell, James B. (1988). *'Dreadful Pleasures': An Anatomy of Modern Horror* (New York: Oxford University Press).

Twitchell, James B. (1989). *Preposterous Violence: Fables of Aggression in Modern Culture* (Oxford: Oxford University Press).

Tylor, Edward (1871). *Primitive Culture: Researches into the Development of Mythology, Philosophy, Religion, Art and Custom*, 2 vols (London: John Murray).

Tyndal, John (1901). *Fragments of Science 1–3* (New York: P. F. Collier and Son), pp. 266–91.

Valente, Joseph (2002). *Dracula's Crypt: Bram Stoker, Irishness and the Question of Blood* (Urbana and Chicago: University of Illinois Press).

van Baal, J. (1963). 'Magic as a religious phenomenon', *Higher Education and Research in the Netherlands*, 7, 10–21.

van Beek, W. E. A. (1975). 'The religion of everyday life: an investigation into the concepts of religion and magic', W. E. A. van Beek and J. H. Scherer (eds), *Explorations in the Anthropology of Religion* (The Hague), pp. 55–69.

Veeder, William (1988). 'Children of the night: Stevenson and patriarchy', William Veeder and Gordon Hirsch (eds), *Dr Jekyll and Mr. Hyde after One Hundred Years* (Chicago: University of Chicago Press), pp. 107–60.

Wacke, Jennifer (1992). 'Vampiric typewriting: *Dracula* and its media', *English Literary History*, 59, 1, 476–93.

Walkowitz, Judith (1992). *City of Dreadful Delight: Narratives of Sexual Danger in Late-Victorian London* (Chicago: University of Chicago Press).

Walther, LuAnn (1979). 'The invention of childhood in Victorian auto-biography', *Approaches to Victorian Autobiography*, ed. George P. Landon (Athens, OH: Ohio University Press), pp. 64–83.

Walton, James (2007). *Vision and Vacancy: The Fictions of J. S. Le Fanu* (Dublin: University College Dublin Press).

Watt, Ian (1986). 'Time and family in the Gothic novel: *The Castle of Otranto*', *Eighteenth-Century Life*, 10, 3, 159–71.

Weber, Max (1946). 'Religious rejections of the world and their direc-tions', *From Max Weber: Essays in Sociology*, ed. Gerth and Mills (Oxford), pp. 350–1.

Wells, H. G. (1937). *Progress and Poverty* (New York: Schalkenbach).

Wells, H. G. (2005). *The Island of Doctor Moreau*, ed. Patrick Parrinder (London: Penguin).

Wells, H. G. (2005). *The Time Machine*, ed. Patrick Parrinder (London: Penguin).

Wells, H. G. (2005). *The War of the Worlds*, ed. Patrick Parrinder (London: Penguin).

White, Jerry (2007). *London in the Nineteenth Century: 'A Human Awful Wonder of God'* (London: Jonathan Cape).

Wilde, Oscar (2006). *The Picture of Dorian Gray*, ed. Joseph Bristow (Oxford: Oxford University Press).

Williams, Ann (1995). *Art of Darkness: A Poetics of Gothic* (Chicago: University of Chicago Press).

Williams, Kevin (1998). *Get Me a Murder a Day! A History of Mass Communications in Britain* (London: Edward Arnold).

Winter, Alison (1998). *Mesmerized: Powers of the Mind in Victorian Britain* (Chicago: University of Chicago Press).

Wirth, Louis (1938). 'Urbanism as a way of life', *American Journal of Sociology*, XLIV, 1, 1–24.

Wolfreys, Julian (1998). *Writing London: The Trace of the Urban Text from Blake to Dickens* (London: Macmillan).

Wolfreys, Julian (2002). *Victorian Hauntings: Spectrality, Gothic, the Uncanny and Literature* (London: Palgrave).

Woolf, Virginia (1985). *Moments of Being*, ed. Jeanne Schulkind (New York: Harcourt).

Worth, George J. (1972). *William Harrison Ainsworth* (New York: Twayne).

Yates, Nigel (1988). 'Jesuits in disguise? Ritualist confessors and their critics in the 1870s', *Journal of Ecclesiastical History*, 39, 202–16.

Yeats, W. B. (1955). *Autobiographies* (London: Macmillan).

Yeats, W. B. (1986). *The Collected Letters of W. B. Yeats*, vol. 1, 1865–1895, ed. John Kelly, associate ed. Eric Domville (Oxford: Clarendon Press).

Yeats, W. B. (1993). *Writings on Irish Folklore, Legend and Myth*, ed. Robert Welch (London: Penguin).

Yeats, W. B. (1995). *Short Fiction*, ed. G. J. Watson (London: Penguin).

# Index